Literature Among Discourses
The Spanish Golden Age

LITERATURE
AMONG
DISCOURSES
the
Spanish
Golden
Age

Edited and Introduced by

WLAD GODZICH
&
NICHOLAS SPADACCINI

University of Minnesota Press, Minneapolis

The University of Minnesota Press gratefully
acknowledges publication assistance provided by the
Department of Spanish and Portuguese Languages and Literatures
of the University of Minnesota.

Published by the University of Minnesota Press
2037 University Avenue Southeast, Minneapolis MN 55414.
Published simultaneously in Canada
by Fitzhenry & Whiteside Limited, Markham.
Printed in the United States of America.

Library of Congress Cataloging-in-Publication Data
Main entry under title:

Literature among discourses.

Bibliography: p.
Includes index.
1. Spanish literature—Classical period, 1500–1700—
History and criticism—Addresses, essays, lectures.
2. Discourse analysis, Literary—Addresses, essays,
lectures. I. Godzich, Wlad. II. Spadaccini,
Nicholas.
PQ6066.L58 1986   860'.9'003   85-20942
ISBN 0-8166-1456-3
ISBN 0-8166-1457-1 (pbk.)

Contents

Acknowledgments

The editors of this volume gratefully acknowledge assistance from the National Endowment for the Humanities, Division of Conferences; the Department of Spanish and Portuguese Languages and Literatures; the Comparative Literature Program, and the Scholarly Conferences Fund of the College of Liberal Arts, University of Minnesota, towards preparation of this work.

Introduction
Toward a History of 'Literature'
Wlad Godzich and Nicholas Spadaccini

In recent years, literary history has receded somewhat from view in literary studies. To be sure, histories of literature, especially histories of Spanish literature,[1] continue to be written, but they no longer occupy the center-stage position that was once theirs. Their principal pedagogical underpinning, the so-called survey course, has been disappearing from the curriculum as well. To some extent, this is a measure of the success of the work of the great literary historians of the nineteenth and twentieth centuries. Without their broad historical backdrops, rich in taxonomic detail, the close reading of individual texts — whether practiced under the aegis of the New Criticism in the English-speaking world, as *explications de texte* in France, as *werkimmanente Forschung* in the German-speaking lands, or as a form of stylistics à la Dámaso Alonso — could hardly be carried out. Similarly, the more recent studies of structuralist or semiotic orientation have fundamentally retained the classifications and divisions of the literary historians, even when the latter have proved to be something of a hindrance to these studies. The current rise in literary theorization has, however, brought into sharper relief some of the discrepancies that have arisen between the readings and analyses of individual works and the generalizations and characterizations of literary history. Since the latter, almost by definition, lacks the specificity and immediate textual support of the former, it has been found to be the more wanting of the two. As a result, with the notable exception of the *Rezeptionsästhetik* movement,[2] literary history has been treated as if it were more and more irrelevant to the concerns of today's student of literature. Yet, paradoxically, just because it has fallen into a sort of benign neglect, literary history and its traditional schemas have not ceased to exercise a powerful influence on the present conduct of literary studies. One measure of this influence is provided by the fact that most scholars in the field of literature define their professional identity by means of the two central axes of literary history: the generic and the periodic, describing themselves as specialists in nineteenth-century poetry, for example, the whole contained in the framework of a national perspective, such as nineteenth-century Spanish poetry.

The poststructuralist critique of the claim that narrative has explanatory power[3] has addressed more directly the issue of the status of literary history, giving rise in the process to considerable hostility since it tampers with the very institutional identity of literary scholars. But, at the same time, this critique has brought to the fore a rather interesting contradiction inherent in the project of a history of literature. For the latter, variability is the essential condition of transformation and development through time, but this variability is strictly circumscribed: it does not extend to the notion of 'literature' itself, so that this notion, and the institution that it designates, are taken to be selfsame through the ages.

Here is revealed the basis for the secret affinity between literary history and the ahistorical methodologies of recent years: by limiting fluctuation to matters of form, thematics, character depiction, generic evolution, and stylistic innovation, but pointedly excluding the scope of the construct of literature itself, literary history has guaranteed a historically stable object to the scholar interested in the definition of literariness or the elaboration of a model for the production of meaning. The fallacy of the guarantee of such a stability is readily apparent. It suffices to recall that in the High Middle Ages, the term *literatura* referred to that which was composed of *litterae*, that is, to anything written, a usage that present-day English retains when, for example, literature from a travel agency is meant to be synonymous with printed brochures.[4] But the institutionalized study of literature, elaborated in the late eighteenth century and consolidated in the nineteenth, ignores this medieval meaning of the term and imposes its own construct of literature instead, treating a number of medieval verbal practices as instances of literature whereas they certainly would never have been labeled *literatura* in their day since they were either performed or composed orally. Similar problems arise for other periods of Western history; they become even more acute when this transhistorical conception of literature is transposed from the Western culture in which it was born to other, non-Western, cultural settings.

If the term 'literature' does not refer then to an entity fundamentally identical to itself in various cultural milieus across space and time, it must become itself the object of critical, and historical, attention, as must the construct it has represented, and indeed the institution it has spawned. The editors of the present volume have decided to undertake such an examination and to focus it on 'literature' in Spain, for reasons both practical—one of us is a specialist in the field—and theoretical. Foremost among these is the fact that the very project of literary history as it came to be formulated in German Romanticism relied upon a construct of literature that, it was claimed, had actually been achieved in Spain and was yet to obtain in Germany. The strategic location of Spanish literature in the validation of the construct at the time of its emergence suggests that we begin with it. It also suggests that more is to be gained at this time from studies focused on specific national traditions than from broadly comparative ones.

Since all students of literature today have been trained and have been practicing their craft in an environment in which the construct of literature itself has not come under question, no individual would be expected to possess the skills and knowledge necessary for a rigorous interrogation of this construct. We have determined at the outset, then, that our enterprise had to be a collective one, bringing together scholars with similar concerns and possessing the very literary-historical knowledge the well-foundedness of which we wished to examine. The present volume is a first step in this direction.

If the construct of literature—which we will henceforth write without placing it in single quotes—is to be the focus of our inquiry, this inquiry can proceed according to its own structure, a structure that has the value of a periodization: (a) before literature; (b) literature among discourses [the present volume]; (c) the institution of literature; (d) the hegemony of literature; (e) literature under attack. It ought to be said at the outset that such a division, which has been adopted as that of our research, is not meant to suggest that these various stages necessarily obtain in pure form or successively in time. There is little doubt, in fact, that temporal swatches contain more than one of these attitudes, though, just as undoubtedly, some are more dominant at one time than another. In other words, the construct of literature is not a concept, in Hegel's sense, that emerges, develops, produces its own contradiction, and finds itself sublated in a hierarchically superior conceptual entity. Rather, it is a historically attested phenomenon whose very historicity must be restored, and which must be freed from the ideologizing that has accrued around it in the attempt to make it transhistorical.

The history of literature—that is, of the construct of literature—that we are attempting is thus not meant to take its place alongside existing histories of literature, nor is it intended to replace them. Rather, its purpose it to effect a breach in the closure that has been imposed upon the field of literary studies by the definition of literature inherent in literary history, in order to open this field to the study of all verbal practices, their structures, their interaction, and their inscription in the social sphere, including their relation to other signifying practices, artistic or not.

The failure to subject the construct of literature to examination manifests itself in a certain type of "positivism" that is practiced even by many who shun or repudiate the term: what is studied, or included in the scope of what is studied, is the already given, the datum, of the critical tradition. In practice, this has resulted in the concentration of attention upon a few texts, labeled "masterpieces," studied in isolation from others, especially their so-called minor contemporaries. Literary history, especially as the object of a pedagogical enterprise, became a peregrination from one masterpiece to another. This attitude has become so strongly embedded in the profession that it prevails even among those who view themselves as willing to question the old conceptions of literature and of literary history. As we have stated above, this is not surprising since the present institutional setting of the scholar of literature, the profession of literary studies and the university that is its home, are organized in such a way as to define the competency, and the territorial rights, of these scholars in terms of these masterpieces and their position in a generic and periodic taxonomy.

In Spanish literature, a cluster of such masterpieces came to be identified quite early and constituted what the Spaniards call the *siglos de oro*, which we have rendered by the singular but collective English term: the Spanish Golden Age. It is undeniable that the sixteenth and seventeenth centuries in Spain have produced some of the outstanding works of any literature. As we argue in our contribution to this volume, this achievement, and the specific form that it took, was to find a special resonance in German romanticism, especially in the writings of Friedrich Schlegel, and came to be given paradigmatic status for the entire project of literary history. It is for this reason that we have decided to begin our examination of the construct of literature with this period. It ought to be clear, then, that the decision to begin with the Spanish Golden Age is motivated by considerations of its strategic location in the formation and development of the project of literary history, and not upon any a priori judgment of value upon the epoch in question or the fate of literature in it.

Two rather different strategies have recently emerged in the type of endeavor that we are proposing to undertake. The first consists in returning to a specific period and attempting to fill out, through very important and worthy empirical research, the scope of our knowledge of literature in that period. The favored way has been to "discover" and study a "popular literature" alongside the already recognized canonical literature. Far be it from us to disdain these studies. Indeed, without them, our task would be well-nigh impossible. They have provided, after all, a wealth of information about small literary genres, witchcraft, games, ritual and other practices, and so on. But we must acknowledge their limitation: in outlook they are as positivistic as the studies we have seen to be insufficient; they do not question the dominant construct of the object of study of our field; they simply seek to provide a more differentiated backdrop, a more richly woven setting, for its appearance in the limelight.

The second strategy recognizes that there is an interaction between the works that we have come to call literature and the others, and it attempts to gauge the impact of their interaction on the actual composition of the masterpieces. Relying upon an analytic concept borrowed from the Russian literary theoretician Mikhail M. Bakhtin, albeit in considerably modified form, the practitioners of this approach see the texts upon which they focus as the nexus of a network of themes, motifs, verbal devices, narrative models, etc., present in other texts, of whatever status in the epoch, and which they call the intertext. This is a valuable heuristic device for it does help establish what was the treasure trove of available material for the structuring and writing of the text at hand, and thus it permits an analysis of the means by which this storehouse is utilized and converted into the text we ultimately read.

This approach differs from the preceding one by seeking to describe and explain the very constitution of a given work. In principle, this is a methodology that could be used with equal justification and validity in the study of any verbal, and indeed nonverbal cultural, artifact, but in practice, it is destined to be used in the study of masterpieces. After all, the entire conception of the intertext and its relation to the text is governed by the notion that the intertext constitutes a sort of raw material available for, and awaiting, the transformation that the (canonized) text effects upon it.

Both analytic strategies share the presupposition of the masterpiece's centrality, and they also have in common the conception of the totality of a cultural field revolving around that masterpiece. Neither addresses, nor indeed has any notion of, the problem of describing and explaining the processes and means whereby the masterpiece came to occupy the locus that will henceforth appear to be its own. In other words, they fail to take into account the double process of institutionalization that, in a first movement, grants a given work the status of masterpiece and then, in a second gesture that is but a confirmation of the first, makes that work the privileged object of literary analysis.

Without denying the considerable contributions of both of these approaches, we nonetheless cannot adopt them uncritically because of this blindness to their own determination. Our focus shall remain the processes and mechanisms by which specific texts or classes of texts came to be differentiated from other discursive entities and given the label "literature." Hence our title: *Literature among Discourses*. Since the institutionalizing movement has been a two-phased process, our procedures must also be doubly attentive: they must follow the historical process of the institutionalization of literature as well as its disciplinary correlative. This is not always very easy to carry out in practice, even when one has a clear view of what is being sought, and the contributions to this volume testify as much to these difficulties as to the processes they seek to illuminate. For one thing, nearly all the data of literary scholarship that are available to us come in a form that is designed more to occult this issue than to elucidate it.

In this respect, Michael Nerlich's essay in the present collection is exemplary in its courage and in its rigor: Nerlich takes on the most widely accepted views of perhaps the most respected historian of Spanish literature, Ramón Menéndez Pidal, and subjects them to close scrutiny. The result is a recasting of the entire problem of "popular" and "traditional" poetry, a distinction that Menéndez Pidal took well beyond the boundaries of Spanish literature, as, for example, in his discussion of the *Song of Roland*.[5] Eschewing the broad type of generalization that we associate with the project of poetics, Nerlich prefers to focus on the developmental courses of one discourse, the discourse of adventure, and on its productivity, indicating in the process its dialectical relation to the social sphere in which it manifests itself.[6]

This sphere is particularly complex in the case of the Spanish Golden Age. Fortunately, for several years scholars have had the work of José Antonio Maravall to guide them. In his contribution to this volume, Maravall reviews his own evolving views on what he has called "the culture of the Baroque."[7] As a historian of social mentalities, yet fully cognizant of the economic and political determinations of the epoch, Maravall focuses on the perceptions of those who lived through a period of frequently unsettling changes. These changes, at times progressive and at others regressive, liberating but also repressive, ultimately imply a degree of transformation in the system of social mentality, which means as well a degree of uncertainty in the values of rank, prestige, authority, etc., and in the credibility of the discourses associated with them. Literature will move among these various discourses and the gaps that do not fail to occur among them, to become a major instrument of a Baroque culture that is characteristically conservative, urban, directed, and mass-oriented; it is a culture contrived and manipulated by the monarcho-seigneurial sectors of Spanish society when the world is deemed to be upside down and the perception of "crisis" is commonplace among the groups in power and those who identify with them. Maravall argues that the Baroque world of seventeenth-century Spain organizes its resources increasingly for the purpose of conserving and strengthening traditional society and that literature plays a role, though not always an unambiguous one, in this process.

The complexity of the changes is well illustrated in Ronald Sousa's careful examination of the play of discourses in an *Auto* of Gil Vicente. Like many of the plays of the age, this *Auto* provides a representation of two social groups, differentiated by the extension of the discourses that they can wield. The problem arises then with respect to the conciliation or unification of these culturally, and socially, differentiated groups. The traditional paradigm for effecting this unification—the notion of an abstract Christian cultural unity—is assayed and found wanting. In the play, it is the abrupt invocation of state, or court, authority that puts an end to the dilemma, but one cannot fail to notice that the discourse of the play itself, indeed the play as an instance of the nascent institution of literature, holds together the varying discourses, without, seemingly, adjudicating between them, but actually acting as container and arbitrator, that is, as both the space and the rule of that space, two foundational notions of the state.

In our own contribution to this volume, we encounter a similar process when we examine the forms of reading in the *Quijote*. It turns out that the actual reader of that work must adopt the position of the state with respect to the variety of discursive productions and strategies of readerly appropriation. Only from a perspective that must construe itself as detached and above the more partisan and directly implicated participants can the reader exercise the faculties that will make him or her an appreciative observer of the state's role as adjudicator of interests and partisan quarrels.

By contrast, Constance Sullivan focuses on a form of discourse that, she argues, can shed considerable light upon a group that was to be shunted equally by the institutionalized literature and the scholarly enterprise that was to police it: the traditional proverbs of women of the popular classes. Learning to recognize marks of gender in these proverbs, Sullivan brings out the lack of conformity to dominant discourses of the proverbs, thereby suggesting both a more tenuous hegemony than has been commonly believed and a greater marginalization than has been documented.

The highly theoretical contribution of Jenaro Talens and José Luís Canet bases itself solidly in the pioneering work of Paul Zumthor, to whom we owe the impetus for a historicization of poetics,[8] and draws as well upon the work of Mikhail Bakhtin. Talens and Canet attempt to trace the emergence of the Spanish *comedia* against the background of both oral and written verbal productivity. Like Constance Sullivan in her contribution, they open fruitful avenues for further research by recasting a problematic that had become a little too predictable in its concerns.

Finally, in an essay that relies on solid research by both literary critics and social historians—among them José Antonio Maravall, J. Caro Baroja, and P. E. Russell—Javier Herrero shows how items from other forms of discourses (popular magic, witchcraft, proverbs, etc.) are transformed into a metaphorical structure in a discourse that claims for itself the status of literature. Herrero thus provides a vivid illustration of the hegemonic tendency of the discourse of literature.

Thus the essays in this volume do not offer scintillating new readings of old masterpieces, nor do they rescue from the oblivion of the past some masterwork unjustly ignored. Rather they seek to replace the very phenomenon of literature in a larger verbal luxuriance, one in which literature is never given but is constantly being forged through a dynamic of inclusions and exclusions as complex as the social dynamic itself. By the same token, they raise questions about the present orientation of literary studies and indicate ways in which a historical consciousness in the study of literature could be restored to a field that has used literary history to make itself immune to it.

Literature among Discourses
The Spanish Golden Age

Chapter 1
From the Renaissance to the Baroque
The Diphasic Schema of a Social Crisis
José Antonio Maravall
Translated by Terry Cochran

I am becoming increasingly convinced that it is impossible to arrive at an interpretation of the Baroque—a culture experienced by the people of Western
Europe during an epoch coinciding approximately with the seventeenth century—without conceiving of this culture as one phase of a more extensive whole.
Only in this way do the phenomena contemplated in this period appear to offer
the possibility of being explained congruently, accotding to the schema of a nexus that puts them in relation to other preceding phenomena and that allows us,
along this line of interpretation, to grasp the meaning of subsequent ones, if not
to foresee them. It is not a matter of seeking out a genetic linkage between various phenomena, nor even a stringent causal relation. For the historian, to seek
out connections of this type, frequently alluded to in the succession of social
facts, is the same as falling naively into a trap. But we also have to avoid being
trapped by another deceptive way out, which would be to resign ourselves to
an arbitrary proliferation of facts. I am setting out along the lines of those who
seek a connection between the facts included in a historical "situation," and I am
endeavoring to define my work as the establishment of "situational relations" that
refer or connect some phenomena with others, and with them form configurations of structured wholes in the diachronic succession of historical changes. In
such a sense, I believe that this "configuration" or historical "structure" that we
call the Baroque can be understood only in connection with another, earlier
structure—the Renaissance—not because we would have to think that this latter
might have caused or engendered it, but because the conditions that end up being
transformed, that made possible the configuration of the phase which later

unfolds with incorporated innovations, are inherited from the preceding situation. The Baroque inherited from the Renaissance the conditioning that enabled it to be implanted in Western Europe.

As is well known, some economic historians—basing their thinking on a reading of statistical data that refer to the movement of contemporary economic life in different economic sectors (such data as could be collected more than fifty years ago in the United States, England, and France, principally, though with some references from other places)—came to establish an image, which at some point became familiar to us, of periods of change, on a double slope, integrated by two intertwined phases. In the first phase—designated by the letter A—the curve of economic dynamics takes an upward turn, indicating growth and prosperity (not for everybody, to be sure, but for the broad sectors serving as protagonists of the event, as well as in all other areas). The second phase—or phase B—is one of decline and depression (of misery, again, not for everybody but for the broad mass remaining outside history). This schema, so summarily laid out—and for my purpose, nothing more is necessary—bears the name Kondratieff. According to the interpretation that Kondratieff gave to the movement—in two parts (upswing and downturn)—the entire period came to last approximately fifty years, although the author himself cautioned that this was very imprecise, very uncertain; besides, within these periods of rising and declining, other briefer periods could occur, constructed under the same schema, but with less prominence. Finally, what remained as the interpretation of the economic phenomena's march in time was the broad schema of a diphasic character, which was formed, then, by broad upswings and broad cycles.

During the years of growth and development—in the recent decades of the fifties and sixties, which are everywhere still remembered today, for there was scarely a corner where they failed to reach, whether by effects more or less direct or induced—Kondratieff's theory suffered an eclipse under the hopeful image of tomorrow. This image seemed to issue from Keynesian theses, leading one to believe that crises were outmoded phenomena belonging to other times and that what could be looked forward to was another image of the future: a course of sustained and widespread development. Nevertheless, the great economic difficulties that began after 1970 (difficulties that have since become accentuated, although perhaps with an occasional temporary alleviation, despite which a consciousness of crisis is becoming more generalized and more widely affirmed) forced the abandonment—according to many economists' interpretation—of Keynesian formulas; and in confirming that a new phase of depression followed a preceding phase of expansion and boom, Kondratieff's theory of cycles again came to enjoy a certain currency. This has been said by very well-known economic theorists—R. J. Samuelson, J. W. Forrester, etc.; clearly it is not something that originated with me.

But before the current economic situation had, with its sequence of distressing upheavals, pushed its way into the foreground of the present, and before the theory of alternating *A* and *B* phases came into its own (I obviously do not mean before it was enunciated), I realized that I had unknowingly applied a similar schema to interpret the Spanish sixteenth and seventeenth centuries, and very specifically to explain the Baroque. Initially, in my 1944 book *Teoría española del Estado en el siglo XVII* (in which I held that the Baroque was not a mere concept of art history, nor even of spirituality, and still less a concept of style; it was, rather, a *historical concept*, a concept of *epoch*. I already viewed this seventeenth century as a time marked by recession, regression, and conflict (that is, what I am calling a *B* phase), which put an end to the innovation and expansion of the sixteenth century. In contrast, in some minor writings and in my *Carlos V y sus banqueros*, the prior sixteenth century appeared as an innovative, expansive epoch; it was a critical epoch, certainly, but critical because of the drive to seek new solutions. It would correspond, therefore, to what one would call today an *A* phase. As a consequence, I consider it more obvious that there exists a fundamental interrelation and even derivation of one phase with respect to the other, which in turn makes clearer the general qualifications I have applied to them.

I think it is simply impossible to speak of the Baroque—now identified as a phase of decline within a broader period of European culture—without taking into account the prior phase, the sixteenth century (or, more exactly, the century of the Renaissance). What prompted the countries of the Western region to strive to cut off the forward march that was under way? What was to have been firmly closed off and contained? In aiming to avoid what the upper layers of society, the dominant sectors of social "integration," judged to be a threat of collapse, what was to have been maintained? In my opinion it was a matter of containing this expansive movement unleashed at the end of the fifteenth and reinforced in the sixteenth century; of an expansion that, from its own economic suppositions, seemed to have entered into crisis before the end of the century; of a renovating tendency that, before 1580, some thought would bring nothing but ill-fated consequences and lead to disorder and excess among individuals; and to the extent that this tendency advances in the final decade, many considered themselves to be in a general situation that, with the erosion of group interrelations, was threatening to destroy established society.

I am convinced that at present it is impossible to take a decisive step into the problem of comprehending the Renaissance without constructing an image— although it may be provisional, it will be valid along general lines—of the Baroque, just as the inverse is no less certain. (It has always been said—this has been taken as the historian's attitude—that to see what a thing is, one must pay attention to what it has been, to that from which it comes. For my part, I think it can be just as interesting and decisive—on occasion, even more so—to ask what persists within it that has not engendered it, but which did in fact precede it.) Hatzfeld made an observation without hitting upon its importance: there is no Baroque where there has not been beforehand a Renaissance more or less faithful to the Italianizing model; that is why Italy, Spain, France, England, Germany, etc., all had a Baroque. I believe, however, that one must take into account an observation from the opposite direction: the historian-sociologist Lewis Mumford has come to maintain that the Baroque is the principal stage in the historical change of modernity that took place in Europe; the Renaissance would be a prelude to such a change (this is contrary to how Burckhardt began to view it). In any case, if one is to understand the Baroque, it is thus of interest to view the advance toward modernity and, ultimately, the forward movement that is given form and according to which history is contemplated in the sixteenth century.[1]

This double-directed consideration that I have just put forth leads us to think that there is no locus for understanding the Baroque without dealing with the question of the expansive movement of the Renaissance phase, as well as with the judgments and assessments that it arouses, with the feeling of disquiet and insecurity that the same upsurge of growth raises to the point of provoking an adverse state of mind in the privileged classes. These classes translate the rhythm of the positive changes as a threat to the situation in which their primacy and effective power reside. But before arriving at this inversion in assessing the epoch's movement, it may be worthwhile for us to follow the steps by which this growth is thought to link threatening consequences, one after the other.

In 1966, in *Antiguos y modernos*, I proposed to study the aspects of this social movement as reflected in consciousnesses and, consequently, the Spaniards' conception of the movement of history in the first modern century – without failing to include numerous references to England, France, and Italy. In every sphere this inquiry resulted in a schema of a future-oriented, *ascendant* vision, in advance of any validating sign. Later, in the "Tours Colloquia," I summarized this view with some new data under the title "Un humanisme tourné vers le futur" (1976), and even later, in Rome, I put forth what I called the "formula of the Spanish Renaissance," understood as a *Renaissance by emulation* (I believe it is a formula no less applicable to France and England, and to a great extent, even to Italy), as opposed to a *Renaissance by imitation*.

A book with such a thesis – published in 1966 and written, therefore, in the preceding years – turned out to be highly debatable (it contained no more than partial commentaries on Villelón, Bodin, Tassoni, Louis le Roy, and so on). F. Chabod had condemned any attempt to find in the Renaissance a preference for the moderns insofar as he viewed it as dominated by an archeologizing passion toward the past. The book of H. Hauser (*La Modernité du XVIe siècle*) was an early invitation to change this point of view, but it did not offer a consciousness of modernity with enough breadth and generality. Today we have at our disposal several books and articles that apply such a schema even to the same classicist movement in the Italian mode, such as the study of Roubichou-Stretz, relative to "La Pléyade," and that of G. Huppert, on the conception of history in sixteenth-century France.

I have delved into all the sixteenth-century branches of human culture in which an expansion took place, to see whether they were accompanied by an openness toward the future. The answer turned out to be overwhelmingly affirmative. In effect, in as many fields as I could verify where new conquests had been achieved, or where there had been notice of a movement of expansion and improvement, I also verified the presence of a future-oriented perspective: all the way from accounting and architecture to music; from navigation to the warring arts and to the incipient bibliography of culinary recipes; from optics to anatomy and agriculture; and everything coming about through literature, the visual arts, philosophy, jurisprudence.

In 1972, in *Estado moderno y mentalidad social* — of which I had already published a preliminary draft in 1960, in the *Cahiers d'histoire mondiale* — I proposed to try to base the formation of this new political structure that was the modern state, and the correlative changes of a social and economic character that were bound up with it, on this consciousness of privileging assessments oriented toward the present and toward the immediate future.[2] And shortly afterward, in 1973, in the *Mélanges Braudel*, I published a synthesis of the consciousness of expansion that served as the basis for this vision in advance of history, which in many diverse aspects agreed with the forward movement of the epoch.

Of course, in saying "expansionist" — a word that some easily carry to its extremes — I do not mean to refer to anything but an accumulation of changes that are very far from being irreversible and that, in principle, suppose nothing more than the opening up of new, more or less realizable possibilities, deriving from a greater territorial extension, from an expansion of demographics or technology, in terms of the economy or distribution of the internal population. All of this is not sufficient to constitute necessarily an alteration of the basic social structure, nor of the institutional network on which it is based, nor, less still, of the mental fabric that covers it. It is not a radical change unless this current of changes persists for a long period, in which case the structures and even the mentality forms themselves can turn out to be affected, to a greater or lesser extent. But even in such cases one does not escape the framework of traditional society, although it is precisely those most closely linked to this society's interests — those who enjoy its privileges and advantages — who fear, from the moment those changes become present, that everything is beginning to be undermined; that the order will collapse if they do not proceed to shore up its resistance.

And it cannot be denied that, along with every movement of expansion, conservative elements always remain to a very great extent; furthermore, the greater part of those elements setting the new situation into movement are conservative, holdovers from the past, and they are broken only when their elasticity is taken to the extreme, giving way to new forms that, even themselves, do not fail to bear embedded traces or fragments of the past. And this is possible because, as has been shown by ethnologists and sociologists, even in cases of small and backwater groups, traditional society is not purely and simply static, immobilist; in it there occurs a greater or lesser index of dynamism, of change and mobility, all the greater, of course, the more it has already been shaken by preceding changes, and the more some of these have come to be of such intensity that they have made it possible for the power resources of one group to spread to others, which would mean the end of traditional society. But even so, whether controlled or not, some elements that are preserved from the past always remain, thanks to the movements of reproduction and restoration which seem inseparable from any society and which, without fail, can continue to occur.

I have included the preceding observations in order to promote a better understanding of my discussion of the expansion movement that stimulates our early modernity[3] in its first moments, initially in the second half of the fifteenth century, and then in the sixteenth century up to its last decades, when it was overshadowed by crisis – in a panorama that continued to be plagued by hunger, unemployment, misery, adverse sanitary conditions, protests and revolts, punishments, fear.

In a very current *mise au point*, J. Heers writes about the state of the economy at the end of the Middle Ages: "The [economic] growth of Castile is the great event at the end of the Middle Ages."[4] If we take into account that Valencia reaches its peak at the time, that it is the beginning of what with respect to Barcelona Vicéns Vives has called the "redreç," and if we do not forget other aspects such as the work of cultivating the Guadalquivir valley and sowing the muddy lands of the Murcian orchard, we can understand that, without going beyond the dimensions of a society that still has a traditional structure, peninsular growth, as I have said, generalizes an expansive image. Perhaps at this moment the dynamism of Castile, or better said, the dynamism within the scope of the Crown of Castile, stands out as greater. Claude Carrière informs us that the presence of Castilian "boats" in Barcelona's port reached great proportions – they paid the largest volume of landing rights – securing on the whole (above all as a consequence of the war between Barcelona and Pisa) the trade of the Western Mediterranean, Andalusia, and the Atlantic ports.[5] In another one of his works, Heers presents a surprising fact: already at the end of the fourteenth century – thus a long time before the arrival of the first important American shipments – the major portion of African gold entering the port of Genoa originated from the Iberian peninsula, from Seville, principally, and then from Malaga and Alicante.[6]

J. H. Elliott, a historian who knows early Spanish modernity very well and who carefully considers the extent of his affirmations, had no doubts about calling the society of the Catholic Kings an early example of an "open society."[7] And a French historian, Joseph Pérez, has come to speak about "poles of growth" in the Castile of the end of the fifteenth century and the first half of the sixteenth, whose localization is situated along the axes of Burgos-Bilbao and of Valladolid-Salamanca-Segovia-Toledo-Seville.[8] Pérez has also maintained that the most visible consequences of the American conquest—such as the flow of precious metals—are frequently exaggerated and that one tends to view this fact as the ultimate reason for such an extraordinary sixteenth-century economic boom (which we may recognize, although it was somewhat fleeting), forgetting that the Discovery itself required a concentration of resources and, therefore, a favorable conjuncture of circumstances. This thesis ends up being corroborated by F. Mauro, according to whom "it is not the metal from Mexico or Peru that provoked the economic impetus of the sixteenth century; on the contrary, this impetus is what brought about the accompanying discovery and exploitation of these metals"—although, afterward, the growth would not have reached its heights without them.[9]

With his customary rhetoric, P. Chaunu—whose extensive information and knowledge of the theme cannot be denied—has presented the question in this way: it is not that the happenstance of Columbus's arrival in Spain provoked the Discovery but that this arrival was produced by the historical reasons of the moment—it was "un hazard logique"; he would have arrived in Portugal fifty years too late, in France or England a century too soon, but he arrived in the Iberian peninsula at the opportune moment.[10]

R. Carande, J. Vicéns Vives, and N. Salomon are other important historians who have made critical contributions to the renovation of the Spanish sixteenth century; their assessments are implicitly similar to those mentioned above. The first, in explaining the state of Seville's opulent and vitalized development, makes it clear that decades later Seville was a great focal point of Baroque culture, because the Baroque—contrary to V. Tapié's unsupportable thesis—needs, in my opinion, an urban support of such magnitude.[11] The second, in pointing out the increase—perhaps in its moment greater than any other—of the Castilian luxury trade, reveals to us the presence of one of the factors that set loose the social tensions traversing the underside of this culture type.[12] The third, in insisting on changes in the nature of the ownership of land—from being a foundation of prestige and rank to being exploited for profit—brings us nearer to the stratum of structural changes, because such a fact had to affect the groups entering into contact in the relations of production.[13]

One historian, holding primarily to a demographic perspective and from there focusing on economic history, has arrived at some conclusions that are of interest. Jordi Nadal, paying closer attention to the first half of the sixteenth century, thinks that "during the government of Caesar, the Castilian economy would take a vigorous step forward, thanks to the double impulse of an increase in circulating currency, indispensable for the multiplication of commercial transactions, and an increase in the opening of new markets, which also served as a multiplying force. Cultivations were extended and new manufactures were created with a view to supplying the recently discovered Indies and the Spains that were more populated than before. The abundance of money, stemming from transoceanic shipments, allowed for clearing new lands and setting up the necessary industries to offer an adequate response to the demands of a growing consumption. The expansion was very visible in the rural sectors (confirmed today by the curve of agricultural prices, until 1575 always higher than industrial prices). But in the manufacturing sector, the first half of the sixteenth century also appears to be a stage of distinct economic development."[14]

With respect to the economic history of agriculture and of manufacture production, Gonzalo Anes writes: "In the sixteenth century, Castilian agriculture and manufactures experienced a notable development. The profits obtained in the Indies trade, in the letting of Royal Bonds, in military provisions, in public credit transactions, permitted the accumulation of a surplus that could be invested in agriculture. The intensification of commercial relations with the Indies undoubtedly coincides with a period of prosperity. . . . The increase in every sort of demand had to favor the development of agriculture and manufactures."[15]

Demographic expansion—that is, a rather elevated index of demographic growth—had to accompany these transformations, at the same time serving as their impetus; it is maintained until approximately 1560, as Carande confirms;[16] a few years later it comes to a halt and remains steady until 1580, and everything leads one to think that from this latter date it begins to decline (in general terms the process is accepted by Nadal). We may observe that in the *Relaciones de los pueblos de España* we still, with relative frequency, find impressions (concerning 1575–78) that conditions favorable to population increase continue to exist. On the whole, this also depends on the type of people we come across: bureaucrats, educated people, people in government had a pessimistic tone; these were urban people who could have a more extensive and better-informed view. On the other hand, those responses drawn from people in circles of a smaller nucleus were more optimistic, although it still has to be added that pessimism was greatest among people in the smallest and poorest villages. Some cities or towns, at their height for specific reasons—for example, because they were "passenger" towns or towns with heavy traffic—should be set aside as exceptions. But what is certain is that a great deal of population displacement occurred, generally going from the rural locales in the direction of urban centers. This is important to point out here because, as we will soon see, this process of urbanization is a conditioning factor in the formation of the Baroque.

But, when we think about the demographic expansion up to the last decades of the sixteenth century, it seems that H. Kamen is right when, referring in general to this epoch in Europe, he writes: "a period of rising population such as this one was one of adaptation and change, and more outstandingly one of expansion in every branch of human activity."[17] There is no doubt that this demographic direction of expansion overflowed into other lines of growth and fomented the expansive movement in other respects, at the same time that the whole of expansion indirectly favored demographic growth. In my opinion, the ebbing wave of population expansion was the most visible among those factors coming together to provoke the crisis and to impress the minds with a consciousness of it. Undoubtedly this rapid diminution in the volume of inhabitants was due only in a small degree to the expulsion of the Moriscos (as Hamilton already noted and as is understood from H. Lapeyre's studies); nor was the emigration to America a decisive factor. While there is no doubt that these and other factors (war and, above all, plagues—as has been confirmed by the studies of Domínguez Ortiz and Bennassar) must be taken into account, perhaps the difficulties of family life were the most serious cause (the decline of marriages and of births can be observed in the investigations of J. Nadal). This is why Baroque politicians cry out against the pernicious governmental measures that allow the reduction in birthrate to take place. And the political writers addressing economic and even military themes call for a policy that might facilitate relations and prove favorable to a higher rate of procreation. Thus, after repeating, along with so many others who preceded him, that "what your Majesty stands most in need of is people," Alvarez Ossorio writes: "man is the most fruit-bearing tree that the world has."[18] This serves as one of the bases for the Baroque policy that seeks to keep the population firmly in their places.

First, one has to take into account a *geographic expansion* that would allow a place for the population excess which was helped along by increments in agricultural yields. There is an intrapeninsular emigration that, instead of moving from south to north, as it does later, now occurs from the north to the south, without counting the less remote displacements (so observable in the *Relaciones de los pueblos*) within the same central zone. These *Relaciones* frequently speak of people who marry and establish themselves in other localities—in the wife's village—or who feel themselves attracted to change in order to find a way of fulfilling their aspirations and of earning a better daily wage. These demographic transferences are corroborated by effects on far-removed European areas—on Italy, Central Europe, Flanders, etc.—by distant voyages to Guinea, and so on. And, above all, in Spain something occurs which is never again to be repeated: the discovery, followed by settlement and colonization, of the New World. Two commentaries from the epoch give an account of the consideration in which this was held: on the one hand, Luis Vives comments that the planet has been made explicit to men; on the other hand, López de Gómara gleans the notion that the feat of one solitary ship, the *Victoria*, destroying the ignorance of wise Antiquity, permitted the whole planet to be embraced.

Technical expansion is very closely linked to the demographic expansion and has multiple manifestations: such as the application of the compass to altitude navigation; the introduction of the light Nordic caravel that originally made possible the voyage to America; the generalized use of firearms that will so profoundly alter military assessments of classes and individuals; artillery, fortification, the techniques of watchtowers, fortresses, and strongholds; printing, although in relatively modest terms; the improvement of domestic lighting which will change habits of reading and make it more widespread.

Economic expansion also plays a role: there is a considerable increase in the supply of foodstuffs, clothing, luxury objects, housing, and household goods; and rise in demand, which sparks in the rich a zeal for better managing the growth and utilization of riches and for acquring costly goods—not only those goods produced in the country or in neighboring lands, but those brought from distant places as well. Regarding the first item (supply), I have at some point cited, along with other data, the dazzling repertory of merchandise being offered in a market such as the one at Tendilla, which is noted in the corresponding report included in the *Relaciones de los pueblos*. Regarding the second item, I have at another point brought up passages from Alfonso de la Torre's *Visión deleitable de la filosofía*, an amazing attestation to the uncontainable passion to possess and take pleasure in new things. The connection of the two currents—supply and demand, which rarely fail to go together—brings about what we could call a market expansion, of which the already cited case of Tendilla would be an example, and of which, moreover, many other very curious attestations can be found in the pages of writers on economic questions, such as Cristóbal de Villalón and Fray Tomás Mercado, besides others I have cited elsewhere. The theme of the greater utilization of money is a powerful factor in the growth I am referring to, and although some tend to reduce this aspect, two things should be taken into account. The first is to measure its newness by making a comparison with the preceding state of affairs, without failing to notice that letters of exchange, credit, etc., are also money (in the sixteenth century, the use of credit seems widespread, and even more so in Castile. The other thing is to notice how frequently it can be said that in literary works (for example, in *La Celestina*, *La Lozana Andaluza*, the *Quixote*, *Guzmán de Alfarache*, *Pícara Justina*, etc.) the assessment of goods—which their characters in their reciprocal relations obtain in kind (a chain, a dress, a jewel, a house, etc.)—is made immediately and habitually in terms of money, proof that its use as an instrument of exchange has entered the mental fabric.[19] Castile and the majority of the other parts of the peninsula (Barcelona, Valencia, Seville, etc., and others in a lesser capacity, but of no less interest: Alicante, Santander, Bilbao, etc.) develop this expansion preferentially with a mercantile character. And this has social consequences, among others, that from our point of view are of particular interest. The Catholic Kings' documents of an international character, which are published by Antonio de la Torre and by Luis Suárez, reveal that there was interest in the merchants' affairs abroad and help us understand the social significance that the rich businessmen came to have, despite the preservation of the juridical estate order. Such is expressed by many, ranging from Cristóbal de Villalón to Tomás Mercado; even Cervantes attests to it. In the lines of one of his *comedias*, *El Mercader Amante*, Gaspar de Aguilar writes that although this merchant may be "poor of lineage," he has the merit of "descending only from himself," which is what makes him "so respected and loved" by the people.[20] In the Baroque period this is the platform upon which the rich stand to launch themselves on the course of achieving more.

Since the fifteenth century in Europe, those becoming rich through trade tended to invest in land in order to collect a higher income, just as did those who received tithes (Heers). Although Braudel already affirmed it, it was not in reference to the Spanish case but, within a broader radius, to all of Europe, and even more so during the crisis in the making at the end of the sixteenth and during the seventeenth centuries. When Braudel speaks about the "trahison de la bourgeoisie," he is referring to all of Europe and, in a very direct way, to Tuscany. The path leading to noble status was sought because social prestige in itself had its economic yield—it was the gateway to the rich. Land endured the crisis better, and those who accumulated grain for the purpose of renting, tithes, seigniorial rights, etc., ended up increasing their revenues. Braudel observes this phenomenon in Italy, in the ambit of Toscan merchants, in the very circle of the Medicis of subsequent generations. Yet, it is much more extensive and probably of a much greater force than in the Hispanic peninsula. It is important for us to point this out and indicate its range and proportions because it will be the basis of the apparently feudalizing reestablishment of the nobles' privileges and power in the Baroque; it is advantageous to mention the broad continental radius of this phenomenon so as not to make errors concerning the supposedly specific characteristics of the epoch in Spain. I want to call attention to the impropriety of the error that is incomprehensibly reiterated: the error of attributing the ruin of commerce in Spain, which is tied to the country's economic decline, to a presumed characteristic of Spanish society—the tendency toward ennoblement, which would have drawn the rich and powerful away from commercial activity, since the two conditions are incompatible. In no land in Europe does this tendency occur with as much or more zeal than in Spain; this tendency does not in a single instance derive from characteristics peculiar to a group but from economic motivations, which are on the whole common to the seventeenth century, although in some countries they produced consequences that were more serious or of longer duration. And this is the way in which this disturbing situation occurred in Spain, along the lines of those countries surrounding it. But it must be observed that the Baroque epoch is one in which the merchants achieve their greatest prestige and the highest social levels, and in which the rulers become more concerned about their states. What so harshly reduced the possibilities of commerce was a particular situation—primarily overwhelming inflation and diminution of manual labor. It was Olivares, the Baroque ruler par excellence, who, following the notions of other writers and rulers (a Gondomar, a Hurtado de Alcocer, etc.), already noticed in 1624 that one had to rule by "putting forth an effort to turn the Spanish into merchants"; in a 1629 report, in indicating the three calamities that the country was suffering, he pointed to the judicial disorder, the alteration in the currency, and the fact that "business and commerce are totally altered, vice-ridden and almost consumed and reduced to their ultimate ruin"; in 1637 he thought that everything would work better "if we vassals of your Majesty were more merchant-oriented and if one were not reduced to dishonor upon being one." Let us add that in order to overcome the final obstacle, which in fact it was only in part, Olivares had the idea of revamping an old project from the time of Alfonso XI: of creating something similar to the *Orden de la Banda*, a variety of Order based on merit and privilege, which would end up introducing a kind of mercantile nobility.[21] Let us keep in mind that Baroque literature—the novel and the *comedia*—frequently offer us examples of persons who, on the basis of their wealth, the international knowledge provided by their business concerns, and the prestige acquired with them, lead a life in the manner of the nobility.

Expansion of labor. Although it has been known since A. Smith that the growth of the market provokes the division of labor, we are now faced with a division into professions: it is not a matter of several workers contributing to the production of an object, carrying out partial and different operations in the process of obtaining it, but a matter of the artisans and incipient manufacture workers carrying out all the operations of a commodity's production process. However, those who work on one type of commodity are more and more differentiated from those who work on another. In relation to this phenomenon, one finds that in the mid-sixteenth century there is a great demand for workers of different professions, and there is in general a greater necessity for manual labor. In the 1551 Cortes de Madrid, it is said to be "better to fall short of day laborers than daily wages" (petition 120); Juan de Robles and Luis Ortiz pose the question of increasing manual labor by improving the worker's situation; Huarte de San Juan deals with the problem of increasing worker yield by improving worker quality through a more adequate professional adaptation; Sorapán de Rieros, Miguel Sabuco, etc., are concerned with maintaining, through sanitary measures, the conditions of the state and the health of the worker. At bottom, it is a very different end, if one observes attentively, from that pursued by Herrera, Giginta, and Martínez de Mata, whose reflections, as the seventeenth century advances from Pedro de Valencia (1604) to Sancho de Moncada (1619) to Alvarez Ossorio (1686), will be seriously applied to the problem of unemployment, of "forced leisure."

We still must point out one aspect with its own characteristics: *expansion in education.* From Alfonso de Palencia, already in the fifteenth century so critical about the state of affairs of Castile; to Pedro Simón Abril, who anticipates in more than one instance, in the last quarter of the sixteenth century, the questions and theses of the enlightened century; to Calvete de Estrella, who relies on observations made about middle-class Flemish citizens – all hold that education, specifically the learning of mathematics, can be considered an efficacious means to acquire property (*hacienda*). Bartolomé de Solórzano believes that with the knowledge of accounting, businessmen can dedicate themselves to making advantageous deals for the good of the republic and the "great increase of their properties."[22] Pedro Luis Torregrosa, who writes one of the approbations of Solórzano's book, says that its teachings are useful not only to merchants but to "whoever may want to know the accounts of their estates and property with greater clarity and certainty" – therefore to the same people.

The 1548 Cortes of Valladolid recognize that the schools are of great benefit to "the children of common and poor people"; those of Madrid (1548) request a lower regulated price for primers used in schools because the children of workers and poor people destroy them, and they turn out to be a costly expense for the parents. The Cortes and the Councils are concerned about salaries received by teachers, about the (perhaps excessive) number of students admitted, and about effecting the acceptance of poor children in gratuitous openings. All this demonstrates that the education and teaching of elementary notions of sciences and letters spread and occupy more space than in the previous epochs – without, of course, reaching sufficient, satisfactory levels. Palmireno complains that some of those involved in mechanical occupations "neglect their children" with respect to the instruction they should give them. But all this is proof that the wave of expansion has reached these layers of society. And to this will be linked the problematic aspects often condemned by the privileged; given the general zeal toward self-gain (*medro*), which in the Baroque serves as an impetus for individuals of different social strata, one can recognize that the factor of teaching frequently plays a role.

Richard L. Kagan, in applying to Castile the formula that L. Stone had referred to England, makes Stone's formula his own; like Stone, Kagan speaks of an "education revolution," of which he finds an interesting model in Castillian society – it is not a renovation of methods (or it is in only a small part), nor in subject matter, nor in institutions, although without a doubt there are also small changes to point out in such aspects.[23] Rather, it is a matter of a revolution in social role: studies are converted into a channel of great importance for the processes of minority socialization, as much for the selection of those to be distinguished from the general public, as for the formation and selection of professional groups as elites.

This problem of minorities is one of the great problems brought on by social changes at the end of the sixteenth century. Experts appear, and in many and differing branches their preparation is of interest. As I have mentioned else-where,[24] the nobles now leave their estate position to become a *power elite* whose individual members demonstrate a consciousness of belonging to a group endowed with internal cohesion. Yet let us not forget that to ascend socially is the objective of the individual who is carried away with a zeal that in the epoch is called the zeal for "self-gain." For such an individual, study – or in this case, the fiction of study – is a very convenient channel (thus, for example, the frequent appearance of this theme in the world of the picaresque novel).

In sum, all these factors of expansion awaken a strong stimulus in terms of social *aspirations*: this is the decisive point I wanted to reach. At the end of the sixteenth century, these aspirations spark off their attempt to convert themselves into a more combative position, that is to say, into *revindications*, taking place on the basis of so many interindividual and group confrontations, with all the tensions, conflicts, and struggles that are swept along with such revindications. For the time being, I am going to focus on, among other things, the possibility of change which very energetically serves as an impetus for the epoch's phenomenon par excellence: *social mobility*.

This phenomenon, which is dealt with so extensively today, is at the center of the process of changes, although not to the same extent as in the dynamic society of our time, but with an incomparably greater frequency than was offered by the traditional society of the Middle Ages; such a process is found in all the Western European countries on the path leading to modernity. From the perspective of those changes accompanying the formation of the modern world, social mobility, in its diverse manifestations, is going to be marked as one of the most relevant phenomena. And, of course, as one of the most influential in the sociological and historical domain.

I have mentioned its diverse modalities, and I will now discuss three of them (instead of the two mentioned above, whose differentiation is owed to Dahrendorf): *horizontal mobility*, whether territorial or change of position; from it I will separate *professional mobility*, or change of occupations; and obviously I will maintain, distinct from the previous two, *ascendent vertical mobility*, or change of rank.[25] The first – horizontal mobility – is discovered at the base of all the others, and perhaps the Middle Ages, which so tenaciously tried to discredit it, recognized that to hinder it was an efficacious means to close the door to the others. Elsewhere I examine this question and give multiple examples of a social conception of human existence that is completely opposed to renovating displacements, whether in terms of a geographical basis or in modes of living.[26] I do not want to fail to make reference to an attestation that – because of its being ahead of its time and because of the author's significance in other fields – I consider particularly significant. In *Momus; O Del Principe*, a great figure of the Italian Renaissance, Leone Battista Alberti maintains that those who seek to change their places do not possess social worth or value.[27] Thus the fact is that, since the end of the fourteenth century, vagabonds seek to find sustenance through their wanderings. Their throngs increase, spreading their aimless bands throughout Europe in an attempt to find remedies to their begging (the latter movement reaches such proportions as to go well beyond the period of the Thirty Years' War). One must also take into account the attraction to wandering and to changing place that propels the poor, marginalized individual. B. Geremek, who has studied this matter on various occasions, notes the frequency of the anomaly that I have pointed out: to the mobility that I have called professional is juxtaposed the so-called horizontal or territorial mobility. So those abandoning the work they have had until then, or that they have inherited by virtue of family conditions and origins, also tend to leave their place of origin when they launch out in search of another professional occupation. They are given to going from one town or village to another or to a more populous urban center. They usually seek to establish themselves in the capital, although they frequently end up as vagabonds. At least the opinion of the epoch accuses them of this (perhaps to avoid—if they are successful in their displacements—the fomenting of this tendency and the generalization of this longing to achieve more than what one has, which boils down to an increase in salary, in recompense, or in any other type of income for their work). And doubtless it sometimes happened that leaving the position occupied in the beginning could be the means of finding, somewhere else, another position that was longed for, although generally it could lead—and this was the customary destination—to remaining at the margin of society, alone, without means and on the path to crime.[28] From the end of the Middle Ages, vagabondage is seen as a crime and those who engage in this sort of life are not viewed as recommendable subjects. Since the end of the Middle Ages, the vagabond was legally condemned in the cities of Castile, England, and France. That is way L. B. Alberti notes that whoever is tied to nothing is esteemed by no one. Having nothing to lose, it matters little if one leaves one's family occupation to assume another. Yet this should never be undertaken by the resident of a city who counts on the esteem of relatives and fellow citizens, for by so doing that person would incur a loss of worth or esteem.

I cite this last resounding opinion both because it is Alberti's and because of what it signifies: it permits us to evaluate the strong negative reaction—against the practice of vagabondage, on the one hand, and the change of occupation, on the other—that is contemplated by those people integrated into the social regime of the Baroque. There occurs a change in the concept of "worker," who frequently made the decision to abandon family and occupation; from being an element of the family, a worker becomes converted into an outside, foreign element. Remuneration in money, no less than other types of remuneration that are accounted for in monetary terms, leads from the old system of defraying personal expenses (lodging, food, clothing) through incorporation into the family, to a new system fostered by the development of the spirit of calculation, of the frequent use of money, and by an increase in supply: receiving a salary facilitates change of a professional nature for it provides workers with greater flexibility in managing their own pleasures and time. This, however, also changes the character of the relation of work: it provokes a loosening of social bonds (*desvinculación*) and brings with it feeling of opposing interest. But such characteristics appear not only in salaried workers but in all those who are displaced.

One cannot fail to mention the feeling of cosmopolitanism that, in the centuries here under consideration, will be maintained by the humanists and that on the whole will be inherited by the clear exponents of a Baroque mentality. With his own spirit still in the first phase, a humanist like Juan de Mal-Lara will glean and, with full approval, comment on the adage "To the virtuous man, as his country are foreign lands."[29] But this challenge to medieval immobility, which is founded in virtue, will be transformed: the dangerous vagabond, the one who has habitually veered onto the path toward delinquency, and the deceiving picaro who has both a virtuous and delinquent role are the best-known protagonists, both of deamabulatory or horizontal mobility as well as of — implicitly — the mobility in occupations. And the negative assessments that are being generalized about these "dissolute" — in the etymological sense — persons, endure into the seventeenth century. As H. Kamen observes, "what seems to have concerned people most was the *mobility* of the poor, the rising tide of beggary and vagrancy, which threatened to make poverty spill out of its old restricted channels and flood over so as to threaten the security of the upper classes."[30]

Territorial or horizontal mobility readily generates confusion, discord, and disturbance. It is thus that the opinion of the epoch views it, upon the arrival of the years profuse in rebellions and protests. In 1617 Cristóbal Suárez de Figueroa comments that in Europe no order is respected: thus, "from this is born the perturbation of minds, the revolts of the wills. A similar excuse can be put forth by those who, leaving their center, attempt to transfer themselves to another."[31] And Suárez de Figueroa groups this with the phenomenon of those who stop being what they were, striving to dedicate themselves to something else.

But professional mobility may present even greater dangers. The aspiration to achieve more — to earn more, to be worth more, to climb the social ladder (the third and final form of mobility) — becomes even more forceful. In terms of the drawbacks it offered, this took on a serious aspect in Spain: the abandonment of tilling the fields. Its economic conditions are so unfavorable that many flee agriculture (1506 Cortes), and the major source of the Kingdom's riches remains without worker support. Certainly rural exodus is not always agrarian exodus, but perhaps more often than not this is the case. In Avila, we are told, "many of the laborers leave their plowing and become teamsters" — that is, traveling salesmen.[32] If all mobility is socially dangerous, professional mobility, or change of occupation, is particularly so: it brings about disorder in the distribution of population or of resources, and the confusion that it introduces threatens to damage the hierarchical power structure.

Ordinarily one thinks about this only in terms of a remedy that will be repeated by many in the seventeenth century; in the eighteenth century it will frequently be enunciated as the great restoration measure. In 1610 Cristóbal Pérez de Herrera proposed such a remedy when he recommended that professional occupations remain bound to the family: "guide many toward following the occupations of their fathers." When the Royal Council to Philip III and the Council and Reformation Board to Philip IV proposed measures that would force the poor to return to their places of origin, they expected that, once back in their places, the workers would return to their former professional occupations; thus these recommendations—brought up first to one and then to the other sovereign—added that not only would the poor see themselves compelled to abandon the court and the big cities, but also the rich and the nobles, because the former depended on the latter if they were to recover their previously abandoned occupations and the means to support themselves. In this way the big urban centers would be emptied of people who are so "free," restless, and dangerous.[33]

As in every epoch, the sixteenth century may have its resistances to change, and one may encounter, even in the language characterizing it, maxims and proverbs that invite one not to move, not to depart from the social pocket that everyone has assigned; nevertheless, there is a widely recognized opinion that positively esteems the greater or lesser prowess of whoever manages to climb a few steps up the social pyramid. This century, of a much more open character than the one that follows, registers a great many references praising individuals who successfully manage to raise themselves to high social levels. Let us recall words like those of Cristóbal de Villalón: "Everyone, even though no more than a day laborer of the basest sort, has the presumption of advancing beyond others by becoming a noble through business affairs."[34] An estate society does not stop needing *homini novi*, who in select positions take the place of those who have disappeared.[35] In the internal amplification of its European and American undertakings, sixteenth-century peninsular society experienced an abundant need of new personnel to cover bureaucratic, military, ecclesiastical, judicial, and financing services. The consequence was that the sixteenth century called on new people to cover these positions and had to open the door to them. "Church, sea, and royal house" were words—ordinarily very poorly understood when used in this way—that meant: studies, maritime trade, state administrative service; that is, the three great branches standing in need of renovation and augmentation in its cadre of personnel. In them, then, vertical mobility, or mobility of ascension, proved to be more attainable.

This was not a characteristic limited to Spanish society, although here it reached great proportions, owing to the immense territorial and, correlatively, bureaucratic unfolding of the monarchy. It has also been applied to England, since L. Stone coined the phrase "inflation of honors" as an expression of the most common aspiration of the eighteenth-century English. In England, then; in France also, where R. Mousnier, Y. Durand, and Labatut pointed out similar attitudes; in Italy, where Braudel himself observed that in Lombardy the Spanish authorities had to take measures to limit the disorder inherent in these ambitions; and in Naples, where R. Villari studied the relations between the old "baronnaggio" and those recently gaining ascendency. Besides what has already been mentioned, L. Stone, alluding to the social background that has been the object of his study, also insisted that this disjointed aspiration toward elevation, which engendered situations of upheaval and conflict, affected the established social order of the privileged.[36] In Spain, its disordered manifestation was frequently used in the picaresque novel as a means to paint the "mundo al revés," or world upside-down (or to have the reader imagine it in this way), in works like *La Pícara Justina, Teresa de Manzanares, El donado hablador, Vida de don Gregorio Guadaña, El Buscón*; moralists and satirists—Zabaleta, F. Santos, Fernández de Ribera, Liñan y Verdugo, Quevedo—insist on the theme. Years ago, when the study of literature did not focus on these questions, K. Vossler, with unique insight, wrote a commentary on Lope de Vega in which—without applying such terms—he came to recognize the play of aspirations, mobility, and inconsistency in status: "What is irregular and inconstant about his conduct in life arises in great part from the contradictory and doubtful nature of his social position, which, in reality, was not such a position, and many things that one tends to attribute to the disquiet of his temperament and to explain psychologically are, in truth, of a sociological origin or are sociologically conditioned."[37]

A witty writer of the time, Vélez de Guevara, has his astonished character contemplate the world's interiorities; and the devil who accompanies his character comments on the jumbled spectacle unfolding before his eyes: in the "human caldron" of the court, "one can see men and women boiling, some upward and others downward and others crosswise,"[38] which implies confusion, disorder, pain, and shameful ugliness, a view produced by the agitating movement that pressures people to upset their ordered positions.

We have, then—and its seems worthwhile to dwell on it—come upon a deep and serious crisis that is caused by uncontainable aspirations prompted by historical growth and by the empowering of the individual; and these aspirations provoke a deterioration of the established system, inasmuch as this system has been viewed as impotent before the forces of change which are consolidated against it. There is no doubt that something like this did take place and that such crises are what makes the course of events march forward. But it also seems certain—and this is recognizable in all the Western countries—that if, in fact, the contemporary consciousness of such occurrences viewed them in this respect, undoubtedly this view further aggravated the consequences that came to be feared. Everywhere society bore the brunt of innumerable turbulences; but perhaps somewhere it found itself threatened—and not remotely—with a rapid overthrow of its order. Of course, there occurred with a relative frequency cases in which striving to be more, to bring about self-gain (in proportions beyond what was accepted), drew one into illicit, criminal, or semi-criminal conduct, and by means of this situation it could be seen that the inconsistency of *status* engendered social instability. Thus I believe that societies that had this experience, and in which Baroque culture was being developed, denounced a process taking place at the very center of what is here in question. That is the way those societies were seen in their own time.

I must proceed a few steps further to gather the data necessary for posing the problem. The structural, conjunctive conditions of the fifteenth and beginning of the sixteenth centuries promote a process of expansion, which, in turn, promotes social mobility. This mobility brings about a consequence that is both direct and aggressive: Weberian "practical rationalism," that is, individualism. In this way, I am designating—allow me to insist on it—the attitude of the human being who, breaking with the tradition transmitted by society, refuses to be subjected to the position in society that has been predetermined and strives to escape it, naturally so as to achieve a situation with better conditions, but risking the possibility—which so easily takes place—that, in being carried to failure, such an individual becomes humiliated and ejected from the group. In my book *El mundo social de la Celestina* (1964), I dedicated a key chapter to challenges of this nature, specifically those against their lot in the network of social relations; those individuals are dominated by feelings of personal gain as well as by agression toward others. In a subsequent book, *Estado moderno y mentalidad social* (1972), I included a long chapter about what I did not hesitate to call "individualism," connected to the formative process of a protonational feeling. Omitting some other brief references, I should mention that this type of question constitutes the key of my *Cultura del Barroco* (1975). Since then, I have become even more firmly convinced that the question must be posed in this way, drawing further support from the fact that L. Stone uses the same word—I have already drawn attention to it above—to designate a series of similar phenomena.[39] I previously cited a series of sixteenth- and seventeenth-century works that, because of their more forceful depiction of the phenomenon of mobility, permit us to descry at bottom the question of individualism; here we can add a few more: M. Alemán's *Guzmán de Alfarache,* Juan Martí's apocryphal *Guzmán,* B. Gracián's *Criticón,* and so on.

The seeds of this presumed threat, by individualist forces against the socially and hierarchically established order, came from the past: they flower in the fifteenth, develop in the sixteenth, and veer off toward an eroding action in the seventeenth century. Here we can utilize two well-known categories from the German social philosophy of some years ago—and I have the impression they are now reappearing: 'community' and 'society.' The crisis of individualism that I am trying to evoke would be intelligible as a step away from a system inspired by the first (community) toward another system inspired by the second (society) – without lacking traces of each of the two in both moments; furthermore, a social order never historically ends without seeking and empowering new community bonds. Tönnies wrote that in the state of society, "everyone is for oneself only and in a state of tension vis-à-vis everyone else."[40] I believe that with these words Tönnies gives us the blueprint for the social state of affairs in the way that seventeenth-century men, especially those participating in privileged estates, presumed to find it confronting them when they began to elaborate – or order the elaboration of – a formula for an urgent remedy, which was the cultural response of the Baroque. I believe that P. N. Dunn's affirmation turns out to be doubtful in all respects: "the profound social changes of the sixteenth and seventeenth centuries were brought about by an alteration in the conduct of those individuals who constituted it." [41] Nevertheless, in the reflections of moralists, politicians, those who write on economic themes, and even novelists, we can discover clear references to the state of society – -most readily to one facet of society, the family – which indicate that it is not only licit but necessary to deal with the disturbing alterations taking place within daily life; and within the whole of daily life, which is the result and ferment of such alterations, are generated the movements of transformation which are so often repeated and so extensive in the Baroque century, the same century when the copper coin is minted. In each instance individualism definitely signifies a social phenomenon.

This individualism is reflected in the "solitude" manifest in human social existence – but let us not forget that it is always "solitude" in the midst of "competition"; attestations to that solitude are abundantly contained in the French, English, and Spanish literatures, where the multiple versions of moral and social pessimism, which are so well-known in the epoch, find themselves so coldly repeated. At one point I brought out that Gracián's *El Criticón*, a work attesting to a consciousness of a "plotting" individualism, of solitude and aggressive pessimism, was published in 1651, the same year as Hobbe's *Leviathon*, a work that is very similar to it. The rupture of traditional ties – inasmuch as a new invigorated society would establish others – places the individual in a state of "loosened social bonds," as much local as familial, professional, political, ecclesiastical, and even religious; even in Madrid, despite the heavy burden of inquisition persecution, there is talk of atheism. [42] This was a gesture of revolt, of dissolution of the family and abandonment of the monarchical order, whose legitimacy was considered to be essential to the country. This is corroborated by the frenzied words of the Carmelite friar Jerónimo de Gracián, denouncing the evils of the epoch.[43] Revolts and rebellions are born from this feeling of dissolving social bonds, and literature, properly speaking already Baroque, is produced for its effectiveness in repressing such revolts – Alamos de Barrientos, Valle de la

Cerda, and so on. The problem—stated with the same words Porshnev used with respect to the situation in France—is the one brought about in "the loosening of the ideological restraints that held the masses in obedience to the regime."[44] The response to this, tending to resecure the collapsing order, defines the formation of Baroque culture in these countries I have just cited.

Expansion, mobility, in its three spheres, a *loosening of bonds,* and *individualism* constitute a chain of phenomena at the end of which appears the link of *freedom,* a word that in the sixteenth century is charged with echoes of positive valorization, which is preserved in part and for some in the seventeenth century, although in the latter what one notices most is mistrust, fear, even condemnation of it. Naturally this political and social "freedom" has nothing to do with the recommended stoic attitude of freeing oneself from the realm of the passions, nor with the theological notion of the "liberum arbitrium." These two acceptations frequently either go against civil or political freedom or in no way help to strengthen it. Civil, social, or, perhaps better said, political freedom—we should take care not to confuse it with democratic freedom—is the capacity to say *no* to what has been established, to the order. It rejects regulation, subordination with respect to juridical, political, literary, and religious norms, these last two inasmuch as they are social conventions alongside other possible ones.

Since this negation—"not to obey," "not to serve" (which have antecedent evangelical condemnations)—supposes a declared irreverence, and inasmuch as every attitude of this type seeks to shield itself from the attack that consists in attributing unjust modes of conduct to the superiors who would have to be obeyed, it is fitting to ask, What is the extent of this negation? Whom does it reach? It extends to all the upper levels, lords, ecclesiastics, even those occupying the throne. I am not saying that it was exactly like this, since I have previously observed—as others have done with respect to different countries—that the results of mobility did not upset the order, or that it could not have upset it as much as those integrated in the system thought and feared. But what is certain is that the consciousness of the rulers felt itself confronted with a besieging of the rich, the powerful, lords, ministers, king, and God. It is on these grounds that the upper groups proposed to take measures of subjection and insistently appealed to the King to make him see that those striving to climb higher—whether they succeeded or not—were enemies of the monarchy and of the privileged society that necessarily served as its support.

In the summer of 1627, King Philip IV suffered a grave illness; after his recovery, the Conde-Duque of Olivares presented him with an interesting document for his own information: his *"Memorial* to the King, motivated by what took place during his illness." And in it Olivares would have the monarch know: "What was hidden from no one was that never has there been seen the freedom with which was seen and heard speak in discredit and vituperation of the Royal Person, of Your Majesty's habits and privacies, by the general and the individual

of the people and of those who stand above them; that on that occasion the pla-
zas, the streets, the confessionals, and the recesses of the Palace saw and heard,
and may God grant that it may not have also been heard in the antechambers";
only the devil can in such a way have "discredited Your Majesty's government
and made his vassals discontent with his Royal Person, leading them to understand falsely that Your Majesty oppressed them with taxes that are to blame for
the exorbitant prices."[45] A similar attestation is found in the *Crónica* of a person
who also moved in the vicinity of the throne, Matías de Novoa; in commenting
adversely on the measures that turned out to be oppressive for the people, he
writes: "None of these innovations came from the machinations of the King's
favorites, but from the hand of the King himself, and not a one offering relief
or encouragement to the people."[46]

There are frequent accusations, in the most dispassionate and reflective cri-
tiques, against the rulers (all the way from the king to the ministers, although
more directly against the latter): Cellorigo accuses "the neglect of those who
rule" and sees in it the origin of "misfortunes, and the door through which all
injury and evil enter."[47] In Caxa de Leruela, one can see that the ruin of this
peasant population—which, forgetting their attachment to place, forms a great
contingent of those bereft of social bonds—is imputed to the powerful.[48] Viñas
Mey put together an interesting anthology of texts (besides the last one cited,
there are texts from F. Santos, Fernández Navarrete, Pérez del Barrio, etc.),
other than the ones I am including here, in which those of the upper levels are
repeatedly blamed for the evils suffered by the lowly populations.[49]

One could make a long list of persons whom we could today classify as
intellectuals, who reportedly criticized the powers that be and unleashed the rulers' wrath; persons who were persecuted by powerful ministers of the Inquisition, and as a consequence their works came to be confiscated, censored, or pro-
hibited; who were even subject to incarceration, in some cases for an extended
time; who had to escape to foreign countries where neither the civil nor
ecclesiastical jurisdiction of the Spanish monarchy could reach; who remained
in prison until their death or until the eve of their death; who lost their lives or
disappeared without a trace. Eugenio de Narbona, Sancho de Moncada, Alamos
de Barrientos, Mártir Rizo, Juan de Zabaleta, Quevedo, Villamediana, Adam
de la Parra, Antonio López de Vega, Andrés de Almansa y Mendoza, etc., figure among those who suffered one or another of such fates. And there was probably no case in which their criticism, the harsh denouncing of bad
government—which is what they were accused of—failed to extend to the
highest level. I have shown this in cases like Quevedo, Almansa, López de Vega
(and other scholars have given us equivalent information about other cases).[50]
Let us recall, because of its profound interest, López de Vega's passage against
"the sovereignty in which now power, now adulation adorn Kings and which free
republics also arrogate to themselves; not being content to subject the bodies of

their subjects, they extend sovereignty in order to subordinate their subjects' minds as well, and to persuade us that we should obey and serve not only with our limbs but even more with our reason, giving to all decisions the same credence as to divine ones, and often in contradiction with the latter and with the natural law on which they are based."[51] There are cases in which the campaign of persecution against a person close to the king seems to issue from the two above-mentioned groups, and whether they are allied or simply coinciding, they are in either case together in their threatening attitude. One example is the violent campaign against friar Luis de Aliaga (the confessor to Philip III, but whom Philip IV also kept at his side), who was accused—in public writings and in denunciations to the king—of corruption and all sorts of unjust actions.[52] And the "intellectuals" were not alone; the popular mass, more or less copious, accompanied them. In the presence of such cases, there emerged a very strong fear that these writers or ideologues might influence those masses or perhaps even some high person and that, given the occasion, some high noble might put himself at the head of the crowd.[53] Porshnev cites a very interesting document, a letter from Richelieu to a superintendent of finances, warning him that if the Royal Council continues with its pressure politics, "some disturbances similar to those in Spain will surely take place in France"[54]—in this passage the plural *those*, in reference to the upheavals in Spain, is revealing. Domínguez Ortiz studied the alterations and conspiracies in Andalusia; R. Exquerra, in Aragon; J. H. Elliott, in Catalonia; in the concluding essay of my *La oposición política bajo los Austrias*, I brought together a considerable number of references to similar difficulties.

I believe that it is a matter of a general phenomenon in the West, although in Spain it was especially serious. From 1580, approximately, in view of the numbers that these subversive movements reach—following, of course, previous movements of the sixteenth century (A. Fletcher and J. H. Elliott have drawn our attention to this), and whatever may be the nature of the same movements (according to the classification that Forster and Greene have made in their edited volume that consists of essays by various authors)[55]—one thing cannot be doubted, which counts as relevant for my posing of the problem: in all the European countries during the first years of the seventeenth century, the rulers, the individuals of the ruling classes, and the privileged feared that they had gone too far in their tolerance of mobility (ascendant, obviously). For this reason, at the same time that protests are made about the royal concessions of titles, nobility (*hidalguías*), or of equivalent honors, it is thought that those with the ambition of moving up the social ladder, away from those who are down below, must be contained so as to keep the established order from tottering toward its end. In this sense, similar attestations could be obtained from every other country of Western Europe. I will again make reference to the complaints of the French nobility gathered at Troyes (1649-50). And I will once again refer to L.

Stone: "By the early seventeenth century things had gone too far, and the Early Stuarts began anxiously trying to shore up the tottering edifice."[56] The solution, which was everywhere sought with such serious concern, came to be, at bottom, the same: a strengthening of the seigniorial interests and a sublimation of past nobiliary ideals, which are no different in the Western monarchies, at least in the greater part of the picture that is painted of them. In France, Préclin and Tapié observed these ideals years ago.[57] And more recently an Anglo-Saxon investigator confirmed this, relating it to the society that gave rise to Racine's theater.[58]

Also in relation to France, C. Vivanti (commenting on Liublinskaia's *French Absolutism*) maintained that, contrary to the often repeated thesis of the ascendant and progressive character of the bourgeoisie as bourgeoisie, thus affirming its presumed class consciousness, one must recognize "the inclusion of that social group into the nobility (or at least its renunciation of all ethical and political values that would have been able to mark its opposition) and the full acceptance of the process of refeudalization."[59] (We will come across this last term again, but first let us emphasize that a similar phenomenon, so comparable to what we have seen in Spain, has nothing that would restrict it specifically to Spain, and, in the second place, that it is an occurrence—the fact that this striving to ascend changes the State—which derives from the social situation conditioning formation of the Baroque.)

In this way a politics of closure was propagated, which in Spain displayed a very particular seriousness and which contributed to the sclerosis of the social system of estate hierarchies and made more difficult the individuals' step from the lower to the higher levels, a step that always constitutes a renewing and revitalizing necessity for a society, but one which accentuates the internal tension between ossified groups. If, following the revolution theory of V. Pareto, we think about this generally being the consequence of an "obstruction in the elites' circulation,"[60] we can accept that the phenomenon indicated in the Baroque's conflicting situation serves us well in explaining the violence between the social groups of different positions in the seventeenth century's hardened social structure. And we comprehend that behind this complex historical "situation" is the process of "social crisis," which conditions the innovations observed in the modes of life of those peoples under consideration here.

Ordinarily, the historians who, in the course of several years, have been participating in the open discussion in the British journal *Past and Present* have tended to present a general panorama of crisis, which extends approximately throughout the century, although it is most pronounced around the middle of the century. This is the way it was done by Hobsbawm, who initiated the theme with his 1954 article, and also by Trevor-Roper, who renewed it some years later;[61] the same line was followed by others who intervened in the discussion in other journals.[62] Liublinskaia was perhaps the first to reject such a generalized thesis, substituting a discontinuous line of intermittent periods whose dates did not coincide from one country to another. She referred above all to France and England, and her book revealed that she was unaware of the characteristics of the situation in Spain, despite the role it played in the crisis of the Baroque epoch.[63] Felipe Ruiz Martín, who agrees with this thesis of geographic and chronological discontinuity, indicated that a period of reestablishment occurred in Segovia between 1626 and 1630.[64] And G. Anes discussed the thesis of this century's agrarian depression in Castile.[65]

But here it is of interest to introduce the central element of Liublinskaia's argument because it brings out the socio-historical circumstances that support the interpretation of the Baroque that I have been advocating for many years: "The exodus of the rural populations to the cities increased the number of consumers of food products and in the same sense had an effect on the existence of standing armies. Similar phenomena, or rather, the increase in the urban population and the existence of large armies, would have generally been impossible if agriculture had come to a complete standstill and if the yields of agricultural production had continued to be stable. In the demographic sphere, one must take into account not only the quantitative changes but also the qualitative ones."[66] As I have said, Anes also recently revised the above-mentioned thesis of a general economic crisis in the seventeenth century. By means of the fluctuation of prices, principally, as well as by means of partial data on supplies and other data on the payment of tithes and sales taxes, he observed that there must not have been such an agrarian crisis in Castile for long periods, for only this would explain why the demographically growing cities could be fed; except for brief incidental periods (a bad harvest, for example), there was no agrarian depression in Castile during the seventeenth century — sometimes in certain areas there were changes from one cereal to another, for example, from wheat to rye, but there must not have been a reduction in the production of wool and meat. At the same time, one must take into account the increase in the production of wine and olive oil.

In recalling these views that in fundamental respects support my interpretation of the Baroque, I must, on the other hand, emphasize that although the difficulties or upheavals of an *economic crisis* are generally found at the base of a *social crisis*, one should not be confused with the other. The social crisis is broader, comprehends aspects at play in the mental elaboration of the world at large, and, inasmuch as it consequently affects the social mentality of an epoch, is generally much slower in the rhythm of its evolution; and its effects that alter the images and things with which a human group constructs and develops its existence are much more persistent and general. Therefore, when the difference between the two concepts is viewed in this way, one must not refer the Baroque directly and principally to the repercussions of an economic crisis, but to the repercussions of a social crisis that is superposed on the former and that continues overlapping the intermittent periods of economic crisis. While these periods translated into figures of scarcity, they were also dramas of insecurity, whose anxiety-ridden impact took place in the consciousnesses, with feelings of anxiety and fear which persisted so long that they combined with subsequent stages of new economic calamities, joining in the continuous fabric of a social crisis. Thus, without taking into account the possible intermittent improvements, there were engendered the upheavals that entailed waves of violence against goods and persons, the threatening deterioration of the modes of relation between groups and of the bonds between individuals, a strengthening of estate structures (as M. Weber saw), and a reflourishing of magical and mythical beliefs. Consequently, what had perhaps begun as an economic crisis, mentally welding its intermittences, continued in a longer and generally more deeply disturbing social crisis. A social crisis could turn out – as always – to be of a longer duration, with its consequences being more difficult to extirpate than those of an economic crisis, and much more difficult, of course, than those of a political crisis.[67]

In an article in which he comments on the economic crisis that has been of so much concern and even surprise in the past decade, R. L. Heilbroner shows that an economic crisis of relatively slight consequences nonetheless produces upheavals making for the evocation of "aspects of collapse, revolution, of the end of the world," and that even when a new phase is reached in which signs of recuperation begin to occur, there remains in people the suspicion, which is difficult to do away with, that the most serious problems are yet to be solved, that there are underlying difficulties which will again surface to provoke a relapse into depression or will for a long time delay the way out of it, and that one must continue to face factors escaping one's control. Everything is in a persisting state of insecurity which forebodes "changes of a seismic magnitude, changes modifying the system's own institutional pillars"; the trustworthiness of the moral order totters, and the regimen of relation and dependency between individuals, their insertion in the social system, begins to show fissures.[68] Does not all this depict a social crisis, which affects a historical situation much more than do economic alterations? Let us recall that in the seventeenth century it was written more than once that "the structure of the globe is about to collapse."

In sum, a social crisis manifests itself as a permutation of the elements integrating society, as a shifting of individuals in terms of their indicated places. It is effectively a matter of a shifting with respect to the systems that were previously in force, in the internal distribution and ordering of the social whole. A social crisis is something that affects stratification and is deemed to be a disorder, a confusion, inasmuch as it appears as a turbulence that threatens – or is judged to threaten – the schema of internal distribution of the society in which one lives. And, in effect, when one arrives at this level, it means that values, prestige, ranks, authority, and wealth are displaced. It is understood that the coetaneous consciousness of these phenomena contemplates them and probably deems them of a greater magnitude and gravity, much greater in fact than they could have had. If in the seventeenth century it was a matter of hardening and strengthening the means serving to hold up the monarchico-seigniorial order, and, on the other hand, if bitter manifestations of nonconformity with this order take place (manifestations going from the anti-ecclesiastical and political satire to marauding and riots, from lampoons, leaflets, chapbooks, public conversations of protest, to insubordination, revolt, subversion, revolution), we can well derive such reactions from this broad crisis situation, if this persisting "residual feeling of crisis" means that the economic calamities—accompanied on this occasion by military disasters, political failures, a feeling of "decadence," according to the term that Olivares and the king (the former speaking about the decline of the monarchy) begin to use between 1630 and 1636[69]—become mentally established. Barrionuevo, in his *Avisos* (1656), begins discussing the bad situation of businessmen in Andalusia, and, extrapolating this experience to people who had nothing to do with mercantile activities, he writes "the various peoples (*los pueblos y la gente*) see each other with such distress that they walk through the streets as though crazed and under a spell, glaring at each other."[70] There is propagated a critical state of being that has no understanding of what is happening, of how long difficulties will last, of what other blows one must suffer, or of how and to what extent they can be borne.

In this way, one can comprehend the moral state that leads to hate and animosity between people and that becomes accentuated in the Baroque century, an epoch manifesting a very striking lack of solidarity between individuals. It is undoubtedly a result of hunger, for when hunger reigns, egoism curtails the practice of charity (thus the famous Baroque saint and protector of the poor, San Juan de Dios, goes through the streets in Granada asking not for the needy but proclaiming this invitation: "Who wants to do something good for oneself?"; it is a consequence of social neglect, of this consciousness of solitude that Quevedo denounces as having been provoked in the poor; the plague's fierce grip plays its part, and, as a result, the hate between the affluent and the destitute is intensified, since sickness rages more cruelly in the latter; and thus occurs the hate between the "states" or estates, which the 1618 Cortes de Madrid makes mention of in a phrase resembling those found in Saavedra Fajardo and others. It would be inappropriate to speak about a "class struggle," except with E. P. Thompson's expression, witty but nonetheless significant: "classless class struggle." I prefer to speak about "social struggle," which in these first moments of modern society occurs as a struggle of individuals against individuals.

Earlier I mentioned that a social crisis leads to the awakening of magical, extrarational beliefs. Sancho de Moncada, in 1619, in denouncing the ill state and dangers of the monarchy, informs that "some based their fear on the fact that they seemed to have been receiving warnings: from the bell of Velilla and from a recently sighted comet," although the author, "leaving these things aside," follows his rational, critical reflection on the crisis.[71] After referring to serious monetary upheavals, Barrionuevo — although he is writing years later (1654), the intermittent improvements have not eliminated the psychological state — comments on the general situation: "Everything is a confusion, people beating their heads against the wall, without knowing what to do nor being able to make anything come out right," in a spiritual state conducive to belief in extravagances, portents, marvels, miracles, and so on.[72]

The "revolving" consequences of such experiences, considered as seriously dangerous for the continuity of order, promote the diffusion of the image, so often repeated in the seventeenth century, of the "mundo al revés," of the "common style of the world, which proceeds upside down [al revés] in everything," writes Suárez de Figueroa. To confront this threatening situation of upheaval, society segregates the culture that gives birth to the Baroque, which comes about through the tensions and conflicting movements of a new epoch in which some are striving to elaborate an ideology to confront the threatening forces, and others are attempting to make use of the possibilities that are offered, taking advantage of them from their nonconformist position.

R. Mousnier cited a passage from a work of a French author, Robert Mentet's *Histoire des troubles de la Grande Bretagne* (Paris, 1649), which could be held as unequivocal evidence of this state of consciousness which I have been discussing: "I don't want to say a word about the morals of our century. I can really only assure you that it isn't one of the best, being a time of violence and hardship. . . . It is eternally famous for the great and strange revolutions that have taken place. . . . Revolts have been frequent, both in the East and West."[73] Thus is it explained that in the epoch, as I have at one point indicated, an entire literature effective in repression would be developed in the service of the integrated groups. Among its cultivators would be the Tacitists (whom some of the conservatives accuse of being people who, instead, are writing to teach the possible means of insurrection to those who are revolting). Among those who take this stance are, of course, Valle de la Cerda, Vicente Mut, Luis Mur, and so on. Luis Mur writes to bring into view the dimensions of the evil of revolt: "those who are seditious transgress against one who is worthy of higher respect and against the State, upsetting its traquillity and unhinging the axes of its firmness."[74] I also have an attestation that is indicative of many more: in a report against Martínez de Mata and his followers, Martín de Ulloa, a "twenty-four" of Seville, gives us the measure of fear vis-à-vis sedition and of the violence with which one responds to it; after denouncing these men as constituting a tumultuous threat, he adds with singular harshness: Sedition "is a word that when I hear it pronounced in public by someone who is imprudent, although it may be in passing or dealing with events under another sign, I would like to pull out his tongue or string him up."[75] Undoubtedly this irate and brutal supporter of repression was one of his Catholic majesty's subjects who is described in various anonymous letters (published as an appendix to Barrionuevo's *Avisos*); in the one from April 1660, it is said that the good vassals who desire the happiness of their prince belong to the line of "untainted Spaniards, his true vassals."[76]

P. N. Skrine (who, focusing primarily on the English perspective, allows us, with his interpretation, to complete our panorama) arrives at results similar to those I have been putting forth; he emphasizes the social disquiet and political instability that he considers to be underlying Baroque society, exemplifying its expression in two literary works: Wondel's *Lucifer* (1654) and Milton's *Paradise Lost* (1667); the Baroque individual, because of the same feeling of insecurity, gives rebellion some terrifyingly cosmic proportions.[77]

Certain terms—'conservation', 'restoration', 'reestablishment', 'remedy', 'redemption', etc.—appear with great frequency even in the titles of works of economic and political literature or in key passages of their representative works. This fact is easily verified and is loaded with significance in relation to what I have been advancing, for the appearance of these terms expresses the works' relation to the state of the monarchy or kingdom or of the republic insofar as it is a political community. And everywhere, in Spain and in the rest of the states, the solution was always the same: to return society to its previous situation, in which it was submitted to the iron fetters of subordination and obedience. As C. G. Dubois says, Baroque society understood itself as an invulnerable "société d'obéissance,"[78] and, with respect to the political writers of the Richelieu years, Thuau says that they propagated a true "religion de l'obéissance."[79]

I have spoken before about upheavals since the Middle Ages, and today there are many who have written about popular movements during this period. Nevertheless, in the Baroque epoch current opinion was not yet taking the problem into account: in the 1469 Cortes de Ocaña, it is said that the lowly people, the poor, the workers, are not to be feared "because they don't know how to complain nor is it their place to do so." Moreover, the poor are unaware of the use of arms in knightly combat. On the other hand, from the end of the fifteenth century, the situation is different, and the popular armed revolt, although its method may be very irregular, is converted into a well-known phenomenon almost everywhere. Before the turn of the century, warnings about the rebels launching attacks against the powerful in the towns and even in the countryside become more generalized, and it comes to be the primary political problem. Let us recall the revolts in the Valencian, Castilian, and Flemish towns. From then on, royal justice is not an activity dealing with particular cases: it does not have the function of a *iudex*; it is the sovereign, supreme agency of a broadly collective action that has for its object domination and punishment; under this agency's cover, the force of its means is employed in imposing obedience and applying severe repression. Around it, the supporters of and experts in political repression—to whom I have alluded—form an ideological trench. The Carmelite friar Jerónimo de Gracián must be counted among the first to follow along this line and to follow it with the greatest rigor; he never tires of repeating that disobedience and revolt are appropriate to atheists who profess it in all areas, breaking all ties and saying "non serviam" (Jeremiah 20): "to pursue my freedom" is their declaration of insubordination, which in the first place manifests itself against temporal as well as ecclesiastical principles, giving rise to a state of revolt that can begin against the pope but that ends against the kings, princes, and lords. In pushing so vehemently for repression, J. Gracián is in a certain way the founder of the unfortunate idea of the alliance between the throne and the altar, which he presents in both of its faces. Valle de la Cerda is a technical adviser on how to squash revolts and proposes an agency of supreme sovereignty which might be granted the free right to punish the rebellious or seditious with the efficacious and rapid action of arms, omitting all the possible guarantees of a legal procedure.[80] Vicente Mut identifies sedition with evildoing: "evildoers are fomenters of discord because they think in this way they can secure their situation and make themselves feared." And it even comes to be asserted, for example, by Enríquez Gómez (in the sphere of the picaresque novel, but projecting it in general) that "in punishing the many who are evil it is necessary for some who are good to enter into danger, for many times the innocent arm stops the crime committed by the head." A poet in favor of authority (as is customary), Gabriel Bocángel, writes: "punishing was always the reason of State."[81]

We should not forget to mention that there are undoubtedly those who address the powers that be—the power endowed with an insuperable repressive force—with criteria of benignity. Many—ranging from Sancho de Moncada, to Quevedo, to Mártir Rizo, to Saavedra Fajardo, to Alvarez Ossorio[82]—recommend that the prince exercise moderation, limitation, and that he fail to recognize any limits to his clemency. And others, within the politics of submission that is preached by Baroque policy, advise the townspeoples to be compliant and subordinate (given the predominant character of those who propagate such a doctrine, the verb *preach* is not improper). Calderón, coinciding with the general sense of Baroque *comedia*, gives us a clear example: according to him, "to offer obedience" is one of the principal virtues—socially the most worthy of esteem—and, therefore, his virtuous character, representing the man who reaches a state of grace and salvation, is one who, although he agrees to make use of thought, has to be "bridling it, rein and bit,/ with obedience . . . "[83]

We can focus on the Conde-Duque of Olivares as a typical representative of this policy that, in my opinion, characterizes Baroque mentality. In a letter to the Infante don Fernando, Olivares explains that "we Spanish are very good under pressure of rigorous obedience, but in reaching a consensus we are the worst of all." And with regard to a similar conviction, Olivares puts into play a very significant notion: the creation of a repressive agency that would maintain stability in the application of authority (*mando*). In a report to the king about possible revolts, in which he puts forth the appearance of trying to preserve positive assessments of the Spanish state of mind, Olivares leads the king to observe the inconvenience of being absent from the kingdom, which can arouse disobedience. Before the Council of State, the Conde-Duque denounces the lack of obedience on all levels: he warns that "today's lack of obedience, lukewarmness of devotion, and excess of self-interest among the grandees, the lords, and all the rest have the service of his Majesty in such a state that if it is not remedied with great care and attention, everything will founder," and therefore to reestablish obedience is for the minister a key point. "It is necessary to revive the severity" that was maintained during the epoch of the Catholic kings. In such circumstances the king "should have himself feared and obeyed by his vassals."[84] And Matías de Novoa recounts that an "Obedience Board" has been created to take charge of the ways in which obedience will be severely reintroduced.

Criticism against the government is severely persecuted, at times with extreme cruelty. It is certain that the repressive action of the public agencies seldom results in violent deaths by strangulation or other methods, but some cases are known in which such methods are applied to persons previously imprisoned for having spoken badly of the government. Let us recall the words cited from Gabriel Bocángel, a poet inflamed with punitive ardor. And Olivares, in the so-called *Gran Memorial* that he addressed to the king in 1624, makes a tremendous and revealing observation which clarifies for us the new tint taken on by the theme of subordination: "the people, lord, occupy third place, inferior because the individuals of this status are inferior, although one can and must consider the greatest power not only with respect to other strengths (*brazos*) but also comparing it alone to the others together. . . . It is infinitely advisable to keep them under the vigilance of justice, teaching with punishment and *terrifying them* so that they stop short of excess, a means that works on them better that any other, and produces effects which they so readily heed."[85] Already retired from his ruling functions, the Conde-Duque meditates on the question: "When the subjects revolt they have to be oppressed and not given time to arm themselves." There are passages in which one can abserve the authorities' great fear of subversion at this moment (and it might be said in passing that some of the lines I have just gleaned serve in themselves to answer the objections raised against my having attributed a mass character to the culture of the epoch). Thus the culture of the Baroque presented an extremely repressive character, having a bearing on the very broad layers of rural and urban population; only a very small component of the powerful, who were exempt or fiscally and judicially immune, remained apart from those layers and free from the crushing weight of vigilance and punishment, which were as much royal as seigniorial; but though they kept themselves integrated in the system, even they could escape only in relative terms. This position has been verified by investigators concerned with the cases of other monarchies. For example, once again with respect to France, Porshnev: "The first and foremost objective of the seventeenth-century French Absolutism was, then, that of preventing and asphyxiating popular rebellions,"[86] an aspect already underscored by H. Hauser, who has affirmed the preservation of the traditional characteristics of French society under Richelieu, the strengthening of its seigniorial organization, and the imposed subjection of the people, with the repression of their protests;[87] and with respect to England, L. Stone: "Authoritarian reaction and reinforcement of aristocratic privilege seemed to be marching hand in hand."[88]

These observations or documentary attestations that I have just gleaned clearly point out the collaboration between seigniorial and royal or state repression. Mousnier at one time objected that I was overemphasizing the repressive character of the absolute monarchy, since the number of its agents available for such an end, in all the areas of the country, was really meager. Nevertheless, I think that one must add the large number of seigniorial troops to those agents strictly dependent on the Councils or other royal agencies. Richelieu himself had personal troops, and Stone offers information about the existence of such troops in England, to defend the interests of the lords.[89] In Spain, likewise, when a rebellious uprising takes in a town (for example, in the cases that Díaz del Moral acquainted us with, in Córdoba and in Bujalance in the seventeenth century), the nobles squeeze into their armor—or the portion of armor still in use—take their offensive weapons, mount their horses, take out their troops, and go forth to confront and squash the rebelling crowd. There is no need to say that the military forces of the king are also used toward this end: Mateo López Bravo tells us that the national soldiers are to subjugate whoever revolts to whoever commands authority, and weapons are to contain "the insolence of misguided citizens, of which there is always a large number"—the second part of this sentence correlatively reveals that epoch's state of disquiet.[90] Quevedo also says something similar about the possible use of those who are unsuitable for war abroad.[91]

The appearance of the citadel and the urban placement of the barracks complete the system, with the location of these barracks being utilized to form pincers around the city which forcefully move to subdue it in case of insurrection. The *Memorial* of 1637 ("Reformation in Wartime") can be found among the Olivares documents published by Elliott and de la Peña.[92] It includes proposals regarding the means to secure the subjection and order of the capital, and a passage in this text formulates something new about population control, which gives us an idea—similar to other ideas of Pérez de Herrera, Valle de la Cerda, L. Mur, etc., which we have already seen—of the spirit bringing this theme into focus: to keep the undesirable, lazy, vagabond people from invading the court, carrying out their misdeeds, and spreading about the bad example of their disordered living, walls should be raised and fortified around the city, and groups of upstanding (*honrados*) residents should take it upon themselves to guard the doors of every neighborhood, forming a militia directed toward such an end. And they should control any person arriving from outside and inquire where he came from and where he is going, so as to pass address lists on to the authorities, even to the upper councils, in order for the people to be watched and the individual criminals, who exist at court just as everywhere else, to be known, and whoever gives them lodging should make a declaration.

But I should point out yet another aspect of the greatest importance: the agency of ecclesiastical repression in the struggle against heresy, that is, the Inquisition, becomes transformed into an instrument of political repression, extremely adequate for the purpose of dominating consciousnesses, of imposing conformity on the popular masses, and of producing effects through psychological and moral intimidation. I have already given these viewpoints in other places,[93] and now I must add that I find myself in agreement with B. Bennassar's conclusions about this subject. Like him, I think that "the political role of the Inquisition" was "a prodigious instrument of social control in the service of the monarchic State"; it was a "political police" whose dominion was extended over the territory of the peninsula as a whole, against political and internal revolt, although for the most part this control "remained guaranteed by psychological pressure, which was perhaps even more efficacious"; in this way "the narrow tie with the State apparatus, of which it will constitute an element of the greatest importance, and the occupation of space and its imprint on hearts and minds, have secured the Inquisition's fear-provoking efficacy much more than the use of torture, which was relatively infrequent and generally moderate, or recourse to capital punishment, which was out of the ordinary after 1500." This is how, in Spain, the Inquisition turned into an absolute political weapon of the monarchy, intensifying or suspending its repressive action against heretics and acting instead to repress hostile writings or other forms of opposition or threats against the monarchy, which had no religious characteristics whatsoever.[94] This is the way in which the Inquisition proceeded to make itself present in consciousnesses and establish a feeling of fear that was difficult to overcome.

Whether it be by means of the secular arm or the ecclesiastical arm, the growing necessities of physical repression give rise to a new role for the jail; instead of being merely a place to retain the prisoner temporarily, it is converted into a place of punishment, where the convicted live out their penalty — sometimes a judge never passes sentence and, like a true abduction, imprisonment is suffered clandestinely; other times it is like a torture chamber. In the French practice there exists the case of the "lettres de cachet," and in the epoch's *relaciones* one can come across in Spain cases of secret executions. There are documents about what goes on in places of monstrous treatment, a swarming penal colony, a place of forced vices, a setting of hair-raising scenes and in a hallucinatory world in general — documents like the two dealing with the jail of Seville, one by the lawyer Chaves and the other by Pedro de la Puente, the Jesuit missionary in Andalusia, which contain accounts going beyond the most horrible and macabre imagination. In my book *La Cultura del Barroco*, I give some data on the number of inmates and their mode of living in this jail of Seville—where there existed various others—and in the men's jail and in the women's jail, called *La Galera*, in Madrid.[95]

But, along with this physical repression (or basically such), there existed a form of psychological repression that, in some cases at least, is of interest. In one of his *Cartas*, Andrés de Almansa recounts that, because sacriligious acts took place in Madrid on successive days, and ultimately two such acts occurred in one day at different temples, the *comedias* were suppressed for eight days, and "there were not even any public women," that is, the brothels were closed.[96]

The theme of death, which is so frequent in seventeenth-century literature and painting, may intimate a desire to experiment on the human body, the nature of its organs, the biological phenomenon of life; but another theme comes forth just as strongly, one which is in a certain way anti-life, ascetic to an extreme: the insistence on the presence of death annuls many energies and keeps them from being employed in attempts to change a social order made up of things that are ultimately of short duration. In Spain the names of two great painters, Antonio de Pereda and J. Valdés Leal, are very well known. Apart from those paintings representing the figure of Saint Francis or of some other ascetic saint who is meditating beside a skull, the skull's presence in paintings with objects that make up "still lifes" (*"naturalezas muertas"*) generalizes in Europe the "vanitas" pictorial topos. In the exhibition on the "nature morte" genre which took place in Bourdeaux in 1978, seven painters (French, German, Flemish) figured into the catalog; laboring under this severe intention, they presented the skull figure in its fatal annunciatory function. Already some time ago the fact that Charles V attended his own funeral was cited as a macabre Hispanic influence over him. But Rousset cites as well two examples of Parisian bourgeois who, in the seventeenth century, organize and protagonize their own funerals.[97] Combined with this is the socio-historical transformation of the theme of death, studied by M. Vovelle,[98] which converts death into the experience that is felt and inexorably suffered by its personal subject. Death, pain, blood, violence, and shuddering processions of penitents or of the condemned are the object of familiar visions in the Baroque, with an undeniably traditional ascetic purpose, but also with a terrorizing intention that constantly surrounds the people with fear and contributes to diminishing the energies of their will to reform.

From the first moments of the Baroque epoch, Cristóbal Pérez de Herrera proposed to King Philip III a system of control that responds perfectly to this type of repressive, vigilant activity that reduces opposition to social impotence and which was pursued so as to keep a nonconformist and discontent populace from banding together to place authority in critical danger. Pérez de Herrera imagines an organization by virtue of which there are, in towns, villages, and neighborhoods, trustees or censors who are appointed from above and given the assignment of making inquiries and offering denunciations before those who command the inhabitants' conduct. And in saying who, toward what end, and how this universal vigilance is to be assembled, he declares that in this way "all live with suspicion and fear and with the utmost caution, for no one is assured that one's behavior and mode of living will not be found out." The author notes that, in being institutionalized, this odious intruding (perhaps the highest level of Baroque repression), which is to lead to a social existence based on suspicion, and insecurity, would have to be assigned to noblemen (*caballeros*) and other persons "of virtue, rank (*calidad*), and property," revealing to us the social system of physical and psychological domination by those individuals of the privileged estate, by those integrated into the monarchico-seigniorial complex. The entire regimen of personal and social life and of city cohabitation in the Baroque period is devised to prop them up.[99]

The abovementioned means of pacification—means that tend to paralyze, surprise, and instill fear—are not sufficient to control the dangerously restless masses. Other means are used to mold and manipulate the wills of those who must obey, keeping them, by their own will, subject to whoever commands authority. Sermons, for example, serve this purpose when those in control impose many guarded limitations upon preachers; art and literature can perform the same function (it might also be observed that literature about princes and ministers, precisely because it is made public through the press, is not being directed toward a small number of rulers but to a group of learned (*cultos*) people who have taken on the task of reading it and disseminating the image of the perfect lord—and ordinarily one assumes that the lord to be obeyed in practice is a good prince or minister, with a few exceptions, such as those offered us in some of Quevedo's works). And it must be recognized that the fiesta plays a very important role as well. Already contemporaneously it was noted that the fiesta has a narcotic or enrapturing effect. Martínez de Mata, Pascal, and La Bruyère view it in this way. "In republics an old and sure politics is to put the people to sleep with festivals, spectacles, with luxury, ostentation, pleasures, with vanity and the nobility; to have them fill up their emptiness and relish the trifling morsels."[100]

In addition, seigniorial and royal fiestas are the occasion to demonstrate, before the astonished eyes of the multitude, the great power of those who ordered the gathering and possessed the means for it: the great power they can exercise over human beings, over things, over the universe itself. The mechanical ploy—already corresponding to cultivated taste (*gusto*) and to the awestruck "suspense" that the technical inventors provoke in the seventeenth-century urban population—plays such a role: examples include the stage trick or "machine théâtrale" in dramatic representations; the dissimulated mechanism of the aquatic fiestas (that are cultivated to such an extent in the Buen Retiro); the force and brilliance of the fireworks' explosive powder. All of this provokes a pleasing awe and suspension of the mind, two psychological means that are very effective in paralyzing negative feelings toward the greatness of power and in producing a certain sensation of fear. Ordinarily there is no lack of tears in those feeling themselves moved.

But, let us also observe, in conclusion, that in these fiestas a happy and active participation of the people does not ordinarily happen. Bulls, theater, parades, and fireworks require nothing but contemplation and elude the multitude's active mass agglomeration, which could degenerate into dangerous disturbances. Instead, the fiestas produce a sensation of distance between the one who orders them and the one who performs them, on the one hand, and those, more or less withdrawn, who contemplate them; these fiestas serve to redouble the people's conviction that they would never be able to elevate themselves to the height of those capable of ordering them. Fiestas are a thing of lords, but those who are not lords are permitted to be present as spectators. They are realizations made possible by the power of the lords, the rich, the upper ranks, that is, the power of those who derive their right to dominate from the ideology of a system that affirms that domination comes to them by nature: dominating the people as they dominate water, fire, the gravitational weight of bodies, etc., that is to say, dominating the world from the heights where the divine ordering has placed them, for the purpose of maintaining the disposition of creation. This explains the opinion of the Council of State that, at its meeting in Valladolid (February 18, 1603), rejects a contrary proposal and points out the convenience of animatedly maintaining the fiestas, taking into account the political and military state of affairs — the ill state — of the monarchy.[101] In mid-century, when the polemic around the licitness of theatrical and other similar representations flares up again, the opinions of the politicians always favor keeping the fiestas in full force, in order to keep popular concerns from becoming displaced into other areas. Toward the end of the epoch (1678-79), the Royal Council's response to the authorities of Seville is significant: it refuses their petition to prohibit comedias — for reasons of "good government."[102]

In the constraining ideological configuration that the Baroque involves, which constitutes the meaning and explanation of its cultural peculiarity, laws are not sufficient, and neither is force. The rulers and the writers know it; the subjects at the more common levels at least suspect it. Hence there must be a use of other means. And a perfectly reconciled correspondence can be observed among the most significant ministers of the epoch. Richelieu and Olivares know they have to count on the peoples' adherence, which is to be achieved by infiltrating the wills of the subjects. One needs both to incline them toward and to maintain them in obedience. And — apart from forced imposition — there are two ways to do this: with the propaganda that molds minds and with the education that forms (or deforms, perhaps) the intelligences. Richelieu proposes to the king a system of academies to instruct the youth (only those individuals at an estimable social level, of course), who in turn will, through the proper channels, direct everyone else; the old university organization no longer works, and neither do the Renaissance attempts at new, special schools. In that system the precept of basic intellectual education says: "they will learn the four basic principles of arithmetic and will read history." Olivares is informed of the plan and also thinks about setting up a system of academies. For him it is an indispensable reform because otherwise the ill state of affairs, the vice-ridden mores of youth—so he tells the king—will do away with the country. In 1632 he first speaks about it in a letter to the president of Castile, and afterward, in each of the 1632 and 1636 *Memoriales* to the king, he explains his plan: the academies will include exercises of physical agility, military instruction, *belles lettres*, living languages and Latin, writing and counting and mathematical elements; travels and readings of travel accounts that give instruction about the government, customs, and notable public successes of other peoples (I believe that this includes what was called "history").[103] I have often concerned myself with the decisive value, the molding force—a "second nature"—that the Baroque politicians bestow upon education; only their idea of education varies greatly from the traditional idea. Writings ranging from the innumerable treatises about the teaching of princes and lords up to the picaresque novels arise in a world based on this idea. Let us recall the words of Olivares: "To make laws about corporal punishment is not sufficient nor advisable because one can be very wicked and not be comprehended in the penal laws for vices". Ambition, for example, is a vice, and, nonetheless, in the current state of affairs it must be used as a means for the remedy. It is curious to observe that in making us see that this "zeal for self-gain" is a remedy to raise the Spanish Monarchy up from the state of uncontained decadence it is suffering, this "*Memorial* Regarding the Upringing of Spanish Youth," published by J. H. Elliott and J. F. de la Peña, reveals to us that this desire to be more, to being about self-gain, was a psychological force in the epoch; and it helps confirm my thesis that the picaresque was nothing more than a literature inspired in the numerous cases of deviant self-gain that occurred, because it was not always possible to use normal means toward such an end. The Conde-Duque of Olivares notes this unhealthy situation in the country and tries to broaden the social layer of those who are allowed self-gain, and he even wants such groups to see themsevles encouraged in their aspirations. In this way the reins will not be lost, and there will not be a fall into the inferno of disorder, with respect to the regime of strata or estates. Education is the most general, most secure, and most efficacious remedy for such an end. This is why he intends to extend the means of education even to farm laborers, so that in this way they can follow a straight path to arrive at more "for in this way they will not wholly lose the hope of climbing."

Through the harshening of repression, on the one hand, and the use of means compelling the masses' adherence, on the other, the individuals of the Baroque thought they could find a way out of the negative phase of the crisis they were experiencing. And before the seventeenth century ended, the slope came to a turning point—with the pre-enlightenment epoch of the innovators (the "novatores"). In the following century the option for education and fiesta not only was maintained but became stronger (although it has other characteristics). But without the necessary structural changes that should have been undertaken at the same time, the positive effects of the eighteenth-century reforms remained only cosmetic.

Chapter 2
Popular Culture and Spanish Literary History
Wlad Godzich and Nicholas Spadaccini

"Popular Literature in Spain, 1500–1700" is the title of the conference that has brought the contributors to this volume together. It is a title that requires some explanation and justification. To begin with, its evident literary-historical form combines something that is still struggling for legitimate scholarly recognition—popular literature—with a geographical area and a historical period in which that object has not been very much studied, thus inviting an initial perception that the project at hand is conceived as a way of filling a possible lacuna. To that extent, the focus on popular literature would resemble the recent interest of some historians in popular culture. The paradigmatic statement in this area is provided by the distinguished Renaissance scholar Peter Burke in his "Oblique Approaches to the History of Popular Culture."[1] In this article Burke argues that the practice of history has generally followed one of two models: that of Ranke, who was preoccupied with the actions of ruling elites, or that the Burckhardt, who described the culture of that elite, that is, the attitudes and values of the elite as they are embodied in symbolic forms such as paintings and plays. The Rankian political historian followed, or reconstructed, the deeds of kings and statesmen; the Burckhardtian cultural historian, those of artists and intellectuals. In both instances, the lives, perceptions, attitudes, and values of the bulk of the population fell through the cracks of the historian's apparatus. Burke proceeds then to describe a variety of ways through which this "lost" element can be recovered.

In its desire to provide a more complete vision of the past, and in "rehabilitating" as it were the culture of "shopkeepers, craftsmen, beggars, and thieves,"

Burke's project is most laudable; yet there is about it a touching naïveté that perhaps can be maintained by the historian but which is entirely untenable to the literary scholar. It assumes that the enterprise of history itself need not be questioned, that it can go on with only some filling of lacunae, regrettable omissions to be sure, but certainly not fatal to the project. How different the project may look to the literary scholar will become readily apparent.

The past thirty years or so have demonstrated to literary scholars that they need not conceive of their activity in terms of literary history: the New Criticism in the United States, the *Werkimmanente* approach that was its counterpart in Germany, structuralism and its aftermath in France and in the United States have, for better or worse, managed to produce a sizable body of work without explicit relation to the project of literary history. Thus, unlike his historian counterpart, a literary scholar who presently would wish to return to literary history cannot simply resume where things were left and assume that project without at least inquiring into its validity. What is laudable in Burke may be laudable in literature, but that proposition needs to be demonstrated, whereas the historian must gloss it over altogether if s/he is to preserve his/her professional identity.

It may not be useless, therefore, to recall to mind some basic givens. Literary history, born of Romanticism, constitutes, together with generic studies — themselves born of the contemporaneous taxonomic impulse — the privileged mode of study of literature in the institutional settings of the universities from the latter part of the nineteenth century onward. Given our own institutional setting in the United States and its genealogy, it is exceedingly difficult for us to apprehend the fact that it is this setting and this genealogy that have constructed not only our object of study but ourselves as the subjects of that inquiry. (The resistance that projects of reexamination encounter is clearly due to the challenge they pose to our identity.) By opposition to the pre-Romantic period — a deliberately vague appellation — the verbal, in its privileged written form, is elevated by Romanticism to an autonomous object, constituting a separate sphere within the realm of culture. Literary history, from its inception, accepts this Romantic model of the "literary" boundaries of the verbal, but it reaches elsewhere for its methodological inspiration: German *Geistesgeschichte*. The latter, whose links to emergent German nationalist consciousness are too well-known to be recounted here, formulated its object of study as the national spirit, to be distinguished from that of other European nations. For literary history, this spirit manifests itself in an unbroken chain of masterpieces in verse, prose, and drama, and the latter are the proper object of the literary historian.

Literature as a separate object in the sphere of culture, and the national spirit as its internal animator, constitute thus the boundaries of literary history. While such boundaries may have some validity for the epoch — and the countries in which they were formulated — their retroactive importation into other cultures could not be accomplished without some violence. Yet this violence was inflicted in such a manner that it was not perceived, at least not as violence.

It has been increasingly recognized that a major mutation in the status of fiction writers occurred in the eighteenth century. Dependent until then, for the most part, upon the graces and financial support of the courtly nobility or, in somewhat fewer instances, upon the patronage of the Church, writers found themselves suddenly thrust in a rather novel environment: the first of the Moderns to have the product of their labors mechanically reproduced on a large scale by the printing press, they were, perhaps even more important, the first to experience a disjunction between the product of that labor and its eventual consumption. In the France and Germany of the eighteenth century, as with England a century earlier, the written work of fiction was no longer limited, in its distribution, to an audience of which the writer was a member, or indeed whose characteristics s/he knew. Unlike the situation of courtly patronage, in which the horizon of expectation, to borrow Jauss's useful characterization, was ascertained through direct, immediate, daily, and dialectical contact, the writer writing for the abstract reader who would purchase that writer's work in a city unknown to him/her was no longer as certain of the expectation s/he is supposed to either fulfill or contravene. Whereas in England there arose remarkably early a consensus on the nature of that "common reader," as it became known—a consensus that is only now beginning to be shattered—the situation in France, and especially in Germany, was quite different. The political, and seeming cultural, fragmentation could not provide the assurance of any common readership. Worse, such a common readership could only be constructed, that is, formulated, as a project for the future. In other words, the writer of fiction who, for reasons far too complex to be inquired into here, was among the earliest of the cultural workers to see the product of his/her labor achieve a certain degree of autonomy from the previously implicit mode of production, communication, and circulation of his/her activity was faced with two immediate problems: the autonomization of this production had to be recognized and then legitimized.

The emergence of the notion of 'literature' as a designator for the autonomous area of the sphere of culture was a response to the first problem. Here is not the place to recall that the term 'literature' initially applied to all that was written, and that, far from being reduced in scope during the Renaissance, the term, usually in the form of *res literaria* or *litterae humaniores* included not only all written matter, from legal and medical treatises to poetry, including scientific writing, etc., but also works of oratory, whether sacred or profane. Now the term 'literature' is used in a far more restricted way, preserving for itself some of the legitimacy of its prior usage (by not surrendering its claim to all that is previously encompassed) but constituting itself as a separate entity in the realm of culture, an entity that would seek its institutionalization in a rather different way from its previous existence: no longer defined by the material basis of its existence (writing: literature), it would henceforth depend upon its mode of consumption (the aesthetic, the realm of art). The autonomization of art is indeed the great cultural phenomenon of eighteenth-century cultural life, and one can but allude to it here. Yet it must be recognized that, for legitimation purposes, this autonomization must present itself not as a novelty, a new development, but as the recovery of an originary reality, an essence. Such will be the task of philosophical inquiry upon the aesthetic.

Yet the problem of legitimation persists, especially in the contingency of its emergence: what is this new autonomous realm of literature for, now that it is defined as the aesthetic? The artisanal writer working at court did not have this problem: he wrote occasional pieces, for holidays, celebrations, and so on. In addition, the *litterae humaniores*, the *res literaria* made a cognitive claim: they were a form of erudition, in the most positive sense of the term, an erudition of the fundamental texts of wisdom and knowledge in the culture, inherited from antiquity. They required a critical form of cognition. No such claim is made on behalf of what comes to be increasingly known as *belles-lettres*, a notion still dominated by the concept of Eloquence and the exemplary figure of the Orator,[2] and certainly even less in the case of *literature*.

It is here that the link with *Geistesgeshichte* is made. Faced with the only certitude in his/her possession, namely language, the writer will assume a responsibility and a mission vis-à-vis the collectivity that speaks that language: the nation. Yet in the case of the German Romantics this leads to a problem: the German nation is more of a project than a reality, and although the assertion that one's activity contributed to the emergence and constitution of the German nation does provide a most powerful alibi—the social legitimation that was sought—this assertion needs to be bolstered, for, on the face of it, it appears rather improbable. Literary history, or, more precisely, the history of literature as it becomes known, is the instrumentality of that legitimation.

The problem at issue could be presented as follows: if one writes for a German nation yet to be, there is a disjunction between the present of the writing and the future of the reading. Only in the future will there be a reader adequate to what is written, yet such a reader will arise only as a result of what is being written. One has no difficulty in recognizing here the structure of what anthropologists call "magic thought." But magic thought does require some evidence that it is operational, that is, some evidence of success. The latter can be sought only in the past, and, most important for our concerns, it must be so sought outside Germany. To be sure, one can claim that one's own national awareness is the direct result of a past writer's writing, but such a claim can only legitimate an individual consciousness, not a national one. What is required is an example in which a writing can be asserted to be the full *expression* (*Ausdruck*) of its people, in other words, a writing whose presentness will be total, uniting its moment of writing and its moment of reading, and thus providing a fullness of presence.

It is remarkable that the German Romantics, especially Schlegel, located this moment in Spanish literature. At first, the choice is surprising: one would have expected antiquity, preferably Greek antiquity, but a careful study of the early pronouncements in this area shows that Greece, and to a lesser extent, Rome, are unavailable since they are coopted for the purpose of arguing for a *universality* of values and experiences and not for a national base for them. We have here one of the most interesting paradoxes of literary history: the earliest histories of Spanish literature were written by non-Spaniards and as such seem to escape the nationalistic underpinnings of literary history, be they French, German, English, or eventually Italian or Russian. Yet at the same time and precisely for that reason, Spain is the alibi for the nationalistic orientation of all subsequent literary history, and not just any Spain but that which goes from the *Reyes Católicos* to the seventeenth century.

The reasons for that choice are obvious and have not been questioned. This is the period in which Spain achieves, through the completion of the *Reconquista* and the expulsion of Moors and Jews, its territorial, ethnic, and religious identity under the aegis of the first modern state, a state capable of forging a powerful modern cultural apparatus, as J. A. Maravall has shown in his extraordinary *Cultura del Barroco*,[3] at the same time that it launched itself in imperialistic ventures within and without Europe. For the German Romantics, as well as for literary historians since, the figure of Calderón in particular, especially in his auto-sacramentales, achieves examplary status here, so much so that even Walter Benjamin in his *Ursprung der deutschen Trauerspiels*[4] sees him as the last writer of the plenitude of meaning and its presence in our tradition.

Spanish literary history has inherited, though not always understood, the privileging of its own early modern times. It has especially failed to appreciate the fact that this privileging, whose consequences for the remainder of Spanish cultural development would condemn it to a representation of decline and backwardness and a deprivation of inner dynamics, was an alibi for someone else's project: the literary history of the Germans. But literary historians themselves have failed to appreciate the consequences of this decision: all literary histories would henceforth be in search of a classical moment, a moment defined not in literary terms but as the congruence of a cultural development with the emergence of the figure of the modern state. Unbeknownst to them, literary historians, blind to the determinant role played for their endeavor by the German Romantic view of the Spanish Golden Age, are fated to write a narrative that leads to the progressive emergence of a moment in which the national spirit will be seen to actualize itself in the manner in which the Spanish one is asserted to have done, and to describe subsequent developments in the rhetoric of decline, with episodes of inevitable renewal and further downfall as its major peripeteia. It should be clear, then, that the culture of Spain's early modern times constitutes a strategic point of departure for any attempt to rethink the project of literary history on a basis other than the Romantic one. Such is the violence that has been perpetrated.

To attempt this rethinking by a consideration of popular literature is immediately fraught with dangers, for the construct 'popular literature' is as much of a Romantic construct as literary history, and thus, to engage in an operation of recovery of the "genuine" popular cultural expression of this period would contribute to the reinscription of the model we have been discussing. It would, after all, but repeat the gesture of a distinction between *Naturpoesie* and *Kunstpoesie*, believed to be the product of a pure and uncorrupted people, where the first was supposed to embody the soul of the nation. It may be useful to recall in this context that, just as the *Kunstpoesie* of the Spaniards was to provide the grounding of literary history, albeit as alibi, the *Naturpoesie* of the Spaniards, located this time in the national theater and in the ballads, was collected with equal fervor by the German Romantics (Jacob Grimm, *Silva de romances viejos* [Vienna, 1815]; Diez [1818, 1821]; Depping [1817]; Pandin [1823]; Wolf [1841, 1846], and Huber [1844], leading eventually to the collections of Menéndez y Pelayo), as part of their project of validating the notion of a *pueblo poeta: das Volk dichtet*, in Grimm's phrase.[5] Nor should this be surprising: if the claim that Spain represents the perfect embodiment of a culture present to itself is to stand, that presence must be equally realized in both *Naturpoesie* and *Kunstpoesie*. Thus any attempt to "revise" our understanding of the Golden Age that would ground itself on the popular literature of the period without reexamining the mode of inscription of that sphere of culture would but confirm the prevailing model.

An examination of these Romantic texts on what is variously described as popular literature of folklore rapidly shows that the definition of their object is articulated around the following opposition: oral vs. written. Discussions in literary theory of the terms of that opposition have shown us, in recent years, that there is nothing obvious about them and that the opposition itself articulates far more than a temporal ordering within the history of culture. Yet at the purely empirical level, there is little doubt that the period we are interested in witnesses a massive development of the written, thanks mostly to the development of print technology, and that such a development must take place at the expense of the previously dominant oral.[6]

A closer examination, however, reveals a fallacy in this reasoning. The terms 'oral' and 'written' are not symmetrical, and our bias in favor of the written has led us to construct the written in ways that are quite excessive. The term 'written culture' in the opposition 'written vs. oral' refers to both the mode of production and the mode of reception of texts in that culture. We do not distinguish between the writing and the reading part, primarily because, in the age of mechanical reproductibility, to use Benjamin's phrase somewhat anticipatedly, the reception of texts is determined by their (print) status, and their production (writing) represents a limited experiential area in the culture: most people are readers, consumers, of printed texts; few are writers. Yet the terms of the opposition 'written vs. oral' would lead us to believe that, by contrast, in 'oral culture' most people were text producers, and it is precisely upon such a notion that the Romantic idea of a *pueblo poeta* rests. If that were the case, then indeed that mutation from a fully collective and participatory, cocreative culture, as it has been described in the case of the oral, to a privatized, individual consumption and passive reception in the written one would truly represent a major cultural mutation. The reality is somewhat less dramatic: the indiscriminate use of the term 'oral' occults the fact that the vast majority of the population participated in the culture as auditors—recipients and consumers—of verbal artifacts produced by relatively few. To be sure, such an auditive reception does differ significantly from a readerly one, and one should be careful not to fall here into the other extreme of collapsing the difference between the two states of culture.

What we need to consider is the coexistence of the oral and the written in a culture that is primarily auditive, where, in other words, even the written is received for the most part in an aural form. Such a culture, as Luiz Costa Lima has shown in a different context, differs from the more purely oral by no longer relying upon a shared thesaurus of formulas and motifs in the construction of its narratives or upon the collective memory for the composition of other materials; it also differs from the more purely written, that is, from the state of culture dominated by texts written for private reading consumption, but not constructing its texts around logical argumentative structures.[7] Rather, an auditive culture valorizes novelty in contrast to the attachment to the traditional found in oral culture, and it strives for emotional impact as opposed to the more deliberative mode of more purely written culture. In other words, its products will be characterized by a high level of rhetorical fabrication. Although orally delivered, such a text does not seek to establish a dialogical relation with the audience but instead to leave the audience dumbfounded: *boca abierta*. The audience does not participate, nor does it internalize the arguments: it is conquered, subjugated, carried by the persuasive flow of the rhetoric. Such a culture is a culture of persuasion, but, as Costa Lima reminds us, of persuasion without understanding (p. 16); in other words, it is a culture of seductive persuasion, given to theatricality. It lends itself eminently to manipulation.

Such a nonparticipatory (by contrast with the oral) and nondemonstrative (by contrast with the written) culture develops different styles of culture consumption. This is an area that is so little studied (the exception here is Michel de Certeau; see *Arts de faire*)[8] that only very rudimentary indications can be given. If one grants that a majority of the population receives the artifacts of such a culture in the way that they are intended, one must see this majority as being essentially manipulated (we shall see later what are some of the instrumentalities of this manipulation, such as the *literatura de cordel*). In other words, one must presuppose a certain amount of uncritical reception, a reception inattentive to the logical discontinuities of what is being propounded and unaware of the passivity enforced upon its subjects. Such a reception could, by analogy with the more recent phenomena of television advertising, be ascribed to mass culture, and we shall refer to it as mass reception.

But alongside such an uncritical reception, one has to posit the possibility of a critical one, that is, a reception by those who do sense the manipulation. However, as soon as one posits such a critical reception, one must immediately proceed to a further differentiation: a critical reception of what is perceived as manipulatory implies either agreement with, or opposition to, the ends of the manipulation. In other words, one can realize that, let us say, a speech, a sermon, or a play is relying on a structure of emotional, rhetorical, persuasion, and one can agree with the goals of that persuasion, yet by being aware of the fact that it is manipulatory persuasion, one excludes oneself from the intended audience. The constitution of a mass-oriented auditive culture permits thus, by virtue of the structure of its operation, what we shall call an elite reception, in which the receiver, perceiving the manipulation, subtracts himself/herself from it, in order to identify with the goals of the manipulators. Such a receiver need not belong to the class or group doing the manipulation, but culturally s/he seeks to join them. In such a mechanism of ideological identification lie the roots of high culture, which, in our view, should not be constructed as merely the culture of the actual manipulating elite. Almost by definition, such an elite will be quite small and its genuine internal culture quite limited. It should be observed that this mechanism of identification with the goals of the manipulators obviously lends itself to manipulation as well, a fact that should not be overly surprising, for once manipulation enters, it will extend its reach. It should also explain why so-called high culture becomes such a strong ideological vehicle as well, but one that relies on mechanisms of identification to a greater extent than the mechanisms of outright and unreflected absorption of the mass.

There is also the further structural possibility of perceiving the manipulation for oneself and refusing its goals. This is a difficult position to describe because, clearly, it is politically and ideologically the one most fraught with dangers. It is based upon the perception of the attempted subjugation and its refusal, usually in the defense of an alternative, older, cultural order, with the possibility of a strong utopian component as well. Such a process need not be fully conscious or deliberately subversive—it may be even grounded in submission to the dominant socio-political order—but it represents a step beyond passive consumption of the artifacts of mass culture. The latter are then reappropriated and recirculated in ways unanticipated by the purveyors of the mass culture. These artifacts are then blended with or combined with more archaic elements from the older strata of culture. Such a consumption, and further elaboration, we shall consider to be properly popular.

In other words, the distinction between mass, elite, and popular that we are proposing is not based on the inherent formal properties of cultural artifacts but upon patterns of reception and usage of these artifacts. This implies that the very same artifact may be subject to at least three different usages according to our differentiation, certainly a complication that most literary historians fail to envisage.

Let us now proceed to somewhat more concrete considerations for the period that interests us, and let us start with the new print technology.

The emergence of a print culture has definite consequences for the nascent notion of literature, both in terms of its societal status, with the assignment of literary properties, and in terms of its internal self-definition with the intro-duction of criteria of propriety and decorum. It must be appreciated to what extent the severance of a text from its immediate framework of communication (that is, from the framework of oral performance) imposes restrictions on the text: considerations of decorum and property arise in order to prevent certain kinds of reception and to preempt some of the dangers associated with the uncer-tainty surrounding the identity, age, gender, social status, and ideological orien-tation of the reader. In other words, they are attempts at constraining reception and, if not entirely homogenizing it, at least defining its parameters. These con-siderations also represent a form of prior self-censorship by the text producers, and they lead to discussions on the effects produced by texts, discussions that are a foreshadowing, and the birthing ground, of literary criticism and of the eventual institutionalization of literature. But before such a birth can be recorded, the consequences of the emergence of literary property must be examined.

It is known that the right to publish a given text gave rise to competition and introduced issues related to monopoly and piracy (Eisenstein, I, 120). Thus not only did printing force legal definitions of what belonged in the public domain, but it also changed the attitudes of writers to their work. While the concepts of plagiarism and copyright did not exist in the communal culture of the minstrel, the new mode of production initiated by printing instigated the institutionali-zation of those concepts. Printers, in fact, may have been largely responsible "for forcing definitions of literary property rights, for shaping new concepts of authorship, for exploiting bestsellers, for tapping new markets" (Eisenstein, I, 122).

By the early 1500s there began a veritable "communications revolution" as printers' workshops were finding their way into the major municipal centers and were contributing to the reshaping of urban culture. In Spain no fewer than twenty-nine towns had seen presses set up by 1521,[9] some of them by foreign printers—especially German—who contributed immensely to the propagation of old traditional ballads in *pliegos sueltos*.[10]

With the proliferation of printed texts, divergent traditions became more difficult to reconcile and contradictions became more visible. The result was that "the transmission of received opinion could not proceed smoothly" (Eisenstein, I, 74–75). The state's attempt at controlling this new technology was swift but only partially successful, especially during the first quarter of the sixteenth century. The first laws governing the printing and publication of books in Spain appeared as early as 1502 when the Catholic Kings prescribed a system whereby prelates were charged to prevent the printing of "cosas vanas, y sin provecho."[11] Yet in 1525 the scholar-printer Miguel Eguía hinted at the ineffectiveness of such laws and at the lack of self-discipline in the Spanish printing houses, for they were producing "vulgar and even obscene ballads, doggerel and books even more profitless than these" (Bataillon, *Erasmo* . . . , cited by Cruickshank, p. 806).

After the convening of the Council of Trent (1545–63), the Catholic Church was to be especially attuned to heterodox propaganda, so that by the mid-sixteenth century, Spain saw its first official *Index* (1559) and became the battleground of the reaction against the publication of the Bible and commentaries of it in the vernacular. Thus at the trial of Fray Bartolomé Carranza (1559–79), whose *Catechism* (1558) had incorporated no less than two thousand citations from the Bible, the Dominican theologian Fray Domingo de Soto questioned such practices on grounds that they divulged information about heresies. At the same time he went on to reject the very notion of a published Bible in the vernacular because "a work once printed becomes accessible to all people."[12] A few years later, in the "Dedication" to *De los nombres de Cristo* (1583), Fray Luís de León bemoaned the fate that had befallen the *Sacred Scriptures*, "for God—says Fray Luís—had intended the use of the scriptures for all people."[13]

The impact of the new technology of production on the acquisition of culture by different socio-economic groups was also alluded to by the Spanish humanist Thamara in a "Preface" to the *Libro de Polidoro Virgilio que tractaba de la invención y principio de todas las cosas* (Antwerp, 1550). Thamara's "Preface"—published, ironically, on the eve of what was to be the beginning of a long process of censorship of printed texts[14]—talks about

> esta nueva manera de escribir que en nuestro tiempo avemos visto y alcançado. Por la qual *un día se imprime y estampa por un solo hombre quantos apenas en* un año muchos podrían escrevir, por causa de lo cual tanta abundancia de libros ha salido y se ha derramado por todo el mundo que *ninguna obra que quiera pueda faltar a ningún hombre por más pobre que sea*.

(this new way of writing that we have seen and achieved in our time. By means of which a single person can print in a single day what many could barely transcribe in a whole year. As a result, so many books have been published and scattered throughout the world that, no matter how poor a person might be, no work is outside his reach if he desires it.) (our translation)

Literacy is seen here as a form of technological competence that is not limited to a particular class.

It is clear, therefore, that disjunctions have occurred between the new mode of production and the old modes of consumption. The traditional sense of community which entailed gatherings to receive a message was undercut by the new technology which made possible the fragmentation of directions. The reading public was now more dispersed, atomistic, and fragmented than the readers of script had been. This movement toward a heterogeneity of audiences led to a diversity of discourses which, in turn, allowed for the manipulation of culture. Ultimately the very consolidation of the modern state was bound up with this new technology (Eisenstein) and the problem of culture became increasingly a project of the state.

While the accessibility to, and the acquisition of, literary culture began to expand significantly through printed texts in the early 1500s, it is important to keep in mind that the culture of the great majority of the population in early modern Spain was oral, aural, and visual and that life was informed by a body of beliefs that was shaped to a large extent by catechism, confessions, religious feasts, and religious art, i.e., the various *retablos* and *pasos* depicting episodes of the Old and New Testaments.[15]

The interactions of learned culture and traditional oral culture were made easier by chapbooks, an early form of what Dwight Macdonald calls "mid-cult," a form that "is situated between the great and little traditions and drawing on both."[16] This fact is practically overlooked by traditional literary histories and has been all but forgotten by recent social histories of literature. Despite the fact that, on the diachronic level, a social history of literature must take into account the physical means of transmission and transform itself at some point into a social history of writing and reading, "no history of literature has as yet taken into account the means of transmission of texts, nor offered statistics, where possible, of the diffusion of works, as if the life of a work were not strongly conditioned by such extra-literary factors."[17]

One of the first Hispanists to call attention to this situation was Don Antonio Rodríguez Moñino, who in 1968 lamented the fact that virtually all histories of Spanish lyric poetry provided a chronological evolution of that genre, a neat classification by schools, a biography of the principal poets, and an assessment of the authors' interdependence.[18] His reservations about such histories rested on two grounds: for assuming that the Spanish public of the sixteenth and seventeenth centuries possessed a "horizon of information" regarding poetry that is similar to what we possess today; and for not taking into account the circulation of an important body of printed materials and manuscripts (17). To underscore the seriousness of the situation, he pointed out that between 1588 and 1621, of some forty-five major poets writing in Spain, only a dozen—most of them minor writers—had books of poetry published (19-23).

Thanks to the empirical work of A. Rodríguez Moñino, E. M. Wilson, María Cruz García de Enterría, and others,[19] we have become more fully aware that, besides isolated poems which circulated freely in manuscript form and often found their way into anthologies (*Poesías varias o Rimas de varios ingenios*), thousands of poems became available to the public through poetical chapbooks, that is, through single quarto gatherings, generally consisting of a single sheet folded twice, known in Spanish as *pliegos sueltos* (Moñino, 45; Wilson, 15; Norton/Wilson, 5). It is estimated that in the sixteenth century more than a million and one-half copies of those *pliegos* were printed and distributed in Spain (for a population of less than eight million). On the basis of these findings one might reasonably assume that, especially in the sixteenth century, at least part of the answer to the problem of transmission of literary culture lies in the chapbooks.

In the greater part of the sixteenth century, chapbooks served as digests of medieval and early Renaissance traditional culture. Those early *pliegos* contained a variety of materials besides ballad texts and were directed to a public that, while not yet differentiated into *vulgos* and *discretos* (i.e., on the basis of whether or not one could exercise judgment in terms of literary criteria), was nevertheless heterogeneous in terms of its expectations. This may explain the fact that in the early sixteenth century it was not uncommon to find within the circuit of the *pliego suelto* learned as well as popular materials. This fact is attested to by a list of some five hundred chapbooks ("obrezillas pequeñas") that Ferdinand Columbus, the son of the admiral, was supposed to have had in his library upon his death in 1539.[20] E. M. Wilson provides a useful overview of the content of the body of chapbooks published from the early 1500s until the last quarter of the sixteenth century. Those texts included

> poems, chiefly amorous, from the *Cancionero general of 1511*, religious poems by Fray Antonio Montesinos, love poems by Juan del Encina . . . , diatribes against women by Cristóbal de Castillejo, bawdy poems by Rodrigo de Reinosa, and even the . . . coplas of Jorge Manrique on his father's death. From the start poems by famous poets filtered down into these humble prints, where they occur alongside lives of criminals, burlesque testaments of asses, cocks, and foxes, narratives of cap-

tivity among the Moors such as the She-Renegade of Valladolid, survivals from the Middle Ages like Diego de San Pedro's poem of the Passion, dialogues between the body and the soul or between man and his purse, or Spanish versifications of the Creed, the Lord's Prayer, the Ave, or the Salve Regina. (Wilson, 16)

One cannot overestimate the role played by printers in the decisions to include or to exclude materials for public consumption. Thus while they were instrumental for the accessibility of poets such as Juan del Encina, Fray Antonio de Montesinos, Cristóbal de Castillejo, and Rodrigo de Reinosa, they may also have been responsible for the exclusion of "champions of the new Italian metrics: Garcilaso, Cetina or the Divine Herrera" (Wilson, 16). One can argue, of course, that the people were attuned to listening to ballads so that the *romance*, which consists of a vowel assonance in every alternate octosyllabic verse, may have "enabled the uneducated in Spain to accept the lyrics and narrative of the cultivated" (Wilson, 16). Yet the question remains as to the status of what those early *pliegos* chose not to transmit. If one were to venture an educated guess, one could come to the conclusion that for practical reasons the printers of *pliegos* were for a time in the camp of the proponents of traditional metrics, whose champion, Cristóbal de Castillejo, had fueled the controversy with his famous *Reprensión contra los poetas españoles que escriben en verso italiano.*[21] In his *Reprensión* Castillejo calls on eminent poets from the past to speak in favor of tradition. Among the latter is Jorge Manrique:

> Don Jorge dixo: No veo
> Nescesidad ni razón
> De vestir nuevo deseo
> De coplas que por *rodeo*
> Van diciendo su intención
> (our italics)

> (Don Jorge said: I see
> Neither necessity nor reason
> To cater to this new deisre
> For verses that, in a *roundabout* way,
> Express this intention.)
> (our translation)

Apparently the printers and editors of chapbooks knew their markets well and used the new technology in the service of old cultural products, which, as opposed to the "rodeos" of italianate poetry, spoke with less aesthetic pretension and therefore appealed to a wider public.[22]

Thanks to the new technology of production which changed the text-addressee relations, those materials became accessible to different publics and, for that reason, had the potential of serving two different functions: the high and the low. For unlike the situation in many tribal societies, where everyone has the same culture,[23] or the model of medieval society, where "man . . . counts socially in that he is a part of a group and as such also has the function of representing that group, of serving as its sign" (Lotman, quoted by Corti, loc. cit., 17), in early modern Europe (in our case, Spain) there was "cultural as well as social stratification. There was a minority who could read and write as well as a majority who could not, and some of the literate minority knew Latin, the language of the Learned" (Burke, ibid., 23). Thus the *pliegos* were accessible to "readers" no matter where they were located within the cultural and social spheres. All readers, literate and semi-literate, as well as illiterate listeners who were tuned into the voices of blindmen who sang and graphically advertised their poems in the streets of the cities and at fairs, were familiar with the poems' general content and story line. A case in point is a chapbook of c. 1514–19 that includes in the traditional Spanish ballad meter, the *romance*, the general plot summary of *Amadís de Gaula*. The books of *Amadís* had been published in 1508 in a version composed by Garci Rodríguez de Montalvo and had been aimed essentially at the learned, aristocratic urban gentry (*caballeros*). The printer of the chapbook — probably Juan de Burgos, Fadrique de Basilea, or Alonso de Melgar (Norton/ Wilson, 13–14) — seized upon the success and popularity of the extended prose fiction and decided to turn a quick profit by trivializing the story of Amadís's deeds while deemphasizing its high usage: the effects of those deeds on the knight errant's winning of his lady's love. The aristocratic public of the early sixteenth century could, of course, enjoy the *pliego* version, and might have been entertained by its oral performance at the hands of a lowly blindman. But a *caballero* could only identify with another text: the books of *Amadís de Gaula*; the text that brought before his eyes the fantasmagoric world of the knight errant, a world that did not acknowledge the existence of the city, i.e., the space where financial transactions took place and where the economic activities of merchants and other progressive groups were perceived as undermining the universal values with which those aristocrats sought to identify: honor, beauty, and so on.[24] The *caballero's* expectations differ considerably from those of the semi-literate readers of the chapbook and from the expectations of an illiterate audience that hears the same poem as it is narrated or recited in song.

In a culture that is no longer signlike or communal, messages become fragmented because the addressee is no longer homogeneous. A century later Cervantes focuses on the multiplicity of receptions that could be accorded printed texts. Ironically, the type of book that he chooses as the centerpiece of that discussion is the romance of chivalry, the line of prose fiction that was set in vogue in Spain by *Amadís de Gaula*. That type of literature, we are told, had so caught the fancy of a poor rural hidalgo (Alonso Quijano) that he went mad and, in his madness, assumed the identity of a knight errant (Don Quijote). Now it is precisely the purported consequences of those readings that precipitate a variety of reactions in the text. Those reactions, in turn, illustrate the degree of fragmentation that exists among the consumers of culture.

The debate over the multiplicity of receptions given to books of chivalry takes place, significantly, in a rural inn and is prompted by a learned priest's remark that the readings of those books "had turned Don Quijote's brain" (I, 32). The first to react to that statement is the innkeeper, Juan Palomeque, who defends those readings quite passionately on grounds that they had put life into him as well as into plenty of others: "For at harvest time—he says—a lot of reapers come in here in the mid-day heat. There is always one of them who can read, and he takes up one of these books. Then as many as thirty of us sit round him, and we enjoy listening so much that it saves us countless gray hairs." The innkeeper admits that he looks for a particular trait in those stories; he is especially captivated by the blows and is so immersed in the fictions of battles that—he says—"I get the fancy to strike a few [blows] myself. And I could go on listening night and day." The innkeeper's wife does not listen to those stories, yet she also finds their recital useful. The reason given is a practical one: when her husband is occupied listening to someone read them, he forgets about nagging and scolding her. A fourth commentator is a prostitute named Maritornes. She also gets pleasure listening to those readings, but her attention focuses on those "parts when some lady or other is lying in her knight's embraces." A fifth viewpoint is offered by the innkeeper's daughter in response to a query by the priest: "I listen too—she says—and, really, though I don't understand it, I do enjoy it. But I don't like the fighting that pleases my father so much. I prefer the complaints the knights make when they're away from their ladies. Sometimes they actually *make me cry*. I pity them so much."

In essense one might say that, in 1605, the subject of Cervantes's discussion of the books of chivalry is how different fictions from within the same type of story have become imprinted on the consciousness of "readers" and "listeners" who bring their expectations (personal as well as collective) to the act of reception. What emerges is that all those listeners are oblivious to the totality of the work. As opposed to the priest, they are not concerned with questions that go beyond certain aspects of plot. They do not understand that "blows," "embraces," "sighs," etc., are interdependent. Unlike the learned priest, the illiterate consumers of romances of chivalry cannot be concerned with aesthetic and moral issues; they are not preoccupied, as were the learned moralists, with questions of "truthfulness" and "responsibility." What emerges from the discussion in *Don Quijote* (I, 32) is that a largely illiterate, lower-class audience has at least partial access to books that a century earlier had been the pastime of aristocratic readers. For the occasional, lower-class consumers, listening to stories of knights errant had a practical function: to find solace from the trials of daily life.

For them, listening to stories that expressed aristocratic values was not a way of consecrating idleness; it was merely a respite from labor and toil.

In a sense one might conclude that we are faced with an example of the "sinking theory," which holds that "the culture of the lower classes (*Unterschicht*) is an out-of-date imitation of the culture of the upper classes (*Oberschicht*) (Burke, ibid., 58). One must also keep in mind, however, that popular culture is not simply a body of texts but a way of using them (See de Certeau), that is, we must understand problems of transmission and horizons of expectation.

We have taken this apparent detour from the chapbooks because, ultimately, it is the novel that establishes popular culture practice in the realm of high culture; it is the novel that incorporates the fictions of literature (high and low), the fictions of daily life, and the fictions of ideological discourses at a time when private readers become fully differentiated into *vulgos* and *discretos*. At the same time that the novel begins to take into account a multiplicity of addressees, chapbook literature begins to aim at a class reader, thus reversing the process that had characterized it throughout most of the sixteenth century when it did not take into account only a "particular class of reader but a public that was still homogeneous and undifferentiated."[25] The changing patterns in the production and consumption of chapbooks can be said to have been tied to a number of factors. Among them, one can highlight the changing conditions of the printing industry around 1600; an ever increasing resistance of the writers of the establishment to that medium; and, ultimately, the marginalization of the consumers of chapbooks by the same writers, along social and intellectual lines.

The crisis of the printing industry in Spain dates back to the late sixteenth century. It seems that as capital investment declined, and as printers came to rely more and more on jobbing to survive, they turned increasingly to the production of chapbooks. Since chapbooks could be produced inexpensively and the modest investments required could be recovered in a matter of days, printers viewed an expanded market in chapbooks as a way of overcoming their economic difficulties. In order to expand their markets, printers were forced to cater to an "increasingly less 'literary' (and less literate) public" (Cruickshank, 809). In effect, the chapbooks were to be directed to a particular class of reader.

The content of chapbooks changed substantially after 1600, when the shorter traditional ballads disappeared from circulation. In their place there appeared "learned historical ballads, derived from chronicles, collected by Lucas Rodríguez and Lorenzo Sepúlveda; . . . selections from the art-ballads of the *Romancero general* of 1600 and its sequels; isolated poems by Lope de Vega, José de Valdivielso and even verse satires of Don Francisco de Quevedo. The old plebeian pieces (the She-Renegade, the verse testament of animals, the narratives of captivity) remained popular. Jácaras, new poems in thieves' cant, had considerable vogue; some were by Quevedo, others by less talented imitators" (Wilson, 16). But despite the availability of new cultural products—especially the new-art ballads that were often marketed in the form of mini-anthologies of four- and eight-page octavo (Wilson, 16) – the new pattern of *pliego* production pointed toward a more identifiable consumer: the lower classes or the so-called *classi subalterne* (Di Stefano, 92; cf. Gramsci). While the interaction between works of high usage and those of low usage continued in some ways (we are thinking here of the *pliegos de cordel*), their content became increasingly more vulgar and less literary. That is, in the first quarter of the sixteenth century the *pliegos* showed a marked deemphasis of high usage from the earlier period.

To the proliferation of the trivial *romances de ciegos* throughout the seventeenth century (García de Enterría, 144), one can add the significant increases in accounts of events published or "relaciones de sucesos,"[26] so that the chapbook clearly became the mass-oriented vehicle that, despite its increasing lack of prestige among the intellectual establishment, was to perform an important function as a vehicle of entertainment and as a tool of political and social propaganda. While it is clear that in the early 1600s print was not the dominant form of ideological control, it is equally evident that print media were being used increasingly for manipulative purposes. Thus the subjects covered by chapbooks in the early 1600s included religious festivals, canonizations of saints, the nativity and passion of Christ, poems dedicated to the Virgin's Immaculate Conception, versified catechisms (with questions and answers and acts of contrition). There were also poems directed against marginalized groups such as Jews, Moors, Blacks, and Gypsies – the very groups that were the objects of many *Autos de Fe*, i.e., those official spectacles of institutional repression against all perceived deviations from the dominant values. Then there were pieces on *bandoleros*, whose freedom from social conventions and obligations generally landed them on the gallows. There were sensationalized accounts of urban crimes, the kind condemned by Lope de Vega in his *Memorial* (1615) to the king: "hombres que en las ciudades de España fuerçan sus hijas, matan sus madres" (men who violate their daughters and kill their mothers in the cities of Spain) (cf. "Que no se vendan coplan por las calles").[27] In addition, there were substantial numbers of chapbooks that included propaganda pieces dealing with current political events: the expulsion of the Moriscos by Philip III between 1609 and 1614: the rebellion of Catalonia (1640); the successful campaigns of the Spanish armies at various moments of the Thirty Years War. In virtually all instances the chapbooks related the official version of those events: the Moriscos are thrown out of Spain for being enemy traitors ("El Rey los echa de españa/por traydores enemigos"); the Kingdoms of Spain are loyal and united against the rebels in Catalonia, ("Echan bandos generales,/A cuyos Regios preceptos/todos los Reynos de España/leales obedecieron"); the Spanish armies are fighting mercilessly against the enemies of Spain and of Catholicism (García de Enterría, *Sociedad*, 298). And so on.

In the early 1600s print media were no less suspect that they had been in the previous century. Yet some aspects of them were incorporated into the state's plan to manipulate culture. That is, no less than the *comedia* (which used the simplicity of rural life and, with it, the songs and lyrics of the people for recuperative purposes) or the *autos-sacramentales* (which were, after all, sermons meant to dramatize on stage and at religious festivals the central teachings of the Church) or other manifestations of audio-visual culture (see Maravall, *La Cultura del Barroco*), the printed chapbooks became one more instrument in the propaganda campaign that was undertaken to consolidate the monarchic-seigneurial interests at a time when the world was deemed to be topsy-turvy and the perception of crisis and decline was commonplace among the groups in power and the intelligensia who served them.

It is significant, for example, that the official ban on the printing of novels and plays which took place on March 6, 1625, did not extend to the chapbooks. Thus, if there was an attempt to marginalize a literature that was viewed as being increasingly vulgar and banal, that attempt came at the hands of professional writers such as Lope de Vega, who, while continuing to argue for greater official control of the *pliegos* on aesthetic, social, and moral grounds, were ultimately aiming at safeguarding property rights and at maintaining powers of monopoly over the production of literary culture (see Lope de Vega, "Memorial").

Let us clarify further our notion of use in culture by looking at who is the (reading) subject of the novel. The emergence of the novel raises a number of important issues, many of which have been adequately studied. There is one issue that has not received sufficient attention, and yet it is of crucial importance to our notion of use in culture: who is the reader of the novel, or, more properly, who is the reading subject of the novel? The latter formulation should indicate that a theoretical answer must be sought before an empirical one can be searched for. It also implies that the appearance of the novel signals a mutation in the reception of texts and that a different subject must emerge. The question, then, is: who or what is this subject for the novel?

It will be recalled from the earlier discussion of the different readings that the *Amadís* receives in the episode of the *Quijote* that the reception of the *Amadís* is fragmented, representing different modes of appropriation, or different modes of using the *Amadís*. A hundred years after the publication of the original, Cervantes shows that the *Amadís* is no longer read as a totality. But one can turn the question to Cervantes's text as well: who can read it? In other words, who can read the fragmentation in such a way that it will be perceived in its fragmentary reception and yet somehow be added up, totalized. An answer to this question requires a more precise characterization of the interaction in that scene. Each of the participants (the priest, the innkeeper, his wife, the prostitute, and the daughter) not only represent a reader with a different horizon of expectation, but also a different discursive circuit. If we take the text of the original *Amadís* as discursively homogeneous, in that its diction, themes, subject matter, and allusive structure constitute a describable system of implication, the break up of that system, and the appropriation of its diverse parts into other discursive circuits, can be taken as emblematic of a larger cultural process that occurs in the period of transition from the Middle Ages to the beginnings of our modernity.

This issue can be illuminated by extending somewhat Bakhtin's pioneering work in this area. The medieval discursive system was based on the existence of relatively autonomous linguistic entities. Beside the great opposition between Latin and the vulgar tongues, various professional groups, such as the guilds, had their own discourses, the apprenticeship of which was part and parcel of initiation into the profession. Each such discourse was self-sufficient and auto-regulated. The latter feature is important because it ensured a high degree of functionality for the discourse and made it answerable only to its own functional demands. Discourses existed for interaction with other groups, and, in those instances where such was not the case, the discourses in presence negotiated from positions of equality. Their coexistence in the discursive system was not hierarchized in the sense that it did not involve passage through a mediator. In somewhat parallel fashion, though at a different level of the society, the relative sedentariness characteristic of the Middle Ages, owing to the agricultural economic base, ensured the development of differentiable local dialects, that is, once again, of immediately functional linguistic constructs. In the realm of what we call literature, and making allowances for the anachronism of the appellation, it is clear that with its reliance upon verse forms, that, by definition, are oriented toward closure (rhyme, rhythm, length), the medieval differentiation of genres is based upon the mutual separability of these, with no single genre containing or absorbing the others.

In early modern times, major changes take place: urbanization brings together speakers from different linguistic areas, either to transact commercial exchanges or in its patterns of residential settlement. The various professional groups become increasingly regulated by the state apparatus and thus become answerable to it. The emergent state bureaucracy, having abandoned Latin, favors one sociolect, and, within it, one discourse (or style as it is known at the time), and makes all others answerable to it. Henceforth all dealings that involve interdiscursive crossing must be mediated by the dominant discourse. The state, in other words, has arrogated unto itself the capacity of containing all the discourses used on its territory, and is making them all answerable to itself, in its own preferred discourse, imposing the latter for all interdiscursive activity. The individual discourses lose their autonomy and, as a result of being integrated into the state's totalization, their self-sufficiency as well. They are now fragments of a much larger whole, patches of a great quilt. Their speakers also lose autonomy and self-sufficiency, and must recognize that they are speakers of fragmentary discourses which can never be totalized. Only the state can achieve this totalization—at least such is the claim.

There is a striking similarity between this claim and what the novel does. *Don Quijote* is paradigmatic in this respect. Its famous dialogical structure represents an attempt to inscribe as many discourses as possible within its frame. The question is who can read them. In a sense, the answer is: the state. Only the totalizing state can claim to be the adequate subject for reading a novel like the *Quijote*, for only the state has attempted to inventory and totalize all these discourses. In practice this means that such a novel serves to provide its readers with an experience of what it is to look at things from the perspective of the state, that is, to perceive the limitations of each of the individual discourses and the configuration of their addition. At the same time, it demonstrates powerfully the inordinateness of the state's claim and the impossibility of its realization. Yet it is an impossibility that both the state and the novel will attempt to overcome, the first through increased regulative structures, the latter through a search for the perfect style, a search that will dominate the development of the novel well into our century.

The view of Spanish culture in the years 1500–1700 we have been advancing is a dynamic one, based upon the recognition that this is a transitional phase from the more static medieval culture to the more consolidated and rigid culture of Neoclassicism.

The major transformation is the entry of the state upon the stage of culture as its major force. Henceforth one must distinguish between official, or state-sanctioned, culture and unofficial, or barely tolerated and potentially oppositional or subversive, culture. Official culture itself consists of two distinct realms: an elite culture that is ideologically consonant with the goals of the state's ruling groups and dedicated to their promotion and realization, and a mass culture that is manipulated and purveyed on behalf of the state to a broad audience. Whereas elite culture presupposes a critical awareness but a conscious espousal of the state's programmatic views, mass culture rests on uncritical reception. The content of both these realms consists of recyclable elements of a fragmented and progressively disappearing medieval culture, as well as original creations and contemporary foreign imports adapted for local consumption.

Unofficial culture consists, first of all, of the excluded materials: medieval material, or remnants of even more archaic cultural strata, that cannot be integrated and reused in official culture; materials associated with banished populations (Moors, Jews, heretics). But it consists as well of the reinscribing and nonstate-serving practices that we labeled as the proper realm of popular culture: the mode of consumption of the products of official culture that detaches the latter from the goals of their purveyors and thus establishes a realm, however fleeting its extent, of autonomous and alternative cultural production.

In this respect, it must be noted how complex the position of the novel is: inconceivable without the kind of cultural fragmentation that occurs in this period, it is at once the most adequate expression of the ideological role of the state and its most obvious challenger. In fact, whereas the state can assert its hegemony over the realm of culture through gestures of exclusion from that realm of those elements it wishes to proscribe, the novel by including all the elements of official culture (both the elite and the mass) as well as the excluded elements of unofficial culture, almost by definition engages in the practices we have called popular. The state's claim to totalization proceeded on the basis of exclusion, whereas the novel's relied upon inclusion, for unlike the state, the novel was not endangered by inner tensions and contradictions. Yet the search for a homogenizing style, which has dominated the subsequent history of the novel, shows that the novel itself was not immune to these forces and that as its practitioners came to identify themselves more with the goals of the ruling elites, the novel became increasingly part of the elite official culture and abandoned its popular grounds.

Chapter 3
Toward a Nonliterary Understanding of Literature
Reflections on the Notion of the "Popular"
Michael Nerlich
Translated by Colleen Donagher

Invited to state my views on the problem of "popular literature" in sixteenth- and seventeenth-century Spain, I find myself—after a moment of immediate enthusiasm generated by the memory of some previous studies I made of such matters as the picaresque and chivalric novels—facing serious problems of definition and methodology: for not only does the term 'popular' carry a multitude of ideological questions, as is well known,[1] but the same is true of the term 'literature'. For what can "popular literature" mean for a period—the Golden Age—in which the great majority of the population (at least 80 percent[2]) could not write or read?[3] In which even the novels that critics usually call "popular" (for example, the famous *Lazarillo de Tormes*) were not read, could not be read, and have not been read by the masses?[4] Let us understand clearly (setting aside the problem of the meaning of 'literature' itself)[5]: we know perfectly well that the literature of that period could not be written or read by the masses. But does this mean that it cannot be popular? Let us say it *via negationis*: if by 'popular literature' we mean literature written by "the people" (*pueblo*) (or by "plebeian" authors) or literature written to be read by the masses during the same period in which it was generated, there was no "popular literature" in sixteenth- and seventeenth-century Spain.

If for these reasons the literature written in the Golden Age cannot, in the ways mentioned above, be considered popular, we still have the so-called oral literature. Let us here also set aside the problems of definition:[6] besides the classic oral "genres"[7] (popular lyric poetry,[8] romances,[9] proverbs,[10] and *cuentecillos*),[11] we could consider as part of oral literature the texts that were read

62

publicly (about which we unfortunately know far too little) and the theatrical representations attended by an audience of different social provenance.[12] For, as is well known, there were many novels and comedies written between *Lazarillo* and *Fuenteovejuna* that make use of traditional forms, elements of the so-called popular genres (ballads, lyric poetry, proverbs, and *cuentecillos*). Two questions, however, immediately arise. First, does not the integration into a work of art that, in itself, is not popular alter the character, meaning, and function of the integrated popular element, so that it ceases to be popular? Second, if the popular element, by the mere fact of being integrated into a nonpopular work of art, is transformed, does the popular public understand it in its new aesthetic and social function, thereby making it popular?

Since at present we cannot, it seems to me, give an answer to these questions, it would be wise to limit the term 'popular'—if by it we wish to indicate that immediate and direct relation between the masses and literature of which we spoke at the beginning—to the literary genres (ballads, popular lyric poetry, proverbs, *cuentecillos*) that we know with some degree of certainty to have been transmitted orally for a long time, a good index of their popularity. And it is true that these genres played an important, even an extraordinary role in the Spanish literary culture of the sixteenth and seventeenth centuries. Research has explained this phenomenon through a supposed popular culture common to all the Spanish people of this period: "in that period," writes Maxime Chevalier, "all Spaniards—peasants, artesans, public officials, burghers, clerics, and aristocrats—possess a common oral culture, a seamless mantle that was to be rent by the Enlightenment."[13]

Arguments of this sort sound very good and seem to be backed up by evidence. But appearances are often deceiving, or—to say it with a proverb—we should never judge a book by its cover. We know that, in the centuries before the Golden Age, the so-called popular genres were remarkable for their almost total absence from written literature, or—to say it another way—by their absolutely secondary role in learned literary production. We know, in fact, that these genres were actually disdained by learned authors, as is shown by the famous quote from the Marquis of Santillana in his *Prohemio e carta*, in which he explains the difference between the "sublime and mediocre" styles and the "lowest" style: "The lowest are those that, without order, rule, or plot, compose these ballads and songs which delight the people of base and servile condition."[14] Without arguing here whether this quotation gives convincing evidence of an already-manifest cultural dichotomy, as has sometimes been asserted, we can nevertheless conclude that intellectuals before the Golden Age did not have this "common oral culture," or that they did not know they had it, or that having it was unimportant to them. Naturally the possibility still exists that the members of the upper levels of society, particularly the intellectuals, artists, *literati*, and poets, secretly continued to wear that "seamless mantel," that is, to belong latently to the community of that "common oral culture," and that the normality of Spanish culture was to be restored in the sixteenth and seventeenth centuries, as the image used by Dámaso Alonso suggests: "The *cancionero* and *romancero* form a totality of popular and semi-popular (that which we have called "traditional") poetry. . . . The treasure troves of both learned and traditional poetry are to merge in those same two centuries, the sixteenth and seventeenth."[15] But all of this clearly shows what the research has unanimously indicated, and which Maxime Chevalier recapitulates, though he contradicts himself elsewhere: "It becomes evident . . . that the attitude of learned Spaniards towards these humble products of ingenuity changed radically with the Renaissance. We know that the people of the Renaissance aligned themselves with all art that was 'popular' and spontaneous."[16]

Although I would not deny that the idea of spontaneity plays a certain role in Renaissance speculations—for example, in the ideas on natural writing ("I write as I speak," says Juan de Valdés[17])—it is somewhat dangerous to suggest a correlation between 'popular art' and 'spontaneity'. Much caution is needed with this material, as we can see very clearly in the question of the proverbs, considered so often as the most direct expression of "popular" feeling and thought. Juan de Valdés's *Diálogo de la lengua*, often cited as proof of the vitality of the proverb during that period, does not bear close scrutiny in this regard. As is well known, Valdés uses Castilian proverbs as linguistic examples, distinguishing them from Latin and Greek adages: "the Castilian ones are taken from vulgar sayings, most of them born and raised among old women sitting around the fire and spinning, and the Greek and Latin ones, as you know, were born among learned persons and are celebrated in erudite books. But, with respect to the properties of the Spanish language, what is best about the proverbs, is that they were born in the vulgar."[18] This famous passage has been quoted and discussed many times, but rarely interpreted in the context that shows its true meaning. Without examining here whether the passage refers to the *Proverbs of Old Women around the Fire* collected by the Marquis of Santillana, the image of the old women in Valdés's text indicates an archetypical storytelling situation (legends, tales, etc.). For Valdés, proverbs are produced "in the vulgar," not by all people, but rather by some people and under very precise circumstances: the makers of proverbs are old and somewhat isolated, outside common daily activity. And, in fact, the proverbs replace for Valdés the literature that he finds lacking in Spain and that should be the authority in matters of language. In this function as literary authority, the proverbs acquire for Valdés greater importance than Greek and Latin adages, not as a common way of speaking, but as examples of the old way of speaking and telling stories. Not "of the vulgar," but "born in the vulgar," certifying their authority because of their age ("Coriolano: 'Do you have a printed book of them?' Valdés: 'Not of all of them, but, as a young man, I remember having seen one with some of them, badly glossed.'"[19], by which the proverbs also attain the dignity of old documents, as Greek and Latin adages have. Because of this, Marcio, one of his interlocutors, says to Valdés: "If you do not have books in Castilian, with whose authority we could satisfy ourselves regarding that which we shall ask you from your letters, at least satisfy us with the reasons why you write some things differently from others, because these might be worth as much as the authority of books; more so since, it seems to me, you could for many things make use of the collection of Spanish proverbs that you told me you collected among friends, when you were in Rome, at the request of some Roman nobleman."[20] And we can see even more clearly that this is an archaeological project by Pacheco's response to Valdés about the proverbs "born in the vulgar": "I promise you, if it were not contrary to my profession, that I would have, some days ago, determinedly begun a book in the Castilian language like the one Erasmus is said to have done in Latin, collecting all available proverbs and explaining them the best way I could, because I have thought that this would render a signal service to the Castilian language."[21]

I certainly do not wish to put forward the nonsensical proposition that proverbs were not spoken among the "people"; but systematic collections of cultural artifacts are usually made when historic consciousness collides with a phenomenon that is historically important but threatened with disappearance; when aesthetic consciousness runs into something aesthetically interesting, rare, strange, beautiful; when a scholarly consciousness comes across something unknown, lost, exotic, and so on. It is clear that all these reasons (and others) can combine, and it is also clear that there were social, cultural, and linguistic relations among the different levels of society at that time, permitting communication through (some) proverbs (for others, erudite commentaries were needed, as we can read in Valdés). Nevertheless, it is certain that the search for old documents that could serve as authorities equal to the Greek and Roman ones, a search greatly inspired by the ideas of Erasmus (whose influence in Spain has been studies by Américo Castro and Marcel Bataillon), comes from an attitude that is dynamically archaeological, as José Antonio Maravall indicates: "Let us bear in mind that if we study and admire antiquity, the proverbs come to be, some believe, the oldest and purest philosophy of antiquity. Some attribute this idea to Socrates. . . . And the connection this supposes between popular wisdom and the exquisite wisdom of the classics is symptomatic, as is the case with one of our most typical humanists, Hernán Núñez. The proverbs are, therefore, antiquity. They are, Mal-Lara tells us, true 'relics of antiquity,' which 'reveal all ancient wisdom.'"[22]

I do not wish to claim, either, that the proverbs and the other popular "genres," once rediscovered, were not rejuvenated or revived, whether by direct resurrection or by imitation or by the integration of "popular" elements in modern artistic works (for that reason I spoke of "dynamically archaeological"); but essentially the same thing occurs with popular lyric poetry as with the proverbs:

"Humanism and then the Renaissance, with their exaltation of the Natural, were necessary in order for these little songs to be admired and imitated by the courtiers," writes José María Blecua: "At the same time that the proverbs were gaining respect, the old ballads were being glossed, and even children's games were considered interesting, the popular and traditional lyric flees the fields and the streets and ennobles itself at the Court."[23] And Menéndez Pidal establishes that "the ballads began to be heard in the palaces as early as 1445."[24]

This evidence puts very much into question the image of the "two treasure troves" uniting as equivalent currents in the bed of a "common oral culture." If intellectuals at about the middle of the fifteenth century began to return to cultural forms then considered vulgar, it is because the society of that day had reached a stage of development in which intellectual curiosity was directed toward everything unknown, alien, foreign, and exotic: there are discovered even the exotic world of the festive practices of the lower levels of one's own society, as well as ways of thinking and poetic forms called vulgar: "Humanism opened the eyes of the educated to a finer understanding of the human spirit in all its manifestations, and the popular received a more fitting and intelligent attention than ever before," writes Menéndez Pidal.[25] Thus, as the cultural forms of antiquity and the Italian Renaissance were integrated into the Spanish vanguard art of that time and transformed it, so were integrated the materials offered by the festive practices and ways of thinking of the lower levels of society: the author (or authors) of *La Celestina* thus discover(s) this other exotic orb of the surrounding world,[26] in the double sense of discovering it for themselves and of revealing it to a public that could understand aesthetic and ideological intellectual information in a new literary form (whose originality has been studied by María Rosa Lida[27]). *La Celestina*, with its combination of classical, medieval, and Renaissance elements, is an exemplary work of high and perfect literary culture and—despite the use of proverbs, for example—not at all "popular," in the same unpolished sense as the truly popular genres: the ballads, lyric poetry, *cuentecillos*, and proverbs.

Was *La Celestina*, then, a nonpopular work? On the contrary, I think it was in fact a very popular work.[28] But if *La Celestina* or *Lazarillo de Tormes* or the comedies of Lope de Vega were popular, it was not because they used or incorporated elements of the popular oral genres, especially since—as stated above—that incorporation must have profoundly altered those elements. I find this view confirmed by what Menéndez Pidal says about the fate of the ballads in the sixteenth century because of his reference to the alteration of the popular materials: "the adaptation of the *Romancero* to the tastes of the educated classes in the sixteenth century . . . brought to the old songs a singular stylistic perfection: the old ballads were repeated and varied by the most learned talents of that Golden Age, educated in the best courtly tastes and equally full of traditional spirit; in those variants, collected and fixed by sixteenth century printing, the *Romancero* was permeated with the most natural, and at the same time the most refined, of Hispanic art, and thus acquired that labored simplicity, that difficult facility for which it is admired."[29]

Here, however, we find ourselves facing another problem: do the ballads not cease to be popular after being reworked and refined by those poets "educated in the best courtly taste?" According to Menéndez Pidal, the opposite occurs: "In no way should we see in the *Romancero* an undifferentiated mixture of aristocratic and plebeian elements. Both elements are present in it, but perfectly distinguished: the versions of one ballad that today can be found in the tradition clearly manifest their origin, whether it be of the educated or uneducated classes; the versions reworked in traditional ways among the learned classes during the Golden Age are the true *Romancero* that we all know; and thus the *Romancero* is popular in the high sense of the word, not vulgar and base; noble for its epic-heroic origins, it continues to be noble for having been reworked and fixed mainly during the Renaissance."[30] Let us state the matter clearly: the amalgam is of Menéndez Pidal's making, an amalgam based on social valorization, founded in a dubious harmonic vision of society grounded also on aesthetic evaluation, full of unstaked assumptions. But setting this amalgam aside for the moment: even if we accept the idea of noble popularity (or popular nobility) of the ballads because of their "epic-heroic origins," what was the popularity, then, of primitive Castilian (and Galician) lyric poetry that did not have noble "origins" and that, nevertheless, and according to Menéndez Pidal himself, was "the true lyric poetry . . . the only one cultivated by the Spanish people"?[31] Was it popular in the "low" sense of the word (that is, in the modern sense of the term 'vulgar' as Menéndez Pidal uses it), until the poets "educated in the best courtly taste" of the fifteenth, sixteenth, and seventeenth centuries ennobled it, thus giving it authentic popularity "in the high sense of the word"?

It will perhaps be retorted to us that one cannot discuss the ideas of Menéndez Pidal about the whole matter of popular poetry without keeping in mind his distinction between popular and traditional poetry; and it is true that one cannot advance anything in the discussion of Spanish popular literature during the Middle Ages and the Golden Age without meeting the shade of his imposing authority. But although in the eyes of some Hispanists it will certainly be a sacrilege, we should ask if one must not begin to question some of Menéndez Pidal's deepest convictions, the truths he pronounces with the most dogmatic certainty. One of these truths, repeated during some fifty years, is precisely the fundamental distinction between popular and traditional poetry, as he established it in his famous lecture at Oxford, in 1922, and to which he referred even in the last years of his life. Starting with the conviction that the term *"popular poetry,* generally used, has an extremely confused vagueness," he wrote in that year: "what we have said will make clear the need to distinguish among the various types of poetry two foremost categories: that of the strictly *popular* and that of the *traditional*. Any work that has the special qualities that make it pleasing to everyone, so that it is often repeated and persists in the public taste for a long time, is a popular work; to a greater or lesser extent the works of distinguished poets, such as Zorrilla's *Tenorio* and Becquer's *Golondrinas*, are as popular as other works whose author one does not wish to remember, such as the song of the *Relicario*, which now is going out of fashion in the streets of Madrid. The people listen to, or repeat, these verses without changing, or revising, them; they are conscious of the fact that the poems come from the outside, and so must be respected in the repetition. But there exists another class of poetry, born in tradition, more deeply rooted in everyone's memory, remembered and repeated more extensively; the people have received this poetry as their own, deeming it their own intellectual treasure; they do not repeat it faithfully, almost passively, as in the other case, but, feeling it to be theirs, finding it incorporated into their own imagination, reproduce it emotionally and imaginatively, altering it in varying degrees, considering themselves to be in part the author. This poetry that is altered with each repetition, that is recast in each of its variants — all of which live and extend themselves in collective waves, within a particular group of people and over a determined space — is the true *traditional* poetry, quite distinct from the other, which is merely popular."[32] Let us note in passing Menéndez Pidal's apparent indifference to the content or themes of the poetic forms: his basic error is to present a specific form of something as the fundamental opposite of this very thing. With such a logic, one could distinguish between an automotive vehicle and a vehicle made in a factory, forgetting that the latter is also an automobile. That is to say: the "traditional poetry" of which Menéndez Pidal speaks, because it is "plurindividual" (as Maravall happily calls it[33]), does not cease to be *popular*, as Maravall himself states: "Art of an anonymous period, which lives in new versions and variants, which is not characterized by being uncultivated and unconscious, but rather popular, and the fruit of plurindividual collaboration."[34]

We can now conclude from the formulation "true *traditional* poetry, quite distinct from the other, which is merely *popular*" that Menéndez Pidal is aware of the problem in his rigorous distinction between "popular poetry" and "traditional poetry," but even in his master work, *Romancero hispánico (hispano-portugués, americano y sefardí). Teoría e historia*, published in 1953, he writes: "Our studies demand a preciseness comparable to that of the experimental sciences; in the contemporary *romancero* we can achieve something similar, since we can experiment as much as we wish, on a hundred, on five hundred oral versions, to our full satisfaction, and this brings us to the conclusion that for the deeply rooted concept and name *popular poetry* we should substitute the scientific concept and name *traditional poetry*, though most either do not know, or have rejected, it."[35] "For the concept and name": clearly this does not work, since one cannot "substitute" the *essence* of a thing for its *particular state of being*. Consequently, in all his works, carrying on the polemic against the term 'popular,' Menéndez Pidal continues to give traditional poetry, as he defines it—in all that relates to its (presumed) essence—for example, the same treatment that the Romantics gave to the poetry they considered popular. It is true that from time to time there is a moment of enlightenment in his works, as when he writes, for example, in his *Romancero hispánico*: "All traditional poetry was originally mere popular poetry. Between the two categories there is, then, a quantitative difference, because traditional presupposes a prolonged, continuous, and more extensive popularity; but there is also a qualitative difference, since the traditional work, when assimilated by the people, is reworked in its transmission and thereby acquires the characteristics of traditional style; it is not only anonymous, but also impersonal."[36] But only in one of his last works, the preface to the 1957 edition of *Poesía juglaresca*, does he seem to approach a more critical understanding of his scientific-ideological position. He again explains that the Romantic "concept of anonymous *popular poetry*, the poetry of an entire people, was confusing and nebulous" and, correctly, that because of this it "provoked an individualist reaction in defense of the idea that all poetic creation is solely an individual work." Nonetheless, the "individualist reaction" was also incorrect. It is true that "we should reject the term *popular*," and that "we must exile the adjective *popular*" and substitute for it the more exact one, traditional poetry"; but: "The exaggerated anti-Romantic *individualist* reaction cries out for a *traditionalist* counterreaction, that is, a sort of neoromanticism, that would help us reach the essence and life of popular-traditional poetry. I wish to contribute to such a reaction with this book, as I have with others."[37]

Since the Romantic origins of Menéndez Pidal's ideas on traditional poetry have recently been demonstrated,[38] we must here show the aesthetic and ideological consequencs of the internal contradiction in his ideas: the combination of the most advanced and rigorous philological research (origins, development, metrics, language, style, critical editions, etc.) with post-Romantic judgments of the most banal sort. This paradoxical combination of rigorous and essentially positivist philological method with *a priori* post-Romantic judgments that are in fact alien to the scientific method explains, on the one hand, the perpetual contradictions in his work and, on the other, his ecstatic tone when speaking about the moral and aesthetic qualities of primitive Spanish poetry: it is a rhetoric of persuasion. But the contradictions have their justification in his intention to save the Romantic-nationalistic ideals by "applying philological methods to the problem": "The exceptional character of popular poetry again reappears, but the so-called Romantic myth, the *Volksgeist*, can be rationalized: the poetizing 'People' is therefore a reality, and the work is a collective one by many authors who, it is clear, do not work simultaneously, but rather successively."[39] And a little later he declares: "Herder's phrase has not died out, although the Romantic myth may be dead; rationally we can hear in traditional poetry 'the living voice of the people,' we can listen to the voice of the Hispanic people in their *romancero*, purer, more natural, and more unanimous than in any other of their greatest literary production."[40]

This explains why we find critical and ironic commentaries on the ideas of Herder and Grimm about the "happy childhood of the people" as *aetas aurea* of primitive popular poetry,[41] and why we read in Menéndez Pidal himself: "The vulgar literatures are born and grant respect to their texts as an urgent necessity for the vulgar language, which remains excluded from Latin culture. This compelling necessity is satisfied mainly by poetic works repeated from one time period to another. As children never tire of hearing the same song a hundred times, a people in its infancy enjoys hearing the same story a hundred times. Thus, the anonymous jongleur inherits from his anonymous predecessors a delightful repertory which he repeats in his fashion, making his contribution by transmitting it to his successors; once in a while he revises it substantially, improving or mutilating it according to his own taste and ability."[42] As everyone knows, children are "simple and innocent,"[43] that is to say, good and uncorrupted; consequently, one of the essential qualities of the art of those children must be the "simplicity" of which Menéndez Pidal speaks in all his works.[44] And this "simplicity" is not only a question of metric form — (cf: "with the greatest simplicity of means, with a simple base of natural elements, he attempts everything"[45]) — it is also a quality of the "Spanish soul": "This psychological sobriety [of the 'Spanish soul'] implies an inclination toward simplicity in all manifestations of life. In art it uses those conceptual and expressive forms that the spirit gains from a vigorous intuition of reality; usually it is a natural simplicity."[46]

Since "childhood"/"simplicity of soul" and premeditation are mutually exclusive, "traditional" Spanish art according to Menéndez Pidal should be an artless art, one that is spontaneous and natural: "the lyric," he wrote in 1919, "before being mere literature, was something else: the flower that spontaneously opens to the warmth of all vital emotion,"[47] and in 1953 he said, speaking of traditional poetry (which he here calls popular, as if some pages before he had not chosen to substitute for this term the "scientific name of *traditional poetry*"), that one can observe "in the masterworks of popular poetry," "that immaculate naturalness, well understood by the Romantic critics as being absolutely free of the smallest shadow of affectation and artifice: using no form that does not lead to the complete spontaneity of all."[48] It is clear that all this is contradicted by Menéndez Pidal's own analysis of the poems, and we therefore are constantly finding new modifications of his positions (or better, *ad hoc* adaptations of his convictions that relate to particular goals in particular contexts). Thus he said in 1953: "we cannot deny art, in the general aesthetic sense, to popular poetry; and even if we believed it to contain only unconscious and spontaneous art, not the art of study and rules, well, there are also many 'artistic' poets who know nothing of rules and technique, nor do they wish to know anything about them."[49] We will not start here a discussion of the contradictory term 'spontaneous art': elsewhere, in 1943, Menéndez Pidal even denied that popular ("traditional") poetry has "the character of non-learned or primary poetry, poetry that is elemental, spontaneous, or anything limited to a state or modality of a poet's soul."[50] And, ten years later, vacillating between his eagerness to see all the "Romantic" qualities in those products of "traditional" art and the recognition that they do not have these qualities, he declared that "the poetic tradition arrives at simplicity through an energetic and purifying force; it extends the veil of simplicity over what had before been complex, covering it up."[51] The explanation for all these contradictions is that Menéndez Pidal wants to keep his Romantic ideas about the "Spanish soul" despite the contradictory reality of the poetic material he analyzes: "Because Spanish man is impetuous, or nothing at all; distinguished by action, disencumbered of perfection. . . . The tendency toward the most spontaneous expression, less restrained by the school-taught techniques, is shown most clearly in versified language. True Spanish versification . . . tends toward metric forms that are devoid of care and artifice."[52]

What is worse, Menéndez Pidal misuses his philological investigations in order to mystify, to "rationalize" the "Romantic myth" of the "*Volksgeist*"; he is undoubtedly correct when he describes the variants of a popular ("traditional") poem as each being reworked anonymously by an individual, with a sort of "collective" creation resulting from the reworking: "This affirmation of the permanence of a song because of its being reworked through generations is the nucleus of Pidal's doctrine of 'traditionalism,'" writes José Antonio Maravall.[53] But Maravall is mistaken: it is not the "nucleus," but the positivist skeleton of the true "nucleus": a Romantic (nationalist) myth that Maravall himself rationalizes (or hides) with his term 'plurindividualism.'[54] It is true that the term well defines the phenomenon and can in fact be a scientific term, but Menéndez Pidal's term is a different one: 'ultraindividualism.' And this is something else again: "Traditionalism," writes Menéndez Pidal, "is actually an ultra-individualism, much more individualistic than the limited sense of the term."[55] The "ultra-individual" is nonetheless the imagined "collectivity" of which he habitually writes: it is the Spanish giant, the Spanish people in their innocent childhood: "*Traditional poetry* is the poetry of a people that makes itself an author."[56] Consequently, the *romancero* is for Menéndez Pidal "the poetry in which the Spanish people has most placed its soul."[57] With this shell game Menéndez Pidal arrives at such definitions of 'naturalness' as the following: "In the continuous working of the variants—ceaseless selection, acceptance, rejection, reworking—the poetic song is molded to the most natural manner of the collectivity; nothing remains that does not respond to the most effective and spontaneous mode of expression; no artificiality covers up the purest emotion."[58]

Let me make myself perfectly clear: I do not here wish to operate as an iconoclast. On the contrary. And so that there will be no doubt I shall state that I agree with all the results of the great Hispanist's *philological* research, but that I consider tragic his own deplorable ideologization of his work.[59] Not only have his studies become outdated because of this, but it is that paradoxical, absurd quality (with respect to philological method), piled up in baroque quantity, that, it seems to me, has blocked Hispanic discussion of popular art in Spain, and prevents international discussion from appreciating Menéndez Pidal's philological investigations, as is shown (as Alvaro Galmes de Fuentes has clearly demonstrated[60]) by the works of Claude Bremond, Gérard Genette, Julia Kristeva, Tzvetan Todorov, and, above all, Paul Zumthor with his brilliant *Essai de poétique médiévale* of 1972. In brief, it is true that the popular poetry that Menéndez Pidal calls traditional is elaborated as he says it is: by a collection of individuals during a certain time who create variants — although it is doubtful that they tend toward simplicity, or, more exactly, toward simplification.[61] But to say what it is about this elaboration that induces Menéndez Pidal to say that "the poematic song is molded to the most natural manner of the collectivity," even to speak of the "naturalness" of this song, the opposite of the "artificiality that covers up pure emotion," it is necessary to define the term 'naturalness.' Perhaps by accepting the Marxist definition of humanity, according to which human nature is social, one may be able to accept Pidal's concept of naturalness. It seems to me, however, that this would more accurately be a play on words. "Traditional" poetry, of which Menéndez Pidal argues, is in effect collective and, for that reason, an absolutely social form: of the "natural," as conceived by Menéndez Pidal, it has nothing. An art, a poetry of which certain works are reworked in innumerable variants during centuries, can be neither "spontaneous" art nor an "expression of spontaneity"; nor can it be the expression or vehicle of "pure emotion." To say that "the epic-traditional style" (or the traditional lyric style) "tends toward an intuitive, immediate, instantaneous vision"[62] is a manifest and inconceivable contradiction. An even more absurd contradiction if one remembers that Menéndez Pidal himself quite correctly points out the "impersonality"[63] of traditional poetry. To arrive at this vision of an impersonal poetry, reworked during decades or centuries, a poetry that would at the same time be a "spontaneous expression" or the expression of "pure emotion," one must pass through the concept of the supraindividual: the people or the nation. "Tradition, step by step leaving behind all that is transitory in individual art," writes Menéndez Pidal, "reaches an atemporal beauty of the greatest stability, of the simplest and most powerful efficiency, that enchants us and relieves the fatigue of our souls, like a perennially cool drink of water."[64]

It could not be farther from my intention to cast doubt on the particular beauty of Spanish traditional poetry (although I do have my doubts about any eternizing idea of eternity), but what Menéndez Pidal — despite his philological studies — did not see, or did not want to see, was the stereotypical character, or, more exactly, the "recurrent"[65] or — to speak with Lévi-Strauss — "serial" (thematic-formal) character of this poetry. As far as the "spontaneous expression" of some "emotion" on the part of the "producer" goes, any poem of the most detested "artificiality" by the poet most hated by Menéndez Pidal is more effective than traditional poetry: "The formulaic style is the specific form of literary expression in the oral tradition," writes Gian-Luigi Beccaria: "The popular text contains repetitive sequences of a 'naive' appearance. . . . It is a ritual whose style is elaborated and transmitted orally by a collectivity and not by an individual. . . . The text does not seek originality of expression but the variation of the identical, the impersonal formula. The code dominates individual choice. The distribution of variables is continuous but the variation is contained within rigorous limits."[66] Nonetheless, in another sense, "emotion" and "spontaneity" do relate to traditional poetry. Since they are repetitive poetic formulas, "serial" and absolutely neutral,[67] the fact that these formulas are perfectly impersonal and anti-spontaneous, along with their apparently simple nature, allows the people of a certain period to construct a sort of poetic thesaurus that is continually available for *emotional and spontaneous use*. "This *impersonalization* of oral discourse allows the listener to take it more easily into account; to identify what he hears with what he is told," says Paul Zumthor.[68] And it is true: by using the stereotypical forms of *traditional poetry* the individual can achieve his/her desire for aesthetic celebration or mourning. One can change emotion spontaneously in forms that are neutral, empty of any alien individuality.

Now I do not wish to claim that *traditional poetry*, as Menéndez Pidal defines it philologically, is "the" oral or popular poetry (Paul Zumthor's recent book *Introduction à la poésie orale* gives us an idea of the multiplicity of its types and variants), nor do I wish to adhere too closely to the study of the Spanish *romancero*.[69] My own research interests lead in another direction, where Menéndez Pidal's successes and failures are of equal use and where Spanish traditional poetry seems to me a perfect example. I therefore repeat: I fully accept the term that, at the end of his life, Menéndez Pidal used in the preface to *Poesía juglaresca: poesía popular-tradicional*. I have already shown that 'popular poetry' in his work was not essentially opposed to 'traditional poetry', although Menéndez Pidal unfortunately used to make this claim. In reality, traditional poetry is a special type of popular poetry: a type that is particularly popular, as Menéndez Pidal is forced to recognize in his *Romancero hispánico*: "All traditional poetry was at first mere popular poetry. Between the two categories there is, then, a quantitative difference, because tradition supposes a continuous, prolonged, and more extensive popularity."[70] Again, I do not claim that *popular-traditional poetry* is equivalent to popular poetry, but that it is definitely popular, philologically well-described and analyzed in its origin,[71] development, variants, metric, language, and themes. In its more exemplary versions, therefore, this popular poetry agrees perfectly with what the research has shown; Beccaria writes, "It has been established that popular song is made up of fixed formulas:

rhythms and cadences that also seem to show a fixity and ideological inertia. The world is accepted as it is and as it has always been, without the bite or urgency of an overt 'ideology,' evident in the content."[72] It is clear that Beccaria's description depends (again, a vicious circle) on the definition of the term 'popular'; let us be content, however, with the evidence that holds for our 'popular-traditional poetry'. But if it is valid for our 'popular-traditional poetry', the existence of this noncognitive and *nonrevindicative* popular poetry destroys many ontological definitions of popular literature (and of popular art and culture).

In his famous essay *The Dehumanization of Art*, Ortega y Gasset, for example, distinguishes two types of art: an *artistic* art (the art of the twentieth-century avant-garde) that he calls not only "nonpopular" but "anti-popular";[73] and another (which he judges "impure"), "popular" because it is realistic. This is because the masses, says Ortega y Gasset, seek in art only the recognition of themselves and the real world in which they move: "for the majority of people aesthetic pleasure is not a spiritual attitude essentially different from the one they normally adopt in the rest of their lives . . . they will call 'art' the collective means through which they receive contact with human matters. . . . It is natural; they know no other attitude toward objects than the practical, that which arouses us to become passionately and sentimentally involved with them."[74] Consequently, Ortega y Gasset judges the realistic art of the twentieth century ("Romanticism and Naturalism, seen from the vantage point of today, approach each other and reveal their common realistic root."[75]) as being of lower quality and especially popular: "It is understandable, then, that nineteenth-century art has been so popular: it was made for the differentiated masses to the extent to which it is not art but bits and pieces of life. Remember that in all periods that have had two different kinds of art, one for a minority and another for the majority, the latter was always realistic." Even more interesting for us is his note at the bottom of the page: "For example, in the Middle Ages. Corresponding to the binary structure of the society, divided into two social groups: the nobles and the plebeians, there was a noble art, which was 'conventional' and 'idealistic'—that is, artistic—and a popular art, which was realistic and satirical."[76]

Naturally we could object that from its very own perspective, the Middle Ages was tripartite, not bipartite,[77] and, that for a serious understanding of medieval society even that tripartite vision no longer suffices. But we shall return later to the sociological aspect. What interests us most here is the idea of the realism of popular medieval art. It is an idea so commonly accepted that we find it even in the studies of modern specialists in Spanish popular literature. Louis Combet writes in his book on proverbs: "Popular lyricism retains this character of simplicity and realism that has often been recognized in the Castilian worldview."[78] Popular-traditional lyric poetry realistic?[79] Perhaps the encounter of the shepherdess and the knight is realistic? Or the *"malmaridada?"*

I suspect that there is a misunderstanding here, and that the so-called simplicity of the artistic forms, vocabulary, rudiments of thought, emotions, and "themes" of popular-traditional lyric poetry is mistaken for the correlative in the expression of the ("simple") soul of the ("simple") people. Again Menéndez Pidal confirms this suspicion. He writes in 1948, having cited some non-especially-brilliant lines from a *"romance* on the wedding of the Cid": "The traditional part, the *realistic simplicity* with which familial hates are resolved . . . revives the nostalgia for a golden age, whose patriarchal simplicity is expressed in a sustained and gracious description of the clothes that Rodrigo and Jimena receive at the wedding feast."[80] It would seem that the people of the Middle Ages felt, thought, and spoke simply.

It occurs to me that research often confuses the Middle Ages with the Neanderthal Age. It seems impossible that in those centuries of which we are speaking when we discuss popular-traditional poetry, the people who, according to the erudite, felt, thought, and spoke (and also sang) like children were, with their practices, revolutionizing the world, erecting the foundation of the modern world, a task as complicated as it was arduous and bloody. In other words, when they acted, they did not think or speak "simply," and although it may be quite correct (as shown by the modern research on mentalities) that they did not feel as we do, this is no reason to believe that they thought in a "simple" or less "complicated" (rich) manner. And because the people of that time worked, thought, spoke, and felt like people who transform the world, when they were tired they needed rest and celebration. Since the means of entertainment were not as abundant as they are today, common popular song was quite important. But we must keep things in perspective: common popular song was an element in celebrations and in the other occasions and ceremonies at which there was habitually singing. That popular song was considered an essential element of these occasions can be concluded from the *Cancionero* of Juan Alfonso de Baena (1445), in which even the reading of books is associated with games and other entertainments such as "bullfights, fencing and fighting, ball, chess, dice, and cards."[81] Where could common popular song fit in except in these celebrations and ceremonies? But these, in turn, are only elements (although important ones) in the whole sphere of social activity. Although comparison is difficult, it seems to me that in their function as "serial" aesthetic forms, "repetitive" and free of individuality (suitable for changing "emotions"), limited with reference to variants, the medieval popular songs, sung at festivals, accompanied or "interpreted" by dance, are more similar to a football game, especially if the game is accompanied by common "spontaneous" songs (for example in the ULS., but also at soccer games, which are often accompanied by choral songs, particularly in Brazil, Scotland, England, and Germany).[82]

Naturally this comparison between "popular-traditional poetry" will scandalize some readers, but let us not forget that as late as 1953 Menéndez Pidal was scandalized by the gypsy "themes" in the *Romancero* of García Lorca.[83] But I do not want to press the comparison, especially since I wished to compare the functions of two social institutions, offering possibilities for the more-or-less spontaneous (collective) inversion of emotions.[84] In historical-social reality, these institutions do not constitute more than (more or less) important elements among an infinite network of factors, with which the institutions share a dialectical relation: to judge the mentality, judgment, and aesthetic competence of medieval people by "popular-traditional poetry" is like judging the mentality, judgment, and aesthetic powers of modern people by their attendance at football games. The arrogance of certain "intellectuals" toward popular poetry, of which Beccaria complains, is identical to that of those same or other "intellectuals" toward football, sports in general, and all the other "popular" entertainments of today: it arises from an ignorance of life and a disdain for others.

With his superb study on oral poetry, Paul Zumthor hurled a gargantuan weight of living cultural forms at the feet of literary research: it is a challenge "pure and simple." From the Finnish *Kalevala*, passing through Bantu Izipongo and Piaf to Woody Guthrie, Jacques Brel, Victor Jarra, Bob Dylan, and Joan Baez (without forgetting *The Song of Roland*), Zumthor shows the vitality of oral poetry in the past and present without concerning himself with the aesthetic values admitted in academic scholarship, and in a case of strange bedfellows, by the modern literary vanguard: "Writing lasts and stagnates; voice abounds. The first holds its own and preserves itself, the second overflows and destroys itself. The first convinces, the second calls out. . . . Just as the Africa of today manufactures its shoes out of our old tires, and uses its genius to recover and instill new life into the debris of our technology, our literatures and our musics, it is high time that we too recycle (bricoler) with the breath of our voices and in the energy of our bodies, the immense and incoherent inheritance of these centuries of writing. In the main square of McLuhan's 'global village', to re-establish an equilibrium between the eye and the ear so that the voice might soon be able to go through the surrounding opacity that we take to be reality. . . . Not in order to go back to a zero state that, by definition, does not obtain, but in order to thematize the traditions of vocal poetry, to have them recognized, repertoried, domesticated, and relived in accordance with the daily requirements of beings such as ourselves, squatters for a life on a piece of our external age."[85] Daily necessities are what count! To value judgments (on high and low culture and literature, or on the triviality of song), Zumthor opposes the necessity of oral poetic creation, the truth of that incredible, powerful practice of oral poetry that cannot be explained or understood through intra-literary reasons, but exclusively through social activity.[86]

But let us consider whether Zumthor is correct when he writes: "The medias seem to bring us back to the archaic situation: they require genres with fixed rules: the thriller, the western, the commercial. That is a tendency of all 'popular' art meant for quantitatively limitless consumption. The absence of any differenciation is therefore the more remarkable in the only exclusively oral art to be transmitted by the media: song. Only its musical style can sometimes give it a specific designation, more often it is the name of a star performer: otherwise, nothing that would lead to the definition of a class felt to have regularities."[87] For me, the problem lies not in his analysis of the *functional* similarity or identity between archaic forms of popular poetry and the modern genres that have "fixed rules," such as the thriller. In this I agree entirely: the "seriality" of forms that lack individuality and that have fixed rules, predictable endings, and standard plots, the whole devoid of "realism" (in the sense of either Ortega y Gasset of Lukács or Brecht), is not only typical of some television programs, but the essense of so-called trivial literature in general, according to specialized research.[88] We could demonstrate the relationship between these forms and archaic cultural forms (for example, popular-traditional poetry) easily enough. I am not convinced, however, that it is correct to speak of a "return" to the "archaic situation." It is true that seriality, recurrence, and the absence of innovation are essential for the art of archaic societies, but it seems to me that one cannot conclude from this that there is no serial art in nonarchaic societies. On the contrary, there are or were very advanced societies in whose cultures innovation plays and played a very subordinate role, and the survival of serial cultural forms does not seem to me explicable as a step backward in social development (the cultural regression of certain classes, for example), or as an interruption of cultural development that would cause a "return" toward archaic forms. Although modern European culture may have arisen from archaic forms, it rather seems to me that these so-called archaic forms (serial, noncognitive nonrevindicative) belong to the social essence of the human in history, that is to say, "to the *whole* of social relations" (Marx). Lévi-Strauss's idea that there is no dichotomy between the "serial" and "innovative" types of culture, but that there is "specialization,"[89] seems to me very important. I think, in fact, that we must modify this idea of a dichotomy between "popular" and "elite" forms of culture":[90] the desire for cultural preservation and repetition and the desire for innovation and the negation of the traditional are constitutive elements of human beings in their historical reality. The predominance of one or the other can be explained by concrete social conditions, but to suppress one to the advantage of the other would constitute a barbaric mutilation of humanity.

Even Zumthor has his doubts about thinking in dichotomies: "A dictionary never amounts to an explanation; there is no great 'divide' . . . and the practice of binary oppositions most often leads to pathetic idealist reductions. The idea of discontinuity is of value only if it is integrated into a dialectical movement. Everything is historical, therefore in motion."[91] For that reason, it surprises me that—perhaps out of necessity—at the end of his book he again falls into a sort of dichotomy between "oral poetry" and "writing." If the production and consumption of oral poetry (or, rather, of poesies or oral poems) corresponds to and obeys a social preference (or, rather, social-aesthetic preference, necessities and social requirements arising from social practices), then written literary production also corresponds to and obeys necessities. Watching television or a football game; going jogging, to the theater, or to a party; listening to the Beatles and Ligetti; singing *Auprès de ma blonde* or *Lo tiré al pozo* and reading Beckett or Mallarmé, watching an erotic movie, and looking at paintings by Michelangelo or Kandinsky or Pollock or Giotto di Bondone (etc., etc.) are not contradictory or concurrent activities, but rather complementary ones. Being able to choose among them constitutes the cultural richness of life. Thinking in dichotomies brings the risk of idealistic reduction, says Zumthor, and he is right. But the worst is that idealistic reductions are the bases of all dogmatisms. To judge, for example, the literature called "low" because of what it lacks in order to be "high" or to condemn certain literary forms as "trivial" compared to the so-called high literature always presupposes the idea of a literature that is socially and/or morally and/or aesthetically "good." But who decides what is good? Such an idea also presupposes that people should read: why should they? We know that the majority of people do not read. I allow myself to state that this has always been true. But I also dare to say that it will always be true. And why not? For what reason should people read? Why should they not play a musical instrument? Why should they not paint or draw? Why should they not dance? Why should they not become theater actors? Why should they not play football? Lévi-Strauss says that we do not know why one begins to compose music. And why does one begin to paint or to write poems (or to play football)? The majority of people do not read. I make an abstraction of the people who even for social reasons—because they are too poor or do not know how—do not read (this would not have to be the reason in socialist states; nonetheless, there also there are many people who do not read); I propose that the proportion is more-or-less equal among all levels of society. And this is natural because whether one reads or not depends on the meeting of the individual inclination with one's societal situation. Nor does one want to read all the time: there are moments when one reads and others when one does not wish to. There are times when one wants to read *Astérix*, others when one prefers Paul Valéry or George Simenon.

Whether one reads does not depend on having learned to read. The taste for reading does not come from reading or literature. It comes from the meeting between one's societal situation, individual inclination, and the presence of suitable texts. And who would dare say that the taste resulting from this meeting is always a fortunate one? Cervantes understood this problem.

We know little or nothing of how people read.[92] But we do know where the faculty for reading comes from: from the whole of social experience.[93] Contrary to what Ortega y Gasset thought, we all arrive at art and reading from practice (which also includes literature).

We are now back at the beginning of this essay: the problem of "popular literature" in the Golden Age. There is no reason to believe that people then arrived at reading by any other road than that of the meeting of individual inclination, one's social situation, and suitable texts. Certainly there can be and were material impediments for the poor (incomparably greater than today), but once having overcome the obstacles, the taste for reading did not (and does not) depend on one's social level. Belonging to a certain class could (and can) orient one's particular interests, but it does not necessarily direct them, and even less necessarily does it direct them *toward one's own class*. Reading (especially fiction) is an act of curiosity, directed by curiosity. The reader is less interested in discovering what "prose" s/he speaks personally than with knowing what *the other* thinks and says. Having seen the essence of popular-traditional poetry, the "serialness" of formal and thematic stereotypes, and the ritual function of this poetry, we should ask if, for the real or virtual reader of the sixteenth and seventeenth century, popular-traditional poetry could be of much interest. One could say paradoxically that the popular-traditional poetry of the Middle Ages could not have been very popular reading for the popular readers (burghers, artesans, etc.) in the Golden Age. Certainly—like all the traditional cultural structures— popular-traditional poetry continued to serve its function as an element of ritual in celebrations and other ceremonies, although it lost much of its importance as more and more cities were founded with the urbane entertainments they had to offer. It would be naive to think—as Menéndez Pidal apparently does[94]—that popular-traditional poesies (but also *cuentecillos* and proverbs) still serve the same social function after being incorporated into innovative, cognitive, and revindicating literature. They have left their function as part of celebration. To understand what happens to popular-traditional poetry, we must abandon the perspective of literary history: the link established by Menéndez Pidal and later by Dámaso Alonso (from Galician poetry or the *jarchas* to Lope de Vega) ignores this basic change in function.[95] Instead of writing histories of literary forms, we would have to write the history of aesthetic necessities and functions. What festive activities, institutions, and genres replace the "serial" art of popular-traditional poetry in the Golden Age (and afterward)? How quickly does this serial art disappear and where? Where does it survive, and why?

We must undoubtedly write the history of artistic forms (literary and others) starting from their functions in the whole of social practice, though this would force us to stop thinking in terms of intracultural dichotomies. But we would thereby restore to art and literature its (aesthetic) social importance, its seriousness: "we must effectively liberate ourselves from a concept of literature that draws its suppositions from a cultural ideology," I wrote in 1977; "we must understand and analyze the *whole* of literary production from the point of view of its function in history or of the historicity of its dialectic, aesthetic, social and political unity, without restrictions or sacred *a priori's*. Only this can be the base on which we can make value judgments, but not through a system of *a priori* norms, even one like Lukács's, which excluded almost all effective literary production in history."[96]

To different interests, necessities, and desires correspond different cultural, artistic, and literary forms. The horizons are in principle unlimited. Why restrict them, introducing the limitation of the term 'popular'? I propose with Menéndez Pidal that we abandon this term, though I do so for different reasons. Should "popular" be considered the "simple" form? And why should the people not also acquire the more complicated forms? And, once acquired, would they not be "popular"? Brecht is correct when he speaks of the unbearable paternalism behind the notion of popular art. (Who accepts this notion? Always the well-intentioned intellectual, the teacher, the professor, giving lessons to the childish "people": censorship begins the same way.) But let us leave the categories of "popularity" and return to people in their social practice to find the history and practice of art and literature.

Is this a premature attempt? What attempt would not be premature? On the other hand, historiography, especially social history and the history of mentalities, has given us a wealth of unexpected data and knowledge. Could they not form the basis for a social history of aesthetic forms? Perhaps they could, but I think there is a danger of losing one's orientation in the sea of this disorganized, chaotic information. We would consequently have to look for a system of categories that would allow us to coordinate materials in nonarbitrary ways. To find it, I think we must return to the Middle Ages, to that period when the modern world was starting definitively to rid itself of the social and cultural forms of organization that ethnology calls primitive and archaic. This was the moment when the modern system of capitalism developed. Even more important: at this crucial moment in human history, the genesis of capitalism engendered and was engendered by two ideological events of worldwide importance. Independent of capitalist activity had developed the system that thought of life as privileged and dangerous: the ideology of knightly adventure. This ideology put at the disposal of the merchants an ideological system of self-justification for the (dangerous) life of merchants. They adopted it, integrated it into their praxis, and transformed it: leaving home, seeking the unknown, taking risks, making a profit, going home, and bringing about change in the process were all aspects of chivalric thought that coud easily be adapted to the activities of merchants. And the second fact unprecedented in history: Rome, the capital of the Christian world, in need of money, looked for it, logically, where it was: with the merchants. But the merchants' activity did not conform to the Bible: making money in order to become wealthy. On the other hand, if the Church had condemned this economic practice, where could it have found money later? The Church found the solution to the problem: to give its blessing to commerce when it involved risk. The three factors—the birth of capitalism, the ideologization of commercial activity with the ideology of knightly adventure, and the beatification of risk in capitalistic venture—were to change the world as never before: even today they are changing it. From then on, the ways of thinking movement (adventure) would penetrate all human activities, all systems of thought, feelings, and mentality; curiosity, mobility, departure, journeys, the far-away as an *a priori* value, the unknown . . . novelty and innovation became the hub of human life. Art did not avoid this dynamism: its fundamental principle would be innovation and novelty.[97]

In 1977 I published the first two volumes of a history of thinking innovation, mobility, and movement: in other words, adventure.[98] I examined also some political-cultural structures in Spain, but I admit that the most important work remains to be done. "Any desire for novelty is extinguished," wrote Menéndez Pidal of popular-traditional poetry,[99] thus indicating one of the essential characteristics of archaic societies. But it does not stop there: thinking in terms of movement, change, and adventure also permeates Spain, orienting human material and nonmaterial practice. We must henceforth write our history of artistic forms in terms of their social function, and we now have the material to do so: the magnificent and unfortunately little-known book of José Antonio Maravall *Antiguos y modernos. La idea de progreso en el desarrollo inicial de una sociedad*, the history of thinking in terms of innovation in Spain from the Middle Ages to the Renaissance: "Only in a changing world is it possible to make a comparative judgment between the past and the present at each transformation, and the change can consequently be evaluated positively or negatively."[100] Thus it is: the history of revolutionary practice and thought gives us not only the possibility of writing the history of art in terms of its social function, but also the possibility of making judgments that are different from more-or-less arbitrary intracultural ones. For these judgments, it is clear, we must know social history so that we can judge another "popularity"—whether it brings reasonable or pernicious progress for the masses, the subjective and objective interests of these masses, and so on. I do not wish to approach this problem here, however (for that we would have to bring in the ideas of Gramsci and especially of Brecht): by doing so we would leave the popular-traditional literature that is "serial," "noncognitive," and nonrevindicating for literary forms that are innovative and cognitive ("realistic" and revindicating).[101] In this context we would also have to seek the solution to the problem of "popular literature" in the Golden Age. For finding this solution, thinking in terms of adventure would be extremely helpful, as is known by the *Diálogo de la lengua* of Juan de Valdés, which very concisely points to the innovative space of the social and cultural vanguard: "From *ventures* we have made a very gallant word with which I, out of respect, am quite enamored; it is: *to adventure*, which occurs in the proverb 'Nothing ventured, nothing gained' (*Quien no aventura, no gana*); from *adventuring*, we also have the 'adventurer,' the one who seeks ventures, and our fictional works written in Romance are full of such people."[102]

Chapter 4
Gender Markers in Traditional Spanish Proverbs
Constance Sullivan

The study of proverbs in any culture is a study of tense linguistic structures that express cultural truisms in short, sententious, often witty form, sometimes containing a metaphor in its literal terms, frequently metaphorical in use, and characterized by mnemonic devices like rhyme, alliteration, parallelism, and other rhythmic elements. Once coined by someone and picked up by other speakers as clever or memorable, a proverb usually maintains fairly accurately its expressive terms, its metaphor if it has one, and its formal characteristics — what I call the core proverb — although individuals and groups over time invent slight variations on the form of specific proverb texts. The search for the origins of a particular saying frustrates and fascinates at the same time; many Western proverbs can be traced to ancient texts, like the Book of Proverbs of Solomon or classical Greek, Roman, or Arabic writings, and more recent individual phrasemakers. In many cases there remains the question whether the "known" author lifted a saying from popular sources and made it his own by writing it down in the context of his own discourse.

It is not my purpose here to attempt yet another lengthy, only partly successful definition of the various types of aphoristic expression. Many paremiologists and writers of dictionaries have tried to distinguish between maxims, adages, *dichos*, aphorisms, apothegms, *sentencias*, axioms, proverbs, Wellerisms, *dialogismos*, and *refranes*, arriving at vague differentiations and contradictions.[1] I do, however, wish to emphasize one important distinction that apparently holds true for literary historians, folklorists, anthropologists, ethnographers, sociologists, historians, and students of human communication:

a proverb can only be called a *popular* proverb if its use in speech becomes widespread, if it is common conversational and cultural currency at a given historical moment. In other words, a popular proverb is not defined by its having been written down, either in a collection of proverbs and proverbial sayings or in a literary work. It is characterized by conversational use by the people who form the particular community in question. Popular proverbs are part, therefore, of oral culture, of and by the people, rather than for the people, and they exist in the speech patterns of a society despite the level of that society's literacy.[2] Proverbs express generally conservative views by reiterating in a rigid form the attitudes of a group, which ostensibly carry the sanction of long and common experience in that group.[3] Their didactic nature can be stressed in certain contexts, and reliance on them for authoritative argumentation is an exercise in rigid thought patterns: they are neat, clever, "common knowledge" units that even when used for humorous purposes tend to cut off debate, eliminate potential disagreement, and end discussion. This is true of all aphoristic style.

The functional importance of popular proverbs tends to diminish as a society becomes more generally literate, when less of the accumulated structuring knowledge or wisdom of that society or culture must be memorized for it to be transmitted to succeeding generations. In relatively unchanging, or stable, societies, oral culture becomes a central pillar of traditional culture, just as other structural elements like ceremonies, ritual, learned patterns of behavior, and thought become traditional through group-reaffirming repetition. Until very recently Spain has been a traditional and predominantly rural Mediterranean society with a preliterate population (a population that knows itself to be illiterate in a structure dominated by literate elites). Consequently Spain's people have retained a vibrant oral culture that, in the case of proverb use, has had only sporadic contact with the hegemonic cultural apparatus and its scribes, interpreters, and pedagogues.[4] Consideration of demographics, literacy levels, mobility, presence or absence of audio-visual media of communication, work patterns, community structures, and what anthropologists call the "social contracts" in the small, relatively isolated towns and villages of the Iberian peninsula indicates that for the greater part of that human mass all too casually referred to as *el pueblo* (the common people), real changes of traditional patterns and the disruption of many time-honored value systems began to occur in the last several generations, or the post-Civil War period.[5]

The genres of oral culture that entail a high performance level—with performer, audience, appropriate situation—disappear more rapidly in times of great change than do the joke, the riddle, and the proverbial saying. In Spain's oral culture the *romance viejo* (traditional ballad) has all but died out, and despite the fact that students of Spain's traditional balladry have been lamenting the same incipient phenomenon for 100 to 150 years without there being a definitive demise of the genre, this time—by the 1980s—the presence of television, radio, and film, greater dependence on printed versions of the *romances viejos*, and the demise or changed composition and attitudes of the many small rural communities in Spain have cut the number of traditional ballad performers to a tiny portion of what apparently existed in earlier periods. The same is happening to the folktale of traditional origin: people now read books and magazines, watch television, or go to the movies instead of gathering to entertain each other by telling stories or singing old ballads. Even traditional popular festivals and corporate ceremonies in the towns have been distorted in the artificial renderings now given or enacted primarily for tourists.[6]

We still have no evidence on which to base a conclusion about the state of the use of proverbs in everyday speech in Spain today, about the proportion of proverbs that are indeed the traditional *refranes* of the past or their variants, and about the degree to which modern slang and new popular expressions have taken their place. Some scholars and writers have claimed that the Spanish peasant population continues to rely heavily on proverbial expression in speech, but it would be of immense help to have a methodical investigation of such assertions.[7] Such an undertaking by contemporary sociolinguists, linguistic and cultural anthropologists, students of human communication, ethnographers, and social historians will require that they devote some work to the written texts of old proverbs in order to distinguish with any accuracy a traditional proverb from a new proverbial expression. To date they have shown little inclination to put in the time it takes to gain familiarity with the collections, even in the United States and with regard to American English or with regard to Moroccan or East African or Polynesian proverbs.[8] In fact, one school of contemporary folklorists all but categorically denies any importance to the bibliographical history of paremiology, disdaining "collections" at the same time that their own theorizings about proverb meanings and use, the structure of proverbs, the nature of proverb metaphors and metaphorical linkages seem both unnecessarily naive and flawed by ignorance of history. It is these social scientists studying folklore who reject the idea that proverbs express the values of a particular society and that one can characterize a culture's specificity on the basis of proverb content, form, and use.[9] An example of this new disdain is the introduction by Alan Dundes and Wolfgang Mieder in their 1981 *The Wisdom of Many: Essays on the Proverb*, to Alexander Parker's 1963 essay "The Humor of Spanish Proverbs":

> Parker seeks to describe the elusive element of humor as he finds it expressed in Spanish proverbial form. However, the more general question raised by this paper is, as in the preceding paper [by Alfred Lister, "Chinese Proverbs and Their Lessons"], to what extent, if any, can peculiar or specific features of one cultural group be delineated through the analysis of the proverbs of that group? Can Spanish proverbs or the Spanish versions of international proverbs yield insights into Spanish thought

patterns, philosophy, or worldview? In terms of humor, the question might be rephrased as: does what a people laugh at reveal their attitudes toward life? The obvious answer would appear to be yes, but the actual documentation necessary to support such an assertion is not always so easy to provide.[10]

These folklorists from the social sciences, the group commonly referred to as "contextualists," attack the proverb scholarship conducted prior to the 1960s for not "consulting informants about the philosophical implications of their proverbs," and for generalizing on the basis of "contextless collections" about "the alleged wisdom or character of a people."[11] Of course, if one limits one's inquiries to the here and now, to explanations offered by contemporary users of proverbs, the "informants," one precludes the possibility of any historical study, which is a kind of scholarly investigation by definition much more complex than asking forty captive college students in Texas how they understand "A rolling stone gathers no moss" or "A friend in need is a friend indeed." Any historical questions—what proverbs were used, and how, in the past? what did they mean? who used them?—must be answered by careful comparisons of available written texts, be they proverb collections, literary works, or other manuscripts.[12]

There is still much to be learned from a study of the substance and chronological development in Spain of traditional oral culture as it was "frozen" into print at various points in time, with the caution bred by our knowledge that the men who wrote down the oral culture of the common people were *not* the common people, nor were these men dependent on oral culture for their own knowledge or wisdom or artistic products in any sense of those words. In the absence of sociolinguistic samples of the speech of everyday Spaniards of any past moment, we have the learned elite's versions and mediations of popular oral culture. Indeed, the whole history of Spanish paremiology is composed of the products of the curiosity of an intellectual elite who studied the language of *el pueblo* (the people), an entity to which none of them purported to belong. In effect, Spanish collectors who transcribed proverbs for publication or transmission in writing, and the literary creators who sprinkled popular proverbs throughout their "high culture" discourses, were involved in a process of reification of popular speech. Their perspective on the people's culture (variously termed popular culture, the people's voice, vulgar philosophy, or wisdom) was from the vantage point of another class stratum. This characterization is valid for all proverb collections and all Spanish authors and interpreters of popular culture, from the first to those of today.[13]

Louis Combet, whose 1971 *Recherches sur le "refranero" castillan* is the best single book on Spanish proverbial expression to date, asserts that all European proverbs are medieval forms and reflect medieval attitudes and thought processes, and he relates proverbial expression to the sophists and their reliance on written or oral authority in argumentation. According to Combet and others, the late Middle Ages in Europe saw the full blooming among the masses of people of proverb forms that we later began to call traditional. The people called *el pueblo* or *el vulgo* in Spain used the *refranes* before authors like the Archpriest of Hita began to use them in literary works. Furthermore, while it is quite clear that the *Adagiorum* of Erasmus did seem to have legitimized the study of popular proverbs for sixteenth-century scholars in Europe, several fifteenth-century proverb collections in Spain predated Erasmus's model.[14] The *Seniloquium*, with a probable date in the 1480s, contained 498 popular proverbs accompanied by obtuse glosses or explanations in Latin, but the most famous fifteenth-century written collection of popular proverbs in Castilian remains the *Refranes que dizen las viejas tras el huego* (Proverbs that old women say at fireside) that has been attributed to the Marqués de Santillana.[15] The Santillana collection contains 750 popular proverbs in its posthumous 1508 edition; some anonymous editor added the brief glosses for the 1541 edition, and most subsequent editions contained those. The *Refranes que dizen las viejas . . .* was a bestseller in sixteenth-century Spain: it went through thirty editions in a hundred years. But we might ask why Santillana, who also published a series of moral maxims in verse format in the volume *Proverbios* (Zaragoza, 1490), collected popular sayings? Ostensibly this Castilian nobleman collected them for his king, at the king's request, as curiosities from the realm of people of low and servile condition. In what may be an overstatement, Americo Castro described the sixteenth century as a period when "se llega a la dignificación de lo popular en una época que desprecia soberanamente al vulgo, como incapaz de juicio y razonar propio. El Renacimiento rinde culto a lo popular, como objeto de reflexión, pero lo desdeña como sujeto operante" (the popular was given dignified status in an age that haughtily looked down on the common people, who were considered incapable of judgment and adequate reasoning. The Renaissance worshiped popular culture, as an object of reflection, but it disdained the popular as portraying ways to act).[16]

During the Spanish Renaissance popular *refranes* were printed in three forms: in simple lists of the items, in glossed lists where interpretations were attempted, and as part of literary discourses of all genres. Scholars of Spanish literature are more generally aware of the third of these modes, where the *refranes* in the texts were clearly understood to belong to, or have been lifted from, another level of discourse, that of the everyday speech of their day. As for the lists, which are not as widely familiar, the humanists who collected proverbs increasingly preferred to explain, and not just list, popular sayings, no doubt because of the Erasmian model that so deeply influenced the intellectuals of Spain in the sixteenth century.[17] Aside from the Latin translations, several very significant lists of *refranes* in the vernacular language were published without glosses, most notably the *Refranes o proverbios en romance* (Salamanca, 1555) by Hernán Núñez, but the Comendador, as he was called, died before he could accomplish the task of explaining and discussing them. Pedro Vallés had limited glosses in his collection, but the most extensive attempts at explanation of context, origins, and use of the *refranes* were those adduced to one thousand sayings in the *Filosofía vulgar*, published by Juan de Mal Lara in 1568.[18] Gonzalo Correas's massive collection, completed by 1627 but not published until 1906, incorporated the *refranes* and proverbial phrases that he discovered as well as those of his predecessors, with whom he, in the fine scholarly fashion of his day, frequently disagreed and argued in his manuscript.[19]

What seems to be forgotten or considered a commonplace unworthy of comment by modern paremiologists is that the major collectors of Spanish *refranes* in the sixteenth century up to and including Correas were all male members of that era's intellectual/scholarly elites: most of them were professors, latinists and helenists at Seville, Salamanca, Alcalá, and so forth. The intellectual communicative vehicle of the time was Latin, and many of these scholars also knew Hebrew and Arabic, all of which facilitated their moving easily within the European intellectual world of their time, in terms of physical contact and in print or writing. For them, the use of the vernacular language, *romance*, seems to have been of philological interest: how do people use this common language? what is it exactly that they say? what do certain words and phrases mean? We should keep in mind that Spain's dominant classes of the sixteenth century were involved in forming a new nation, in creating Castilian as the important language in the new political entity called Spain, and in asserting both nationhood and cultural distinctiveness in the face of national rivalries as well as the supremacy of Latin as the European intellectual language. Juan de Valdés used many Castilian *refranes* in his 1535 *Diálogo de la lengua*, where he saw fit to say the "en aquellos refranes se vee mucho bien la puridad de la lengua castellana" (in those popular proverbs one sees very well the pure state of the Castilian language).[20] But this defense by Valdés of the vernacular language of his country occurs in the context of his assertion of a class difference, a difference of relative prestige, between the ancients (and himself) and the *pueblo*:

> los [refranes] castellanos son tomados de dichos vulgares, los mas dellos nacidos y criados entre viejas tras del fuego, hilando sus ruecas, y los griegos y latinos, como sabéis, son nacidos entre personas doctas y están celebrados en libros de mucha doctrina. Pero, para considerar la propiedad de la lengua castellana, lo mejor que los refranes tienen es ser nacidos en el vulgo. (p. 13)

(Castilian proverbs spring from common sayings, most of them born and bred among old women spinning beside the hearth, while the Greek and the Latin, as you know, are created among learned persons and are celebrated in books of great worth. But, for purposes of considering the true likeness of the Castilian language, the best thing about the *refranes* is that they were born among the common folk.)

They are "authentic" and to Valdés's mind, therefore, they provide pure data about a new language he is promoting abroad. Of course, Valdés also used *refranes* as rhetorical devices throughout his book, as authority in his arguments, and, very significantly, as vehicles for humor.

Juan de Valdés was a Spanish diplomat in Naples, so his circumstances were not totally similar to those of the professors of Latin and Greek back in Spain who were busily studying languages and, as part of that study, in many cases spending years compiling lists of popular proverbs, called *refraneros*. To some degree their work with the vernacular language represented an aspect of a transition with which not everyone was equally comfortable. At least a sector of the erudite community in Spain showed reluctance and embarrassment at having to write on occasion in *lengua vulgar* instead of Latin, as in León de Castro's introductory remarks to the 1555 edition of Hernán Núñez's proverb collection:

> De manera que, pues los más sabios de los hombres en tanto tuvieron los refranes, y tanta autoridad les dieron, juzgo que el Comendador Hernán Núñez mi maestro, no se empleó en cosa baxa, como a mí y a otros podía parecer. . . . Hernán Núñez rogó . . . que . . . buscase algún hombre que estas letras supiesse, que pusiesse en un prólogo el valor y estimo del refrán, do parece que tuvo alguna voluntad que yo como su discípulo, hiciesse esto. . . . Pues que yo lo sabía, no pude dezir que no (aunque se me hizo harto de mal), porque bien veo lo que a muchos parecerá a cabo de tantos años de estudio, salir con un prólogo y en romance, pues escrivirlo en latín en obra de romance no quadrava; . . . espero que a mí no me porná en culpa de escribir en lengua vulgar.[21]

(Therefore, because the wisest of men regarded popular proverbs so highly and gave them so much authority, I conclude that the Comendador Hernán Núñez, my teacher, did not spend his time on some mean subject, as I and others may have thought. . . . Hernán Núñez asked that I find a man who knew these writings and would do a proloque about the high value of the *refrán*, and he seemed to want me, as his own disciple, to do it. . . . I knew that and could not say no [although it upset me quite a bit], because I can imagine what it will look like to many people, that after so many years of study, I come out with a prologue, and in the vernacular—it would not be fitting, after all, to write a Latin prologue to a work in the vernacular; . . . I hope no one will criticize me for writing in the vulgar tongue.)

Despite such academic resistance to their efforts, humanistic scholars in Spain's sixteenth-century universities and intellectual circles went on dog-gedly—even competitively—collecting and commenting on the *refrán*. These scholars included Hernán Núñez, Pedro Vallés, Sebastián de Horozco, Juan de Mal Lara, Lorenzo de Palmireno, Francisco de Espinosa, Gonzalo Correas, and others. I do not find most of them so terribly interested in the "moral truths" expressed in the mouths of the common people, truths that Erasmus had guessed there would be in his endorsement of that kind of scholarly object, although many of their commentaries, for reasons of sociopolitical and religious context as well as some personal bent, did stress the connections between the ideas and morality contained in popular *refranes* and those of classical and biblical authori-ties. On the whole, they seem to have been quite intrigued with the language of the popular classes. Thus their obvious desire for inclusiveness and exactitude led them to list rough, obscene, unacceptable, controversial, and immoral proverbs in their collections.[22] Not all the original editions and manuscripts were censored either by the compilers themselves or by the authorities, and their works give the impression of being true scholarly research. There is some hedg-ing of bets by means of adding lengthy explanations and cluckings of tongue over how awful some of these common sayings were. But they seldom left the data out. There are some fascinating verbal and logical gymnastics to be found, like Mal Lara'a lengthy *glosa* to "¡Ay, qué trabajo, vezina; el ciervo muda cada año el penacho y vuestro marido cada día!" (Ay, what a lot of trouble, neighbor; the buck grows a new set of horns every year, and your husband does every day!):

El Comendador declara, que moteja a su vezina, y que cada día ponía nuevo cuerno a su marido. Tres cosas ay en este refrán muy notables. La primera, el dolor que muestra la vezina. La segunda, la semejança que trae natural del ciervo. La tercera, el daño que recibe el marido. Es la verdad que, considerando bien este negocio, no era para escrivirse, pero teniendo entre manos la materia, y viendo que ay de todo en ella, somos obligados a buscar cosas que hasta agora no han tratado muchos, y dízense en nuestra lengua cosas que, pidiendo razón, no se sabe dar. Porque en castellano ay pocos libros curiosos y que aprovechen para saber. He preguntado a muchos, que por qué se llama uno cornudo. Y como el dicho es tan odioso, me responden que si es pulla. Esto dizen los mas alterados. Otros, que no han provocado tal cosa. Otros, que les guarde Dios de tal sobrenombre. Otros, que no es menester saberlo. y assí digo yo, por cierto porné lo que he hallado. Y al fin, si no acertare en ello, téngase por entendido que en este negocio lo mejor es errarse. (ML, II 9–10)

(The Comendador states that this criticizes the neighbor, who put new horns on her husband every day. There are three noteworthy things in this *refrán*. The first, the sorrow the neighbor shows. The second, the natural analogy with the male deer. The third, the harm the husband receives. It is true that, considering this matter carefully, it should not be put in writing, but having the material in hand and seeing that there is a bit of everything in it, we are obliged to look for things that until now not many have discussed, and things are said in our language that no one seems able to explain. For there are few interesting books written in Castilian that are an aid to knowledge. I have asked many people why it is said that a man wears horns. And, because the phrase is so hateful, they ask me if this is a joke. That is what the most disconcerted men say. Others answer that they have not provoked such a thing. Others beg God to keep them from having such a epithet. Still others say that it is not necessary to know the answer. And to that I say that I will certainly put down what I have found out. And after all, if I am not right about it, let it be understood that in matters of this kind it's best to be mistaken).

He then capsulizes some natural history, zoology, alludes to animals in heat to explain the metaphorical analogy, and ends his lengthy comments with a somewhat defensive statement that his intention is to understand the saying with his reason, and one should, of course, always watch the decency of one's language.

Mal Lara's glosses to the thousand *refranes* from Hernán Núñez on which he comments are probably the most chatty of all, and they make Correas, especially, look curt and taciturn by comparison. But these scholars collected as many popular sayings as they could find, using others' written collections, which they normally credit, particularly if they disagree on meaning or even on the form of the sayings, and by actively seeking new sayings on their own. Mal Lara states in his preamble "De la novedad de glosar refranes" (On the novelty of explaining *refranes*) that when he was in Salamanca in 1548 "el Comendador Hernán Núñez juntava refranes y aun los comprava" (ML, I, 11) (the Comendador Hernán Núñez was collecting popular proverbs and even paid for them). According to Miguel Mir's preface to the 1906 edition of the *Vocabulario de refranes y frases proverbiales*, a similar fieldwork technique was used by Correas: "usaba el método de la observación directa, inmediata, *in fraganti*, por decirlo así, de los fenómenos lingüísticos que pretendía estudiar" (he used the method of direct, first-hand, *in fraganti* observation, so to speak, of the linguistic phenomena he was trying to study). Mir elaborates on the particulars of that method, somewhat rhetorically:

Después de explicar en su cátedra del Colegio Trilingüe las arcanidades de la lengua santa, las gracias del habla helénica o los viriles accidentes del hablar romano, el Maestro Correas, dejada su muceta y birrete, salía a las calles y se mezclaba con el vulgo de las gentes, metiéndose por casas, ventas y mesones, siguiendo con anhelosa curiosidad a los niños en sus juegos infantiles, a los mozos y mozas en las lozanías de su edad, a las mujeres en sus faenas caseras, a los varones maduros en sus contratos y mercaderías, a los viejos y viejas en sus debilidades y chocheces.

Pendiente, digámoslo así, de sus labios, asistía a sus tratos y conversaciones, escuchaba sus disputas y querellas y recogía cuantos dichos, frases, refranes, brotaban de las lenguas de todos.[23]

(After explaining from his Chair at the Trilingual College the arcane secrets of the holy language, the gracefulness of Greek or the manly features of Roman speech, Maestro Correas put aside his cap and gown to go out in the streets and mix with the commonest of people, entering houses, inns, and taverns, following with eager curiosity children in their games, young lads and lasss in the exuberance of their years, women in their household tasks, mature men in their contracts and market dealings, old men and women in their dotage and ailments.

Hanging on their every word, one might say, he was present at their dealings and conversations; he listened to their disputes and quarrels, and he gathered all the sayings, proverbial phrases, and popular proverbs that sprang from everyone's mouth.)

Mir goes on to say that Correas rushed home to write down what he heard. This obviously was Mir's attempt to explain the extraordinary richness and variety of the Correas manuscript, but without alluding to sources of his description of method used, which leads us to wonder how much of it Mir simply imagined. There is an earlier source. A letter by Bartolomé José Gallardo, who refers to a Salmantine tradition of the late eighteenth century, put it this way:

El Mro. Correa [sic], hombre de singular humor, es fama en Salamanca que ya en sus últimos años tenía la humorada de hazerse poner los días de mercado un sillón a la cabeza del puente, junto al famoso *Toro* . . . i al charro que le dezía un Refrán que él no tuviese en su Colección, le daba un cuarto por cada uno.[24]

(It is said in Salamanca that Master Correas, a man of singular humor, had the strange idea of having a chair placed for him at the head of the bridge, beside the famous statue of the *Bull* . . . and to any bumpkin who told him a popular proverb that he didn't have in his Collection, he gave a coin for each one.)

Whatever the real details of his method, the Correas collection is impressive and contains many sayings that were definitely anything but moral axioms. To my mind, this in itself indicates that he and his paremiological colleagues gathered data more as linguists and philologists than as moral philosophers or ideologues. Of course, by Correas's time (1627) we already see the ideological phrases so unceasingly repeated by Spanish folklorists of proverbs in later centuries: "Los refranes son evangelios chicos" (The *refranes* are miniature Gospels) and "No hay refrán que no sea verdadero" (There are no untrue *refranes*). But the overwhelming bulk of the evidence available points to the conclusion that despite the moralizing or corrective comments that Correas and other Renaissance paremiologists occasionally inserted into their explanations or prologues, the best of them tried to be all-inclusive and true to their object of study.[25]

In a 1978 article Fernando Lázaro Carreter discussed what he believed to be the difference between folklore—particularly *refranes*—and literature.[26] His essential contrast was that the linguistic forms of *refranes* were imposed by a society on its members as part of an unchanging cultural baggage to be memorized, and that the freedom to break from "el redil tribal" (the tribal sheepfold) by modifying past forms was available only to literature, which he characterized as having originality. At several points he added comments referring to the contemporary loss of folklore's validity, like the following:

La rápida desaparición del Refranero en nuestra actual conciencia colectiva, aun lamentándola muchos, y siendo en ciertos aspectos nostálgicos lamentable, no parece indicio valioso de pérdida de aptitudes idiomáticas por parte de los españoles; existen otros síntomas mucho más graves. Revela sólo que la comunidad hispano-hablante ha perdido docilidad ante esas consignas acuñadas que, formando red, trabaron y configuraron la sociedad tradicional, imponiéndole virtudes reales o falsas, justificando sus buenas y sus malas acciones, inmovilizándola en conformismos, a veces sumamente cínicos. (143)

(The rapid disappearance of the treasure of traditional popular proverbs from our contemporary collective awareness, even though many are sorry about it, and it is lamentable in certain nostalgic aspects, does not seem to be a valid indicator of a decline in the linguistic aptitudes of the Spanish people; there are other much more serious symptoms of that. It reveals only that the Spanish-speaking community has lost its meek acceptance of those fixed phrases that, forming a net, trapped and shaped traditional society, imposing on it real or false virtues, justifying its good and bad actions, locking it firmly into conformities that were often deeply cynical.)

As a structuralist, Lázaro Carreter here views Spanish proverbs as pure form, without wishing (as anthropologists would prefer) to specify which conformities and what good and bad actions he means: he explicitly refuses to consider content and meaning in his objectivizing of proverb structure. Thus he is not viewing proverb texts in context, but as separate little nuggets removed from literary or speech discourse, and from cultural contexts. Proverbs never occur all by themselves, except in collections, and it is the collections, or, rather, the 1967 Combet edition of Correas's *Vocabulario* . . . , that Lázaro Carreter is really commenting on, despite his reference to the verbal aptitudes of today's Spaniards. He ignores here both the conscious use of proverbs as verbal strategies in literature and the realities of the oral tradition. In doing so, he perpetuates the surprisingly monocultural perspective and printed-text orientation of Spanish paremiology of the past two hundred years, where seldom if ever does the simultaneous existence of the same proverbs in other cultural traditions become a problematized issue and no one studies the dynamics of the actual use (which continues today, *pace* Lázaro Carreter) of proverbs.

Roman Jakobson and P. Bogatyrev suggested in 1929 that folklore, like language, was a collective phenomenon with definite regularities of pattern (*langue*), but that there were also particular, idiosyncratic, actual texts of folklore utilized by individuals (*parole*). It is this aspect, the individual variation in use, that Kenneth Burke called the study of proverbs as instruments of verbal strategy, and that Alan Dundes and E. Ojo Arewa labeled "the ethnography of speaking folklore."[27] When we analyze literary works like the *Libro de Buen Amor, Celestina, Lazarillo de Tormes*, and *Don Quijote*, it is not enough to cull the text for aphoristic expressions and list them (Gella Iturriaga has done this time and again and editors of many works include such lists as a helpful aide).[28] We must study the dynamics of their inclusion in the overall discourse for how and why they are used, for what they accomplish in the larger text, just as students of human communication and sociolinguists study the modifications of the meaning of a proverb within a particular conversational setting, examining relationships, power games, and possible ironic up-endings of usual or expected meaning. While we correctly generalize that proverbs "have the function of summing up a situation, passing judgment, recommending a course of action, or serving as secular precedents for present action," that, too, is not enough.[29] We know that the Archpriest of Hita ends his poem in praise of small women with the *refrán* "del mal, el menos" (Take the least of [two] evils). But when he does so, he contradicts the entire force of the appreciation he had so lengthily expressed by reminding us, with the *refrán*, that the small woman is still a woman after all, and if you can't live without women, at least take the smallest of that evil. The saying "del mal, el menos" in itself has nothing to do with women except in that connection established by the context of the poem. Therefore, the context creates the metaphor *mal=mujer* (evil=woman) for the proverb.

This manipulation of proverbs by the discourse context(s) occurs in prose and in speech today as in the past. A curious Renaissance example of that manipulation is the first published book of glossed *refranes* in Spain that is not a pure list in alphabetical order like most of the larger collections: the anonymous *Refranes famosíssimos y glosados* (Burgos, 1509). It contains in twelve short chapters a father's advice to his son, the same framing device used by Santillana in his list of *Proverbios*. Unlike its historical contemporary, *Celestina*, this little volume of prose self-consciously calls itself a *refranero*, or proverb collection, and highlights most of the proverbial expressions with large capital letters and thicker ink, introducing them with phrases like "y bien es" (and true it is), "por eso dize el refrán" (that's why the proverb says), and "por eso se dixo" (that's why it was said). The *refranes* are placed at the end of particular pieces of advice as culmination or proof of a point argued, to claim its accuracy, truth, and sense by appeal to common opinion in the popular phrasing that opinion has found. While the placement pattern and function of the proverb texts here are not untypical of the rhetorical style seen in other Renaissance works and in proverb use generally, we might profit from closer analysis of the interrelationships of the intentionality of the discourse, the choice and curious mix of specific *refranes*, and what happens to the metaphorization of the proverbs.

Chapters 3 and 4 of *Refranes famosíssimos y glosados* constitute probably the first written Spanish *refranero* of the subtopic Woman, within a misogynist surrounding discourse, much like what Martínez Kleiser was still doing in 1931 in his essay *La mujer en el refranero* and José Jara Ortega in 1953 in his more subtly devised book, *Más de 2.500 refranes relatives a la mujer*.[30] The overall discourse of these two chapters has a profoundly antifemale cast, and it colors or modifies the "meaning" of some sayings that have other referents than women, and men's troubles with them.[31] For example, although the heading of chapter 3 is "Que habla de las mugeres" (that talks about women), the discourse actually deals with the son's future wife (who is to be the subject also of the advice in chapter 4). It begins with a firm, extended antifemale statement that makes the rather neutral proverb "Casarás y amansarás" (Marriage will tame you) apply only to the woes marriage will bring to the male. Similar context-specific meaning is applied in this passage to "Quien bien ama, tarde olvida" (One who loves well is late to forget), "Quien hace un cesto hará ciento" (One who makes a single basket will make a hundred), "Al enhornar se hacen los panes tuertos" (The loaves get misshapen when they are put in the oven), "Quien por mal de otro se castiga" and "Del agua mansa te guarda" (Beware of still waters), all of which can refer to women and men alike and to matters other than marriage. This passage of course contains a large proportion of female-specific proverbs too. But beyond that it provides models and examples, even advice on how to use *refranes* as verbal strategies to accomplish certain purposes: women will excuse themselves by saying X, you should answer with Y and Z, and do not say it directly, but to a third party, or tell an anecdote that contains *refranes* A and B in conversational subtext, and so forth. The conflictive tone of these two chapters (and the other ten, for that matter), one that puts clearly the jockeying for power of two people who use proverbs as weapons or tools in their verbal struggle, combines with the humorous effects of the rhetoric itself to make this text a sociolinguistic document of sorts that would bear comparison with the proverb use in *Celestina*.

A great deal of work remains to be done in analyzing Renaissance prose texts of this sort; the advantages to be gained by referring to proverb collections of the period involve the possibility of scrutinizing the proverb texts that were not used in literary discourses, as well, as those that were. Those older collections (on which many modern collections have been based) are richer on specific topics, in levels of decency in language use, in multiplicity of voices and attitudes, and represent an ideology disparate from those of the literary products of their age and later. No discourse-related authorial "selection" presents a mediation of language use, and if we study them in the context of cultural traditions and the relationships between different strata of groups in a society, much can be learned about heretofore silent groups and the true intentionalities of literature.

The particular aspect of cultural value systems that interests me here is that which deals with male and female sex and gender roles, the perception and expression of the relationships between men and women, and the female voices "heard" in the Renaissance *refraneros* that have been muffled, if not silenced, by the cultural intentionality of the dominant classes and the male sex in terms of the denial of access to public voice for women. For instance, one of the Hispanic, indeed Western, "high cultural" clichés that was perpetuated through imaginative literature, as well as by written laws, theology, philosophy, and medicine, is that women are inferior beings.[32] Because of the negative view of women that pervades his published work, Gonzalo Correas has been characterized as a misogynist like other stellar figures of the misogynist Spanish seventeenth century such as Quevedo and Tirso de Molina. Even so, Correas's *Vocabulario de refranes y frases proverbiales* at least includes many aphoristic texts never used in print by Tirso or Quevedo or their literary contemporaries. The proverbial texts I refer to go far beyond those sayings that merely talk *about* women, those that regard them as objects or the quintessential Other, describing women, prescribing acceptable behaviors for them, condemning them as irritating presences in a male world. There are other proverb texts that express female points of view, female experiences, and verbal creativity by women and girls. This kind of proverbial text sometimes contains an implicit disparity between the culture's normative statements and the lived realities of a sector of the nonpower groups that can help us put into context the literary works of a past age. It can also contextualize the documentary evidence, the statistics of social historians, and the structure of custom, ritual, and architecture analyzed by social anthropologists.[33] If, for example, "high cultural" documents of any historical period systematically omit an entire type of proverb text that their contemporaries knew to exist and recorded, we can further refine our concept of the nature of the exercise of social control, that which is effected and maintained by the creation of whole groups of "nonpersons."

I alluded earlier to the fact that most collections or commentaries on women and Spanish proverbs have focused on sayings that mention the female explicitly in her various life stage and roles (women, daughter, maid or virgin, widow, whore, nun, baker's wife, old woman, mother-in-law, daughter-in-law, among others), or on those that contain a feminine pronoun, as in "La que . . . " (She who . . .). When masculine pronouns like "El que . . . " (He who . . .) are used in proverbs, determining the gender referent is problematic: grammarians still insist that the masculine form does not exclude the feminine as referent (*hombre*, or man, equaling *ser humano*, or human being), but sociolinguists and psycholinguists have been proving succssfully that such is not the case, at least when a man uses those terms.[34] For practical purposes here we might accept as a theoretical or abstract possibility that, as traditional male authorities would have it, the masculine pronoun is unmarked for gender. The feminine form, by contrast, never refers to males, and proverbial expressions that contain feminine nouns, pronouns, and adjectives constitute a very large proportion of Spanish *refranes*.

Beyond such direct and explicit third-person allusions to women, there are other Castilian proverbs and sayings with an identified first-person female.[35] These female selves are most readily perceived in the *dialogismos* or Wellerisms like "Kon el vino sano io, marido, con el agua póngome mala" (C, 423) (Wine makes me healthy, husband, and water makes me sick), "Marigüela, ¿fuiste a la boda? – No, madre, mas galana estava la novia" (C, 526) (Mariguela, did you go to the wedding? – No, mother, but the bride looked beautiful), and in *refranes* like "Ke no kiero ser kasada, sino libre y enamorada" (C, 383) (I don't want to be a married woman, but free and in love), "Ke no kiero, no, kasarme, si el marido a de mandarme" (C, 383) (No, I will not marry, if my husband is to rule over me), and "Marido, de la boda vengo, i paz kiero io; otro día iréis vos allá i no rreñiré io" (C, 526) (Husband, I come from the wedding, and I want peace and quiet; some other day you'll go and I won't nag you). The female identity of the first person, or one or both of the voices in a Wellerism or *dialogismo*, often depends on the factors in what Peter Seitel has called the proverb situation:

the relationships and context of what the proverb itself literally portrays.[36] Thus, in the proverbs quoted above a mother and daughter converse, a single woman rejects the constraints of marriage, and a woman speaks to her husband in ironic self-defense. Considered solely as texts, as specific linguistic forms or verbal structures not contained within a larger discourse in which a speaker uses them as a verbal strategy, these proverbs often lack internal metaphors. In such cases the metaphor is created when someone lifts a proverb from a passive repertory and applies it in speech or written discourse to what Seitel terms the interactional context: the dynamics of the situation in which a speaker and listener are involved at that moment.

Some lifting and application of the core proverb require changing the gender referent, and indeed, the Renaissance and Golden Age collections include some *refranes* with variants wherein only the gender of the pertinent nouns, pronouns, or adjectives changes. For example, "Io dígole ke se vaya, i él abáxase las bragas" (C, 161) (I tell him to leave, and he takes his pants down) is otherwise given as "Io dígole ke se vaya, i ella se arremanga las faldas" (I tell her to leave, and she lifts up her skirt); the inopportunity of a sexual gesture or invitation is retained in both variants, but one version has a female speaker, the other a male speaker. But what of other proverbs where the Renaissance collections do not show a variant for the male speaker? Is it merely a case of omission? Juan de Mal Lara declared that all proverbial sayings pertinent to marriage are meant and used literally, but we can try for hypothetical purposes to imagine a masculine version of an expression like "Ke no kiero, no, kasarme, si el marido a de mandarme" (No, I will not marry, if my husband is to rule over me), although I have been unable to find one in the collections. My invention, "Ke no kiero, no, kasarme, si la muxer a de mandarme" (No, I will not marry, if my wife is to rule over me) has no "societal" sense in the Spanish tradition because the expectation of all concerned is that, as he should, the husband will rule the wife, and when he does not, he is regarded as a noxious aberration. But, also hypothetically, one could imagine a joking use of "Ke no kiero, no, kasarme, si el marido a de mandarme" by a man who is perhaps reluctant to join in a task or project where he would be subordinate to another male. The context of conversational use in that case would have to be subtle, the speaker very much in control, and clearly humorous effects intended, because for cultural reasons having to do with male pride, fears of suggesting homosexuality, and male avoidance of any analogy with a female, a Hispanic male might not use that phrase in reference either to himself or to his male listener. My purpose in inventing such a hypothetical verbal strategy is to emphasize that it is in the context of a different overall discourse that metaphorization of a proverb frequently occurs, as well as to underline the situational-use limitations to one sex or the other that I perceive in the texts of many traditional Castilian proverbs.

There is yet a third type of female-related proverb, a type quite discernible to those persons who are consciously aware of the traditional contexts of women's lives, their spheres of activity, their biological functions, their relationships, duties, habits, and proscribed behaviors. It is here that some sophistication regarding European women's history sharpens our eys and ears, in addition to knowledge of cultural anthropology of traditional Mediterranean societies, of traditional architecture, of the history of Western "mentalities," and sociolinguistic research into women's speech patterns and habits.[37] For example, European or Western ideological dictates for women have, among other things, long specified that women should spend all their time and unceasing efforts on domestic tasks within the home, the sort of prescribed behaviors and spheres encapsulated in such proverbs as "La muxer en la kasa, i el hombre en la plaza" (C, 204) (The woman at home, and the man in the plaza), which is a neat expression of the concept of separate public and private spheres and roles for women and men. Logic, then, leads us to the conclusion that men would not say, referring to themselves, "Marikita, daka mi manto, ke no puedo estar encerrad(o) tanto" (C,527) (Mariquita, give me my cloak, I can't stand being shut in so long); the freedom of movement accorded traditionally to the Spanish male would simply make this rather senseless.

Still within this third group or type of female-related proverbs, a significant number of metaphorical proverbs do not mention women explicitly, but rather women-related tasks or objects, and can have therefore at least two very different meanings and uses. Numerous proverbs mention *la olla*, which is the container or stew pot as well as the stew that is cooked in it. Yvonne Verdier, in her book *Façons de dire, façons de faire: La laveuse, la couturière, la cuisinière*, and Martine Segalen, in *Mari et femme dans la société paysanne*, corroborate for France what the Spanish *refranero* reveals of Spanish traditional culture: that women had the cooking responsibilities and that men were never symbolically connected with the slow cooking of the ubiquitous culinary mainstay of traditional life, the stew, except in the eating of it. Thus we find what I call the "recipe proverbs," or instructions about how properly to prepare *la olla*: "Olla ke mucho hierve, sabor pierde" (C, 175) (A stew that boils too much loses its flavor), "Olla sin sal no es manjar" (C, 175) (A stew without salt is not a meal), as well as those *refranes* that make explicit reference to social rules or custom in connecting the woman to the cooking and the man to the privilege of taking the first helping: "Kasarme kiero, komeré kabeza de olla, i sentarme he primero" (C, 374) (I want to marry; I will eat the best of the stew and I will be first at table), and the curious "Pensé ke no tenía marido i komíme la olla" (C, 465) (I forgot I had a husband and I ate [all] the stew). The cultural and expressive identification between the woman and the stew, and between the woman and the stew pot itself, has led to the perception of another analogy or level of metaphor in these proverbs: the woman *is* the *olla*. Thus cultural context leads to the understanding of "Olla sin sal no es manjar" (A stew without salt is not a meal) as referring to an erotically "appetizing" or "unappetizing" female. The metaphor applies to the sexually active or promiscuous woman in "Olla que mucho hierve, sabor pierde" (A stew that boils too much loses its flavor) as much as it does to the idea that sexual activity with the same woman for a long time becomes boring; the metaphor is also clearly present in "La muxer viexa, si no sirve de olla, sirve de kobertera: (C, 207) (If the old woman can no longer be the pot, she can serve as its cover), where the play on the word *cover* alludes to an older woman assisting the secret liaisons of a younger one.

Another frequent internal, or textual, proverb metaphor for the female is the analogy between woman and the *gallina* (hen). The analogy is explained not just by the qualities of stupidity and flightiness generally assigned by tradition to both chickens and women, but also by the fact that in traditional Europe women were in charge of the henhouse, which was considered as being either close to the house or sometimes, actually inside it. Castilian proverbs at times make a completely and simply explicit analogy between the behavior of women and chickens, as in "La muxer i la gallina, por andar se pierden ayna" (C, 205) (If women and hens wander, they get lost out there), and they may allude to the female responsibility for raising and receiving the products of the henhouse with "La gallina de mi vezina pone más huevos ke la mía" (C, 188) (My neighbor's hen lays more eggs than mine does) or "La gallina de mi vezina siempre es más gorda ke la mía" (C, 188) (My neighbor's hen is always fatter than mine is). The metaphor woman = hen is more implicit in other proverbs, like "Cien damas en un korral, todò es un kantar" (C, 300) (A hundred ladies in a courtyard is one big crowing), "En casa del ruin, canta la gallina y el gallo calla" (ML, II, 214) (In the worthless man's house, the hen crows and the rooster is silent), and "La gallina ke en kasa fika, sienpre pika" (C, 188) (The hen who stays at home always nibbles). The last of these refers to some cooks' habit of sampling food all day and not being hungry at mealtime; it, too, took on a sexual connotation that expresses the distrust a man feels when his wife is not in the mood for sex when he comes home at night.

If we are alert to the traditional contexts of women's lives, other *refranes* that may lack direct references to women either as objects or as subjects, or that do not comment on women by metaphorical analogy, are seen to be female-related or even uniquely female proverbs. Women are the childbearers and the raisers of children to about the age of six. Consequently, proverbs that refer to that physiological and social process communicate predominantly, if not exclusively, female concerns: "El niño ke mama i kome, dos kueros pone" (C, 90) (The child who both nurses and eats puts on two hides); "El niño i el becerrito, en mitad de la siesta an frío" (C, 90) (The child and the young calf get chilled in the middle of a nap); "Quien presto endentesce, presto hermanesce" (ML, IV, 12) (One who teeths early will soon have a brother or sister); "Criatura de un año saca la leche del calcaño" (ML, II, 313) (The year-old who nurses sucks the milk from the back of your heels); "La ke presto empieza, presto lo dexa" (C, 193) (She who begins (giving birth) early will be done with it early); "Mala noche, i parir hixa" (C, 531) (Such a bad night, and to give birth to a girl). Furthermore, there are many instructional, or "how-to" proverbs about cooking, cleaning, weaving, spinning, sewing, baking bread, growing and using herbs, nursing the young or the sick, and maintaining relationships within the family and the community that fall within what were deemed to be female domains and roles in traditional society. These are eminently practical expressions in many cases and can be interpreted literally; they pertain clearly to the proverbs of pragmatic instruction that so dismay some modern commentators who are entranced not with culture or the use of language but with metaphors in proverbs.[38] Obviously this type of female-related proverb that lacks an inherent metaphor has been regarded as too everyday, too dull, perhaps too blunt, indecorous, obscene, intimate, or ideologically unacceptable to be highlighted in topical collections similar to José Gella Iturriaga's *Refranero del mar* or Nieves de Hoyos Sancho's *Refranero agrícola*, both of which contain much that is highly "practical" and instructional in nature, but that pertains to what has been seen as a sphere of male activity.[39] Sixteenth- and seventeenth-century Castilian proverb collections virtually teem with female voices, voices that give advice: "A tu marido, muéstrale el koño, mas no del todo" (C, 24) (Show your husband your sex, but not completely), and "Kome kon él, i guarte dél" (C, 430) (Eat with him, but be on guard from him); voices that complain: "Marido tras del lar, dolor de ijar" (C, 526) (A husband in the kitchen is a pain in the side [hip]); voices that argue with other women; "¿Kien me llama puta sino kien me ayuda?" (C, 417) (Who calls me a whore but the one who helps me?), and "Io señora i vos señora, ¿kién kozinará la olla?" (C, 160) (I'm a lady and you're a lady, so who's going to make the stew?); voices that console: "La suerte de la fea, la hermosa la desea" (C, 214) (The beautiful woman would like the ugly woman's good luck) and that criticize: "Vergonzosa es mi hixa, ke tapa la kara kon la falda de la kamisa" (C, 517) (My daughter is bashful and covers her face with the back of her skirt), and "A ti te lo digo, hixuela, entiéndelo tú, mi nuera" (C, 24) (I say it to you, dear daughter, but it is meant for you, daughter-in-law); voices that generally express female views or even their willfulness: "Borracha estáis, Mari García. — La voluntad de Dios sea cumplida" (C, 360) (You're drunk, Mari García. — God's will be done). These are women's voices clearly, women who socialized the young and kept resocializing each other into proper behaviors at the same time that they mildly or sharply protest against their prescribed roles or simply expressed inability or unwillingness to live up to them.

Of course, I have been seeing, or "hearing," contexts to these proverbs, and since their cultural presence has only been recorded in printed collections rather than in literary discourse, much of what one interprets them to mean, or how they could or might have been used in the past, depends on who one is in terms of gender, knowledge, and awareness at the very least. An instance of this perceptual difference stems from Mal Lara's *Filosofá vulgar*, in which all his good intentions (and his other accurate explanations, as with *La criatura de un año saca la leche del calcaño*, II, 313), could not prevent him from showing his ignorance of the intimate details of female reproductive physiology. Correas does not provide an indication of the meaning or application of "La muxer ke kría, ni harta ni limpia" (C, 206) (The nursing woman is always hungry and never clean), but his predecessor, Mal Lara, bravely tried to help in his 1568 collection. He explains at length that this *refrán* states the fact that mothers never take the time to eat or devote efforts to their own grooming and clothes but instead expend all their self-sacrificing energies on cleaning, feeding, and clothing their child. That fits the ideological view of the self-abnegating mother, but when a person with more practical knowledge of female realities reads or hears that *refrán*, she recognizes a description of two aspects of breastfeeding an infant: the greater nutritional or caloric needs of a nursing mother will cause her to lose weight rapidly as she nurses unless she eats more than her normal diet, and the problem of the sour smell on her clothes that is caused by the leakage of milk from her breasts. Naturally, one might use this *refrán* either to console or to criticize, depending on the interactional situation and the strategy involved. But the terms of the proverb do not refer to anything but breastfeeding, and the person spoken *of*, if not necessarily *to*, will always be a woman.

Louis Combet characterized the roughness of many *refranes* collected in the Spanish Renaissance—including those that expressed female points of view—as holdovers from the Middle Ages.[40] Implicit in this assessment is the idea that the rough, obscene, scatalogical expressions in those collections stopped being a part of oral proverb use during, and especially after, the seventeenth century except as printed evidence of the past. The new phrases found in the Rodríguez Marín collections of the twentieth century, even if no one knows where he got them or how he and his colleagues may have "polished" them, indicate that Combet is wrong in that assessment. We need to know whether Yvonne Verdier's rural French women informants of the late 1960s were aberrant in their obscene female-to-female talk, and whether Ramón Sender merely invented the rough language his female characters are said to use in the novel about Asturias, *Requiem para un campesino español*, or whether Spanish women, especially when they are in female groups, continue to use this rough language and sharp, witty, ironic tongues. I think it is a fair bet that they do. We know that women have always talked and that women's talk has been considered highly dangerous in the traditional societies of the Mediterranean area.[41] The *refranero* is full of recommendations that women be silent, and full of complaints about their refusal to comply with this masculine dream; speech was women's only weapon—as the saying goes, "Kuchillo de muxeres, korta si kieres" (C, 452) (Women's knife, cut if you will). Far from being the frivolous, mindless chatter the term 'gossip' seems to imply to many people, women's talk, their gossip, was a structural element in the cohesiveness of traditional society, assuring that everyone behaved as they should, inside and outside the immediate family into the street and the neighborhood. And, although canon and civil law and *refranero* permitted and even advised men to dominate and control their women by violent physical means, as in "La mula i la muxer, a palos se an de venzer" (C, 203) (Mules and women are made to behave with blows from a stick) and "La muxer ke no pare ni empreña, darla de palos, kargarla de leña" (C, 206) (The woman who neither gives birth nor conceives should be struck with a stick and laden with firewood), it is clear from a perusal of the proverb collections, at least, that women kept on sharply disputing verbal dominance.

While we wait for sociolinguistic analyses of proverb use in contemporary Spanish speech contexts and for further documents from the past like the memoirs of Madre Isabel de Jesús recently unearthed by Electra Arenal, we can examine the proverbial expressions salvaged by the Renaissance paremiologist/philologists, for those scholars provided us with extensive data about the speech of the common person of their time, whether or not they agreed philosophically and morally with what they heard and whether or not they were able always to provide accurate explanations of meaning and use. In the Golden Age works accepted into the literary canon, we can see glimpses or shadows of the lives and language of the nonelite classes of Spain, but the peephole through which we can know about the cultural dynamics of the Spanish Renaissance, even the Middle Ages, is enlarged greatly by a careful comparative analysis of the printed proverb collections considered chronologically and in the contest of what we know of the historical realities and the literary works of past eras. One of the salient facts provided by such study is that the old women who were the first named informants for popular Castilian *refranes* in the Santillana volume were no doubt living repositories not merely of what I suggest are female-related proverbs but indeed of much of the entire *refranero tradicional*. The evidence suggests that they did not limit themselves to repeating proverbs, but created them: Spanish women of the remote past may have been denied direct access to the printed word, but they expressed themselves in speech and were recorded in part at least by Renaissance paremiologists.

Chapter 5
Literature versus Theatricality
On the Notion of the "Popular" and the Spanish Culture of the Golden Age
Jenaro Talens and José Luis Canet
Translated by Nicholas Spadaccini

Nietzsche used to say that there are no facts, only interpretations. Echoing this principle, an approach to a topic as complex and as debated as that of "popular culture" in the Spanish Golden Age must begin, therefore, not so much with an analysis of the works or authors in whom the "popular" is manifested as in the questioning of the very concept on which such an analysis seeks to anchor itself. That is, it must focus less on the results of reading than on the mechanisms of the act of reading.

A true reading is a task through which meaning is produced from a given textual space. That task is ever more complex and difficult if the textual space confronting us does not belong to the sphere of our own culture, whether or not such "nonbelonging" refers to the language, space, time, or form of civilization. For that reason, approaching a Golden Age work now, well into the second half of the twentieth century, implies that the productive relation author/reader alters its very nature. The reader and his/her culture (as receivers and as virtual coauthors of the artistic product) do not coincide with their homonyms which are already incorporated in the textuality as threads of its signifying fabric.[1] Because of that lack of connection, they tend to erase or obscure the relationship of mutual implication which constituted that product's mode of existence and which, originally, gave it its specific purpose and organization. Our critical path, therefore, is forced to rely on anchorings that would be superfluous and redundant in the case of contemporary works. However, the diversity of points of view (extrinsic, intrinsic, of historical bent, etc.) is justified to the extent that the consideration of textuality as such precedes it, demands it, dominates it, and, finally, recuperates it.[2] In effect, everything ends up being incorporated, assumed, textualized, even those elements that are not immediately perceptible or that a reader would never have dreamed of attributing to a text. Language is never neutral, and even the most innocent verbal play brings with it the stamp of its social origin.[3] It may be that the predominant modes of cognition in a given social formation are blind to this fact, but the absence of a *conscious* glance does not imply an absence of something to glance at, nor for that matter of a glance. Medieval poetry could, in many instances, be approached as mere play, without greater transcendance.[4] For instance, not until the Albigensian crusade (until a century after the death of the first troubadour), did it occur to the Church to attribute ideological origins and functions to the songs of that period. Of course, that origin and function always did exist, and if they are not accessible to us today (as they were then for the Church) from the same textuality of the poems in question, it is, among other things, *because History cannot inform us about the nature of semantic relationships except by ensuring the inscription of its presence in what we know as forms of the discourse.*

If effect, the text functions as a filter. It draws it sustenance from the problems of daily life, even if it is to negate them; even if its later projection is realized on an imaginary board. That way the text unfolds into two opposing spaces: one *exterior to it* (the circumstances, etc.), another intrinsic to it (what it takes from every day life); and the dialectical confrontation of both produces one of the faces of the text: its historicity, the trace of the material conditions of its process of production. At the same time the text organizes ideological tendencies within its own poetic space, and, because of its relation to those tendencies, it constitutes what Cesare Segre has called *cronotype*;[5] that is, a place of confluence of parallel transmutation of the elements of a culture.

The writer locates himself in language rather than language in the writer. To do so, the writer penetrates it armed with the devices offered by tradition, devices that are given to him, as a differentiated individuality, by his social group. This group, rather than the writer, is in charge of the motivations.[6] The individualized writer merely introduces himself in a world that precedes him, while justifying his presence in that world by restructuring a collective "imaginary" that precedes his existence as a writer and whose elements, already elaborated and in many instances codified, impose certain limits upon his mobility. For this very reason, for example, the question of plagiarism never arose for a medieval writer. The very notions of textual debt, of borrowings etc., do not make much sense since, as such, they are elaborations that arose out of a different mode of production, one that was based on the concept of private property; on the supplantation of use value by exchange value; on the cult of individualism, etc., under the aegis of money. Thus, to confront medieval writing from a conception applicable only to bourgeois artistic production is not only an error of perspective but a kind of falsification. The very notion of author implied that of an artisan-continuator of a tradition. The shift from the feudal to the capitalist mode of production supposes the consolidation of the notion of author as owner of his production, of its meaning and use; in short, as *private* owner of its mechanisms of signification. It is in this opposition, usually one that is hidden under the apparent identity of the same concept, *author*, that the problematic of the *popular* is located if we pretend to define such a notion not in terms of reception (popular—successful with the people) but in terms of discursive devices.

Marx said that history repeats itself only as parody. In a sense, an elite culture is but the reincarnation *sub specie imitationis* of an earlier mass culture. Yet we should not confuse mass culture with what is known ambiguously as popular culture, which in the majority of cases is but a second, degraded, reincarnation of elite culture; a parody of parody. Walter Benjamin commented correctly on this matter:

> The mass is a matrix from which all traditional behavior toward works of art issues today in a new form. Quantity has been transmuted into quality. The greatly increased mass of participants has produced a change in the mode of participation. The fact that the new mode of participation first appeared in a disreputable form must not confuse the spectator.[7]

Although this German thinker's reference was to contemporary art, his words are applicable to our case. Apart from essential differences found in their manner of manifestation, the functioning mechanisms of what we have called elite culture and mass culture continue to be the same. For, ultimately, they refer to a problem as old as History itself: that of the oppression of certain classes at the hands of others. In effect, if a dominant class maintains its economic domination by exploiting and cannibalizing the dominated class (or classes), it proceeds similarly in the field of ideological manifestations, such as culture: it gobbles up the wider repertories of the dominated classes. It assumes them as its own and then returns them (in that falsifying and hypocritical process called the acculturation of the masses) to its point of origin transformed as art. Yet insofar as it is the dominant class that defines art and distinguishes it from what is not to be understood as art, the so-called acculturation is no more than a masked form of defending its own interests and values and of combating those forms of practice that alter its system of signification and, therefore, its dominance in that field, relying upon models of value that it previously elaborated. Elite culture is always a residue (and it is important to make clear that elite is not the same as vanguard), and it becomes art (a superior form) when its strength as mass culture begins to wane. It happened with oral literature after the appearance of printed books. A jongleur earned his living by reciting; now he would perform in theaters or concert halls for the pleasure of experts; he would continue to earn a living, but through his exchange value rather than his use value. That is also what happened to photography with the appearance of cinema and to cinema when television established itself as an alternative medium. However, *art* that is conceived as such, while not forgetting that its natural receiver is the class that produces it rather than the *people*, seeks to attract the people to its sphere. For that reason it is forced to adopt the appearance of being "popular." Such a mask might be effective under certain conditions: if the problem is displaced from the productive device toward the elements in which such a device realizes and manifests itself—that is, from the act of uttering to the utterance—and if, as a corollary, the latter becomes central in art, thus initiating the false epistemological dichotomy: form/content.

This process of transformation/manipulation can be seen clearly if we analyze the development of two differentiated discursive typologies: literature and theater. Those two terms encompass, under a common epigraph, two forms of practice that, in the transition from the feudal to the capitalist mode of production, are not only different but contradictory.

In the first instance, that is, in literature, we might use as an example the process that leads from the medieval story to the constitution of the novel as genre in the seventeenth century. It is important to recall here that unlike Lukács, who viewed the novel as a bourgeois form, M. Bakhtin (in an essay written in 1938— *Epos and the Novel*—and only recently translated into a Western language)[8] saw the genre of the novel as emerging from the artistic and popular celebrations of the Middle Ages (principally the fourteenth century), understanding as such not only what we know as literary forms but also festivals, carnivals, and so on. (This thesis was developed in his splendid book on Rabelais.)[9]

This Soviet writer attributes three characteristics to the novel as it goes through the process of constituting itself as a genre and as it initiates the process of evolution of modern literature (what we properly define as literature):

1. Its three-dimensional stylistic nature connected to the multilingual consciousness that is actualized in that process;
2. the radical transformation of the temporal coordinates of the literary image;
3. a new zone for structuring literary images, one of maximum contact with the present in its open-endedness.

Those three charactertistics are organically interrelated and, at the same time, are determined by a certain break in the history of European society. This rupture is marked by the change from the conditions that characterize a semi-patriarchal, closed system, to those that are implicit in the rise of international and interlinguistic relations.

With reference to the first, Bakhtin refers to one of his previous works (*Discourse in the Novel*)[10] in which he explained that while polyglossia always existed, indeed existed prior to pure or canonical monoglossia, it had never been the center of the process of writing until that moment. Although classical Greek already had the intuition of both the existence of different "languages" and linguistic epochs as well as of the variety of Greek literary dialects, literary production was always realized in pure languages: languages that were closed onto themselves, even while being, in the last analysis, hybrid. During the period in question the tranquil coexistence of national languages, each living in a closed circuit, can be said to come to an end. Now languages interfere with, and influence, one another to the point that one language becomes conscious of itself only to the extent that it aggressively stakes out its reference to other languages. The same can be said of each territorial dialect of each national language, of each literary language, of the language proper to each genre, and so on. In that multilingual reality, a new type of relation is established between each language and its object, with enormous consequences for the so-called literary genres established during the period of monoglossia. The consequences are in all respects far-reaching for the later development of verbal art, on a linguistic as well as on a stylistic level.

With respect to thematics, in relation to the two remaining characteristics cited above, the novel would be defined by the alteration of the constitutive features of the epic. In effect the epic (a) had as its object the national epic past (the absolute past, to use the terminology of Goethe and Schiller), (b) utilized national legend rather than personal experience as a source of inspiration, and (c) found itself separated by absolute epic distance from the presence of the poet and of his/her audience. It is precisely in that sense that the productive impulse of epic "literature" can be considered to be the work of memory rather than the work of knowledge. The novel, on the other hand, starts from experience, from knowledge and from practice (it does not draw sustenance from the past but from a yearning of the future). It is not by chance that the theory of knowledge becomes the fundamental philosophical discipline around the time that the novel becomes the dominant literary genre. Of course the epic past cannot be reduced to time as such but is, simultaneously, a hierarchical category of time and a category of value. Walter Benjamin defined the narrator as he who counsels those who listen; it follows, then, that a characteristic trait of the world of storytellers is an orientation toward practical interests. For that reason, "the storyteller takes what he tells from . . . the experience of those who are listening to his tale."[11] From that comes the idea underlying all narratives (except the novel) of the real possibility of existing beyond fiction, that is, of intervening as such, without mediations, in daily life. An example of this can be found in Orson Wells's *An Immortal Story*, a film that is as lucid as it is ironic (a bitter irony, of course).

This last circumstance carries with it an idea worth stressing: that of becoming the specific feature of narration. Benjamin writes:

the "meaning" of his life is revealed only in his death. But the reader of a novel actually does look for human beings from whom he derives the "meaning of life." Therefore he must, no matter what, know in advance that he will share their experience of death: if need be their figurative death—the end of the novel—but preferably their actual one. (ibid., p. 11)

That is why, what we call narration is not didactic, even though it teaches. At least if by the didactic one means—as is generally the case—the transmission of finished and closed knowledge rather than an ongoing contradictory and dialectical process. Of course death does occur in narrative but in order to eliminate meaning rather than to produce it. Death as an ending presupposes that life takes on meaning when it is considered as a whole closed onto itself. If, on the other hand, life is seen as a continuous flux and not as a closed off entity, a transformational process and not a structure capable of totalization caught between a beginning and an end, then death is only destruction; consequently it cannot dispense meaning. Let use remember how in the *Libro de Buen Amor*, for example, the death of Trotaconventos gives way to one of the major indictments ever written in Spanish against that senseless failure of nature: death.

For that reason, since the storyteller's talent is his own life, and his dignity is being able to narrate it, the narrative never tends to lie or to mystify. Those characteristics are to be found more within the realm of the novel, at least insofar as the narrator's position vis-à-vis his narrative is concerned.

The narration of the medieval text is always a *text en situation*.[12] The relationship between text and listener (which is fundamental in the process of the production of meaning) implies a concrete confrontation, a real dialogue between a giver and a receiver, within sight of one another as well as in spatial and temporal contact with one another.

The Middle Ages did not know what in recent times has been called, ambiguously, *art for art's sake*. Without saying that such a theoretically absurd proposal subsequently existed (behind it there always lies an ideological inscription that is perfectly traceable and evident), we can affirm that a medieval writer's practice as writer or as artist responded to the necessity of intervening in a direct and in an immediate manner in the world around him. From that standpoint, narration, poetry (and, of course, the so-called dramatic texts) possessed a character that approached our current-day *happenings*, or psychodrama. It possessed a spontaneity that was invented in the very act of being produced. That seems to have been, at least initially, the charactertics of courtly poetry. Paul Zumthor has said it convincingly:

The most relevant general characteristic of Medieval poetry is, perhaps, its dramatic aspect. Throughout the Middle Ages texts seem to have been . . . destined to function in theatrical conditions as a form of communication between a singer, a recitant, or a reader, on the one hand, and an audience on the other. The text literally "plays a role" on the stage. (p. 37)

In effect, the text is produced in time and is written in space—at least in the West (Derrida has shown in his indispensable works on writing how the graphic reproduction of the previously spoken temporal chain does not occur in oriental cultures, for example). We read spatially, but the medieval audiences did not read; they listened. And such a reception is temporal. Yet, with the possible exception of the *grand chant courtois*, the medieval text integrated devices that made possible the production of equivalents of spatial perceptions (cf. liturgical plays, stage directions, and so on). That has been the mechanism followed later by playwrights in the writing of their texts (implicit or explicit asides, information on staging, or on the movements of lights, characters, etc.) and what allowed theoreticians such as Julia Kristeva to speak of the possibility of a semiotics of theater beginning with textual inscriptions of the phenomenon of the spectacle in the written text.[13]

The text, then, was written in order to be heard. It came into being in the space between the mouth that uttered it and the ear that heard it. The voice rather than the eye has the monopoly of transmission. The text is addressed to a public conditioned by the so-called representational arts and by rituals, that is, by the glance and the gesture. In such a context the voice is limited to the production of a third dimension. If the text is spoken, it is logical to consider as an immediate corollary the fact that, for the people of the Middle Ages, it did not constitute a simple matter of writing (the way we understand it today, tied to the bourgeois concept of literature) but a form of multiple and complete language.

For us, in the twentieth century, the notion of text is related almost instantaneously to that of book, but for the medieval listener it was an auditive, fluid, and mobile object. The utterance was separable from the act of uttering. Gesture and voice in the individual who recited were but two complementary forms of textual existence, of functioning as an active, real, and palpable presence. It is not by chance that in specific areas of Western Romania the terms 'author' and 'actor' came to be confused on more than one occasion during the fourteenth and fifteenth centuries.

The text, therefore, is no more than the trace of the work.[14] Writing (referred to as spacing by Derrida)[15] is, to express it with the felicitous formulation of Henri Meschonnic, a will to live, manifesting a homogeneity of thinking and of language, of being and of saying. For us, writing explains and justifies the pluridimensional character of the text.[16] Yet, by doing so, it also negates the linear originality of the spoken word that produced it. By definition, a text already fixed abstracts the word from its temporality and, as a result, from the historicity that is constructed and affirmed by the word in the very act of being spoken. The text produces an autonomous space. But, of course, that production is not arbitrary since, as with the medieval text, it derives from a prior spoken word. "It has seldom been realized that the listener's naive relationship to the storyteller is controlled by his interest in retaining what he is told."[17] That is why the structuring of a medieval text counts as more than communication as such. It is significant that medieval narrative (the *fabliaux*, for example) prefers verse (language based on repetition) to prose (whose structuring principle is combination). The extreme, though constant, manifestation of that tendency is verbal virtuosity, and the principal mark of the text's theatricality is the fact that action prevails over commentary.

This theatricality, moreover, manifests itself through a presence rather than through *representation*. In effect the representation indicates a double process of abstraction and reduplication: it designates the constitution of an immediately perceptible equivalence, a similarity revealed through the manifestation of an extreme analogy. Hence the mechanism of comparison. Both the comparison and the similarity, however, are the basis for an aesthetics of the general, indifferent to the particular and unrepeatable aspects of the real. In the Middle Ages the world possessed a global truth, one which differentiated itself by stages, through subdivisions, in such a way that the referential axes are already implicit in each word and in each text. Absolutely nothing new or unpredictable could occur. That is what Lotman has called paradigmatic culture.[18] That is why the system of expression was grounded in a form determined by conventions and topoi. That is what happens in Berceo, for example. Yet when a *popular* writer (or one who seeks to be such) – Juan Ruiz, to cite a clear example – is confronted with that framwork, he effects an opening unto the concreteness of the individual and the particularity of experience, proceeding from typologies. In principle this is something analogous to what takes place, according to Focillon, in the field of sculpture with the transition to anecdote.[19] The concrete and the general coexist. But the latter does not give meaning to, and does not clarify, the former. The didactic, therefore, by its dispensable character underscores its fundamental contingency with its presence. It does not negate a superior essence, but it takes for granted that, in any case, it cannot be what explains the most concrete, ambiguous, and contradictory aspects of individual experience. Hence textual theatricality does not imply the representation of a previous *quod erat demostradum* but the representation of experience as such. The open-endedness inherent in its writing is related to this. Only what is completed is *representable*. What is either left open or incapable of being closed off can only be *presented*.

That is why medieval writing, as popular practice, is defined in terms of theatricality and not in terms of literariness. In our minds the term 'literature' is associated with the concept of book. In effect the significance of writing is modified with the arrival of printing. The book constitutes a retreat and a refuge created by the solitude of the printed pages, from which the writer, already separated from his medium – the spoken word – controls a message he wishes only to produce. From having been one of the elements of a process, the writer now elevates himself into a mediator, indeed the master, of what he says. Reading is a solitary act, and, as such, it negates participation in the theatrical sense of the term. It is clear that each reader interprets (which is already a manner of participation), but the reader's intervention in the process is narrow. The dialectical play of the transformation of the work by the receiver, and of the receiver by the work, functions as a fictitiously real interplay in literature. In popular practice it functions as a genuine interplay, as a *sine qua non* of its discursive existence.

Yet is does not always function in this manner. In Gonzalo de Berceo, for example, theatricality is already literature *avant la lettre*. The world that his *Milagros de Nuestra Señora* put forward to the audience is already closed off, and it possess a meaning that is perfectly delimited beforehand. Everything is seen from the perspective of the end. Death and eternal life beyond death give meaning to lived experience.

As a structural framework, this is the position that will be assumed by the practice of writing when it constitutes itself decisively as literature. As a result, the persistence of the "popular" in the novel of the 1600s is only apparent. The themes remain, but the point of view of the speaker does not—nor does the notion of narration as defined by Benjamin. In the prologue to his *Novelas a Marcia Leonarda*, Lope de Vega pretends to narrate as the populace does. Cervantes, speaking through Sancho Panza, ironizes this problem, underscoring the fact that the *novel* implies a learned elaboration from a framework in which the reader has stopped being a participant and has become a receiver.

This process also occurs, perhaps in a more perceptible manner, in the field of theater (the second of the typologies cited above) in the transition from the Middle Ages to the Golden Centuries. Two guideposts are given for the origins of theater in Spain: the carnival festivals and the religious theater. Each will be designated as follows: (a) *representation of everyday life* and (b) *representation of the mythical*.

The carnival festival bases its functionality on *laughter*—with a superficial structure grounded in the presentation of scenes of daily life and a deep structure consisting of laughter as a common liberating element—and on the absence of a fixed text. Everyday life is, after all, subject to change, and what is presented is a concrete moment of its evolution, all of it being unusable in another context and under different circumstances. This festive ambience encompasses masks as well as certain forms of oral literature (blindmen's songs, popular songs) that are characterized by an open and, therefore, modifiable structure.

The religious (mythical) theater, however, represents that *serious* side of the world, with a superficial structure that manages to incorporate elements of daily life for the exclusive purpose of having them shore up the principal element: the mythical. If at times it utilizes laughter (domesticated, under consolidated forms), it does so for the purpose of moralizing. Thus, in order to reach a greater number of people, pressured by the public, the representation of the liturgy will move out of the churches and on to the public squares, adopting in the process some of the forms of popular festivals. Characteristically, those representations are based on closed, unmodifiable, texts; since ancient times the serious has been molded in the written text (Moses's famous *Tablets*, for example).

Theater as we know it today rose out of the dialectic between those two types of representation. The transition from the first type known to humans (based on the imitation of their own reality; the festival, the carnival, whose purport is reality itself) to the second changes the attitude toward representation in a fundamental way. The functionality of a festival rests on participation. Everyone is at the same time actor and spectator. Everyone can create, modify, and, ultimately, live the representation. In the mythico-religious theater, on the other hand, the text begins to be immovable. Moreover the actor distances himself/herself from the spectator,who becomes a passive element and is consequently left out of the generation of the representation and at the mercy of the ideology that it bears.

In this context, where two differentiated types of performances live side by side, the religious works incorporate a greater number of elements from popular festivals—the vernacular, the introduction of characters with a presumed referent in concrete reality, and so on. At the same time, owing to public pressure for greater participation, and because too many pagan elements have entered into it, the representation is taken out of the Church and onto the streets.

This theatrical form, the appenage of a determinate social group (the Church), imposes itself, increasingly, to the detriment of popular festivals, which see the introduction of the serious and the mythical in their performances. A type of literature appears, partly oral and partly written, to become the fixed element of popular festivals (the songs or elements that recall the tradition). At the same time, however, the mythical representations recuperate, increasingly, elements of popular tradition, producing a certain break between the representation and the ideological element that sustains it: once and for all theater moves out of the ecclesiastical domain (the feasts of Corpus Christi, the Nativity, the Passion, etc.), assuming a mobility that is somewhat characteristic of popular festivals and daily life.

But this theater, being dominated by a social group (the Church) that uses it as a propagandistic element of a certain ideology, shuns a class that is becoming ever more powerful: the nobility. The latter, wanting to impose its dominance, utilizes the former's representative schemes as propagandistic elements for its own ends. The result is a theater that is tied directly to courtly pomp. Those dramas are "text" and "spectacles" at the same time and are tied either to religious festivities (for example, the first pastoral eclogues) or to commemorative ones (*dramas-fasto*, political plays, and so on). Soon, however, an osmosis is produced between both currents.[20] The pastoral eclogues now gravitate toward secular themes, and the illusion of participation of the real increases considerably. This situation gives rise to a series of comic-rustic characters; to shepherds and shepherdesses; to idealized, platonic love between disguised young noblemen and their ladies. These pastoral works are commissioned for specific celebrations—religious or secular—and are elaborated accordingly, depending on the occasion (the latter trait is gathered from popular tradition but reproduces the framework of the mythico-religious representations when it becomes formalized in the written text). At the same time its public is quite small, and the *author-actor-spectator* relationship reiterates on stage the same relation that is given in everyday life. Depending on the nature of the articulating elements of the deep structure of the play—everyday life or mythical—this theater revolves around two great axes. When everyday life is the articulating element, the play refers to things that are recalled (for example, the *Egloga* of Francisco de Madrid, which recalls the invasion of Italy by the French; and the *Egloga de unos Pastores* of M. de Herrera, which recalls the conquest of Orán in Algeria by G. de Córdoba known as Grán Capitán). When the mythical is the articulting element, there occurs a theatricalization of courtly life itself—as happens with many of the *dramas-fasto* of Gil Vicente, Luis de Milán and Fernández de Heredia.

In the middle of the sixteenth century these eclogues and pastoral dramas begin to lose their functionality as a new theatrical practice establishes itself through professional author-actors in the streets and other public places. When that practice is actualized, the textual element loses much of its importance, becoming no more than a script used to support a show that is fundamentally entertaining, that has no moralizing pretensions, and whose staging is geared to the type of public that is witnessing the performance. That practice can utilize learned or mythical elements in private theatrical representations, but it can also use popular elements proceeding from a form of the revel or "mocking games" (*juegos de escarnio*), carnival festivals, etc., for representations in public squares. The main characteristic of the theater of the so-called author-actors— and of the Italian *commedia dell'arte*—is the technical professionality of the actors, which brings with it the possibility of improvisation on stage. In their hands the text loses much of its functionality for it can be actualized in each particular representation, depending on the public's expectations. The displacement of the festive as experience to the festive as technique is one more step in the process of mystification of the medieval popular tradition which is now maintained as mere appearance.

At this time there coexists with it a new theater: a humanistic, jesuitic theater produced mainly in universities and academies. This type of theatrical representation uses a fixed, unchangeable text, and, as opposed to the types already described, it recuperates a new form of theatrical representation based on classical models. It is a theater that emerges under didactic principles: to accustom students to colloquial Latin, to instruct them in rhetoric. It is a theater that is both solemn and entertaining. This type of theater gains in popularity through the introduction and use of the Castilian language, so that its form and part of its content appropriate the forms of daily life. Some of those theatrical representations will become integrated in the ideology of a new social class, one that begins to emerge vis-à-vis a nobility that is in the process of decline and an absolutist monarchy that is becoming ever more powerful.

Hence many of the tragedies of the so-called classicists (Cristóbal de Virués, for example) propose in their deep structures a defense of tyrannicide and a certain criticism toward the absolutist monarchy. But this theater, which is distinguished by a structure that is overly rigid and fixed and incorporating few elements of daily life, could not compete with a more popular kind. For that reason it will not succeed in reaching a substantial audience even if it is to provide certain structural forms to a new dramatic current in its formative stages: Baroque theater.

From a confluence of various dramatic elements in the sixteenth century there arises a new type of theatrical representation, one that supposedly concerns itself with daily life, with stock types (the fool, the shepherd, the moorslayer, the young lover, etc.), with a supposedly real referent, and with a type of plot borrowed from Italian novellas and from the *commedia dell'arte*. Although this type of representation is based to a great extent on the world of daily life, myth still predominates in its deep structure while sustaining its textual rigidity. Yet it does manage to develop a technique originating from popular traditions by incorporating "popular" characters and their whereabouts to attract the largest possible audience for the purpose of moralizing. A perfect but costly symbiosis has been achieved, therefore, between two theatrical forms that initially appeared to be irreconcilable. From this moment on both of these original forms will be banished from the world of theatrical representation. The new theater (the *comedia*) will serve various purposes: religious feasts (*comedias* dealing with religious topics, lives of saints), courtly celebrations (mythological plays, splendidly staged spectacle plays), and popular entertainment (cape and sword plays, sensational plays, with plots and counterplots, and so on).

At the same time this type of theatrical representation contains a great dose of moralization and ideological propaganda that seeks to extol model behavior as well as concrete religious and political attitudes. Clearly the *comedia* serves the political interests of an absolutist monarchy and of a post-Trent, counterreformational Church which backs its power. Hence those earlier types of theatrical representations—the ones referring to feudal or medieval interests—no longer have a reason to exist toward the end of the sixteenth century. That is why the *comedia* of the Baroque period establishes itself decisively, erasing from the world of the theater and from the world of popular festivities any other type of representation. The theater of the seventeenth century, therefore, becomes popularized (that is, it reaches a greater number of people) at the same time that the conception of the world in that theater ceases to be "popular." For the true popular forms of entertainment, in which the world is placed upside down, have disappeared from the history of theatrical representation. From then on the public can act only passively, rewarding or punishing an author with greater or lesser attendance at the place of performance. But the public will no longer be able to participate in the ideological generation of the performance itself.

If Juan Ruiz's theatricality gives way to the literariness of María de Zayas and the carnavalesque undergoes a similar change in Lope de Vega (with both authors — María de Zayas and Lope de Vega — enjoying "mass" appeal), does it make sense to continue speaking of popular culture in the seventeeth century? In the final analysis, that is the question.[21]

Chapter 6
"Vos outros tambem cantai por vosso uso acostumado": Representation of the Popular in Gil Vicente
Ronald Sousa

The words of my title—"Vos outros tambem cantai por vosso uso acostumado" (You too sing, according to your custom)—are said by Fé (Faith), the representation of Christian belief, to the shepherds Bras and Benito at the end of Gil Vicente's *Auto da Fé (Play of the Faith).*[1] The play, a slight one of some 330 lines, was presented to the court of the Portuguese king Manuel after that court had celebrated Christmas matins in the year 1510.[2] Like much of Vicente's early "pastoral-religious" theater, it is in the very strictest of senses occational: much as had been the case with his first play (*Visitação*, or *Monólogo do Vaqueiro* (*Visitation*, or *The Herdsman's Monologue*), of 1502, the central concept of *Auto da Fé* is the two peasants' appearance at the palace chapel where matins had just been said and festive celebration of Christmas is beginning. What is done with that dramatic situation to lead up to the lines reproduced in my title can, and eventually must, be analyzed with regard to the cultural-literary practice from which it arises and which it in many ways subsumes, as well as with regard to Vicente's own prior and subsequent work. For example, the play is the last of his so-called sayagués plays—continuations, in his fashion, of the pastoral-religious theater of the Salamancan playwrights Juan del Encina and Lucas Fernández. (As a result of that precedent, the shepherds of *Auto da Fé* speak sayagués, whereas Faith, by contrast, speaks Portuguese.) The entire dramatic development from Salamanca to Lisbon undoubtedly owes to the peninsular Church miracle and morality plays of which we know primarily by reference in Spanish sources. Before I allow such elements to enter the analysis of *Auto*

116

da Fé, however, I wish to engage in a preliminary reading of a generally technical nature, after which I shall let those other considerations enter slowly, in an
effort to extend that initial reading in what I consider to be useful analytical
directions.

The first item in reading is necessarily an accounting of the situation of the
play's staging. Because of the radically occasional setup, there is in fact minimal
proscenium function in the play, and what there is is highly permeable: the
actors playing the character roles were probably given a small space and were
watched by a more-or-less formally composed audience, while in the world
behind that minimal proscenium they observe in amazement the splendor of the
court and as well the symbols of the Christian faith, both circumstantially present at the site, as though the court were going about its Christmas celebration
unaware of their presence. Thus, while only the peasants and Faith have speaking parts, the nobility/royality/upper-level clergy *is* presented within the text. It
both is represented *in corpore* as an element strongly present in the world of the
play through the permeable proscenium arrangement and also is re-presented —
to itself, as audience — in the language of the play, through the words of Faith
and of the represented peasant figures who comment on its appearance. Thus a
key feature of the play is treatment of a multifaceted juxtaposition of what are
defined as representations of two social groups.

The active element is that represented by the shepherd figures. Bras and
Benito enter the royal chapel and react to what they see. Their initial bedazzled
reactions indicate social inadequacy: they cannot identify much of what they
encounter and bumble around, aware of their inadequacy, providing the material
for a broad verbal humor grounded in social differentiation:

> Ben. Cata, mas ha hi que mirar:
>   qué siñifica esta mesa
>   con tanta retartanilla?
> Bra. Bobo, es cama á for de villa,
>   chaqueada á la francesca.
> Ben. Cuerpo de santa Pipía!
>   sabes mas que tú ni yo.[3]

> (Ben. Look, there's more there to see:
>   What does this table, with so much
>   Stuff atop it mean?
> Bra. Fool, it's a town-bed
>   Decked out French-style.
> Ben. By Santa Pipia's Ghost,
>   You know more than either of us!)

Indeed, those lines manifest a characteristic feature of the play's language: the shepherds metaphorize in a specific, idiosyncratic way about the items they are unable to identify with adequate terminology: "cama á for de villa, chaqueada á la francesa" has analogues throughout the play applied to the people and things that they see in the chapel. In fact, there is soon suggested a standing relationship between the characteristics of the shepherds' diction and the items of upper-class culture — items the terms for which in that culture we are regularly provided with in the stage directions or by Faith, when she finally comes in to help resolve the shepherds' dilemma. The metaphorical or metaphorlike locutions uttered by the shepherds usually incorporate reference to specific objects and social practices, are openly typed as "rustic," are composed periphrastically, and sometimes employ a biographical-experiential dimension reflected in anecdote. Opposed are single, usually referentially abstract terms that regularly come imbedded in an elaborate abstract metaphysics.

Overcome with their verbal-cultural inadequacy, the shepherds wish for a "lletrado, que supiera esto entender" (86) (lettered [i.e., literate/learned] person, who would know how to understand all of this). They need a guide into a culture that they admit is superior to, and has authority over, their own. The guide who appears immediately after the wish is verbalized is Fé, specifically called by them a *lletrada*.[4] Incidentally, she is said by Benito to be dressed "á la morisca" (Moorish-style). Commentators continually repeat that remark as an instance of cultural syncretism,[5] not seeing that what syncretism there is is lexical and that what is at work in the passage is the same sort of culturally based humor as occurs elsewhere in the play: Benito, unable satisfactorily to identify Faith's Christmas finery, again destroys himself culturally as a result, and again is therefore comic.

When the shepherds ask Fé what all this is that they have encountered, her response is:

> A divinal claridade
> seja em vosso entendimento,
> e vos dê conhecimento
> de sua natavidade.   (88)

> (May divine clarity
> Enter your minds,
> And may it give you understanding
> Of your nativity [i.e., nature].)

Her answer is hardly one involving the issue of cultural differentiation, which has been the primary element at work in discourse-shaping up to this point. Instead, she insists that the shepherds are innately capable of understanding all that faces them if abstracting divine light is made to enter their understandings and they thereby become aware of their true identities. She in essence states that the guidance that she can provide will lead to a higher resolution of the problem presented to her. She then goes on to explicate the surroundings in theological terms, turning circumstance into language and, simultaneously, attempting to catechize her two interlocutors.

It becomes clear at this point — if it was not so earlier — that the core problem of the play is the nature of Christian cultural continuity and that what we have before us is a kind of shepherds' play deriving from the Christmas *officium pastorum* — though to be sure an unusual one. At the point where Faith enters, we expect the shepherd figures to begin to play the role of the shepherds of liturgy, to (re)experience the Nativity, leaving behind the state of nature that we can presume their cultural ignorance to betoken, thereby acting as symbols of the transparent, simple sincerity and openness to a metaphysics grounded in faith that is the human soul presumed by traditional Catholicism. In short, we expect a movement in the play's langauge, through transmutation of the status of the shepherd figures, from, according to medieval exegetic hermeneutics, *sensus literalis* to *sensus anagogicus*, and we expect that movement to affirm both universal Christian culture and the language constitutive of that culture, a language ultimately grounded in the Word of God. Indeed, this play of all plays, with the title *Auto da Fé*, promises such a movement: exposition to the soul, through the medium of faith, of the Word as guarantor of unity of culture and language.

What happens, then, is surprising. After Faith majestically introduces herself: "Pastores, eu sam a Fé" (Shepherds, I am Faith), Bras replies: "Ablenuncio Satané! fá ni fé no sé que se es" (I renounce Satan [to be read as a general interjection of surprise]! I don't know what faith is, or even fa). And the play goes on in that vein. Faith explains that the Christian symbols, and the shepherds, comically, metaphorize now not only about the symbols but also about the language of the attempted explanation, in just the same manner as they had previously done. It becomes a battle between hermeneutic literality, given a very tangible culturalist development in the representation of the shepherds, and Faith's constant effort to locate signification at the anagogic level and thereby to unify a discourse whose disunity is becoming more and more apparent as the play goes on. In rhetorical terms, the battle is one involving competing metaphor systems. On the one hand, Faith attempts to establish a set of culturally given metaphors that define a relationship between existence and presumed essence, as when she explains to Bras:

> Aquella he a cruz preciosa,
> pera sempre esclarecida,
> pera os perigos desta vida,
> e nao da salvação nossa.

O homem se chama Jesu,
Messias, Rei, Salvador,
Deos e homem, Redemptor;
(não sei se o entendes tu)
Deos he seu nome maior. (90)

(That is the precious Cross
Forever immanent
Against the perils of this life
And ship of our salvation.
The man is called Jesus,
Messiah, King, Savior,
God and man, Redeemer
(I don't know if you're understanding);
God is his greatest name.)

In contrast, Bras responds with a much less theological formulation of his own, but one with certain trinitarian implications:

Mi amo ha nombre tambien
Pero Alonso, y Pero Matos,
y Perazo lo llaman hartos,
ansí como á mano vien. (90)

(My master is named as well:
Pero Alonso and Pero Matos,
And Perazo many call him,
Whatever comes to hand.)

One is tempted to worry that the third term, 'Perazao', with all its morpho-semantic implications, corresponds to the Holy Ghost. Be that as it may, obviously two discontinuous concepts of master or lord and of the implications of the naming of that personage are at work in the passage, and, again, they describe a struggle between a culturalist literality on the one hand and anagogy on the other.

On the play goes in the same manner, Faith trying to get the shepherds to relive the Nativity, with all that that implies, as behooves shepherds on Christmas (93), but getting the same "concrete," "biographical" responses. In short, instead of the expectable movement from literality to anagogy, the second part of the play involves a dialogue between literalist discourse and anagogic discourse that ultimately is not dialogic but rather merely enacts a process of canvasing a series of key items circumstantially present about which the two sides discourse, each in a code that meets the other only back at the point of departure: in the item itself. Thus the presumed Christmas shepherds' "simplicity"—the vehicle for raising from literality to anagogy—never moves from its original constitution: "simplicity" is worldly "ignorance," or "inferiority," even "stupidity."

The entire situation is gnomically represented in what is a very clever nine-line sequence constituting Bras's reaction to the explanation of the Cross that Faith offers:

> Alla en nuestro lugar
> si no viene lluvia ni vella,
> toman una como aquella
> nuestros amos, á clamar
> *ora pro nubes, ora pro nubes;*
>   y las mugeres ansí
> la que mas gritillo tiene:
> la lluvia ni va ni viene,
> e la cruz estáse ahi. (90)

> (In our land
> If mist and rain don't come
> Our masters put up a Cross
> Like that one, calling
> *Pray for clouds, pray for clouds;*
>   And the women too,
> Especially the ones with the loudest voices;
> Rain doesn't show up
> And there the Cross stands.)

A reading of the lines in immediate contextual terms reveals but another instance of rustic metaphorizing, here articulated by an anecdote containing what amounts to a popular etymology that, humorously, resides in phonic differentiation of only two sounds: *nobis* becomes *nubes*. That small difference serves to set in relief the cultural-linguistic divergence that has been built up to this point, one between referential concreteness and referential abstraction, practicality and idealism, ritual grounded in direct observation and ritual grounded in an elaborate metaphysics. That reading, however, merely sets up background for a series of further, metalinguistic readings. The nine-line sequence constitutes an elaborate chiasmus whose pivot comes between the two halves of the center line, between the two instances of "*ora pro nubes,*" and whose end line—"e la cruz estáse ahi"—proclaims that we have just had a chiasmus, or "cruz," uttered. Thus is traditional rhetoric suggested. Biblical rhetoric, for example, makes great use of chiasmatic structures, from simple chiasmus to entire inverted panels—of which the sequence in question is an example in miniature. If we look upon the sequence with that linking in mind, it can be read as an ironizing of Biblical rhetoric through rehearsal of it with trivial content as a response to the explanation just uttered by Faith. The last line can then be seen to say "That is all that chiasmus can put forth in this situation"—"la cruz estáse ahi." "Cruz" also signifies "burden," and in context "e la cruz estáse ahi," so read, suggests failure of Christian ritual heretofore to produce results, or, analogically in this context, to produce anagogy. Further, "cruz" is cognate and parallel to English "crux," 'a crucial point to be made.' In the light of the other lines of signification that run through the entire nine-line sequence, lines that sum up the nondialogic dialogue that has been taking place, the last line read as "there is the crux of it all," "la cruz estáse ahi," can be seen as a metalinguistic commentary on, and summing up of, the play's problematic to this point. At very minimum, then, the lines release another discourse to play a role in the language of the play: a discourse that resides in rhetoric itself and that posits the existence of metalinguistic commentary on the language of the play. In fact, that rhetorical discourse, here confirmed, has already suggested itself in less obvious ways several times earlier in the text. Its impact within the play is multiple. In traditional "characterization" terms, it keeps the shepherds from being representationally autonomous, for, as in this example, the significance of their words occasionally exceeds their language, to be registered in another discursive system as well—in a manner that is humorous. Their deficiencies are thereby added to in relation with yet another aspect of the text. The presence of the rhetorical discourse thus alludes to the text itself as rhetoric, to a complex communication with the audience, to authorship. In the final analysis, given its role in comic domination of the represented shepherds, it suggests an organizing force within the text that promises throughout a final resolution in favor of upper-level Christian-noble culture. It suggests, in sum, that what is in doubt all along is not "whether or not" but rather "in what manner" that resolution will be effected.

After we reach that "crux" of the play, the movement to resolution—that is, to "how" it will be achieved—is rapid. The nondialogic dialogue moves on for a scant few lines, if only to give Benito the chance to follow out in a limited way Faith's suggestion that the shepherds try to use imagination to reach greater understanding. He follows it at least far enough to contemplate how nice it would be to "ver a nuestro Dios nacer" (see our God born). That is, he contemplates movement toward the expected participation in the *officium pastorum* but ends up asking a factual question about the Nativity instead.

Finally, in answering that factual question, Faith concludes:

> E porque elle [Cristo] é dado a nós,
> cujo imperio he eternal,
> faz esta corte real

a festa que vedes vós.
vos outros tambem cantai
per vosso uso acostumado
como lá cantais co'o gado:
ambos de dous começai. (95)

(And because he [Christ] is given us
Whose Kingdom is eternal,
This royal court prepares
The celebration that you see.
    You too sing
According to your custom
Just as you sing with your herds;
Both together now, begin!)

The argument is key. It moves from Christian "imperio . . . eternal" (Kingdom . . . eternal) to the rhyming "corte real" (royal court), suggesting interrelationship: the royal court celebrates the presence of the eternal empire by having a "festa" (feast, festival, celebration), which, of course, is culturally meaningful precisely because the court is "real." The "festa" is thus a claim for celebrant as well as celebrated. That mutually confirming relationship between the two loci of authority is made clear rhetorically when it is seen in the context of the play, for it has already been emphasized that Christian, upper-level culture is true and socially superior, and it has been promised that this culture will ultimately triumph. And it is from the rhetorical union of noble and Christian that there emerges the imperative that constitutes the title of this chapter. Faith tells the shepherds that they "too" should "sing." In that way, they "too" participate in the observance that anchors the superior social, cultural, and linguistic order, the order that Faith had suggested as universal in her first speech. It is now obvious, however, that the case is quite different from the one she initially proposed. There is now no talk of "claridade" (light) entering "entendimentos" (understanding[s]). The participation suggested instead is a mere formal following-along, since it is quite clear that the shepherds have not been moved into commonality with the dominant culture through movement to anagogic status. Indeed, Faith's immediate addition of "por vosso uso acos-tumado" (according to your custom) confirms precisely that disjuncture. Further, the song that Benito gives us has in itself absolutely no Christian cele-bratory value. It is rustic, associative, culturally inadequate, and therefore comic—as was much of the shepherd language before. After the song, however, Bras thanks Faith for having shown the shepherds "el cielo" (Heaven), and the play ends.

At this point we are left with the problem of understanding what sort of resolution has in fact occurred. There has been no raising to anagogy, no demonstration of a single basis of language and culture. What is left is pure authority, which of course has all along been a part of the claim for Faith's language, but there it is an authority based on the promise of performance, a promise of the power to create unity. At the end of the play, however, Faith simply tells the shepherds to sing, and they sing a song from their "own culture" that has no inherent correspondence to the issues invoked but which participates. It is a resolution that, contrary to the notion of a necessary interrelationship between human nature and Christian faith inherent in the medieval exegetic hermeneutic itself, is grounded in cultural divergence, with union only through an authority principle.

That point is clearly the critical one—for a reading of the play and of its immediate cultural significance as well. Rather than pursue it within the text—a pursuit that will quickly reach a point of diminishing returns—I shall here break off my reading and attempt instead to "surround" it with approaches from several other viewpoints: from a review of other related texts, from a brief consideration of the socio-cultural implications of the song Benito sings, and from an analysis of the implications of the court's presence in the play.

Although it is by no means unequivocally clear, *Auto da Fé* would seem to have been the seventh play of Vicente's career. Of the preceding six, all save the first—which is occasional and involves shepherd figures, but is not devotional—and the last two, are religious festival plays. In the first of those devotional plays, the *Auto Pastoril Castelhano* (Castilian Pastoral Play), written for Christmas matins of 1502, there is Gil Terrón, a sayagués-speaking shepherd who, unlike his companions who in many ways recall Bras and Benito of *Auto da Fé*, is constitutionally called to a contemplative life. It is he to whom the nativity is announced by the Angels and who explains in detail to the other shepherds aspects of doctrine—as Fé does in *Auto da Fé*—and leads them to adore Christ. That this represents a change in his character is observed by another shepherd, who says to him:

> ¡Á Dios plaga con el ruin!
> mudando vas la pelleja:
> Sabes de achaque de ygreja!

> (God be praised by the outcome!
> You are changing your skin:
> You now know the Church inside out!)

And Gil answers:

Ahora lo deprendí. (29)

(It just now came to me.)

The change prompts another of the shepherds, after having been catechized by Gil, to remark:

> Gil Terrón lletrudo está;
> muy hondo te encaramillas.

> (Gil Terrón has become a *lletrado*;
> You've climbed into the depths [of yourself].)

The lines are important as forerunners of the language of *Auto da Fé*: being a *lletrudo* is compared to "climbing into the depths" — of yourself and of presumed devotional and cultural truth. In terms of plot, Gil Terrón undergoes a process of personal/metaphysical anagnorisis. In terms of language, he articulates movement to anagogy. His response to his companions' analyses:

> Dios hace estas maravillas. (31)

> (God performs these miracles.)

As precursor of *Auto da Fé*, then, *Auto Pastoril Castelhano* demonstrates the possibility of the movement from literality to anagogy, with all its implications regarding culture and language, thus indicating what was taken up but very pointedly *not* achieved eight years later in *Auto da Fé*.

The other important early play is *Auto dos Reis Magos* (The Play of the Magi), presented on Epiphany of 1503. In that play, two shepherds come seeking the Christ child. A hermit whom they meet remarks, in a passage that indicates the type of language that he uses throughout:

> Oh bendito y alabado
> y exalzado
> sea nuestro Redentor
> que un rústico pastor
> con amor
> lo busca con gran cuidado. (37)

> (Oh blessed and praised
> And exalted
> Be our Redeemer
> That a simple shepherd

With great love
Should seek him with such dedication.)

The three eventually run across a nobleman who is also seeking Bethlehem; the shepherds and the nobleman get into a quarrel—apparently for no other reason than class conflict. It turns out that the nobleman is a separated member of the Reis Magos' entourage. When the shepherds find that out, they apologize for their "ignorance" in language that resembles that of the shepherds' self-analysis as inferior in *Auto da Fé*. The nobleman responds to the apology by replying to one of the shepherds:

Yo te perdono, pastor,
que el Señor
por cualquier culpa mortal
no pide al al pecador. (47)

(I pardon you, shepherd,
For the Lord
Asks only that of the sinner
For any mortal sin.)

Now the situation is somewhat different from the two Christmas plays, but there are representations of each class defining the other linguistically and entering into opposition. There *is* a culturalist characterization. No move to anagogy occurs, since the setup is different, and the hermit has enacted an explanatory part all along, with the others engaging in complete, meaningful dialogue with him. The resolution of the class-based quarrel, however, coming in a pardon given by the nobleman in the name of greater pardons given to greater transgressions, paves the way for a reaching of Bethlehem. Thus a tiny rift in a presumedly unified culture is quickly patched up in the name of the prime guarantor of cultural unity. Nonetheless, there is in *Auto dos Reis Magos* a hint both of the culturalist analysis that is to come in *Auto da Fé* and also of the universal resolution that will there be denied.

By contrast, no such class-based constitution is given to shepherds, and no such sense of class opposition is to be seen in the work of the Salamancan playwrights from whom Vicente derived these structures (with the exception of a passage in Lucas Fernández's *Comedia de Pravos* (Comedy of Pravos)—and there it comes about and is resolved differently). Instead, the entire situation with the Salamancans is different: by and large, shepherd figures—very clearly, the shepherd and the entire pastoral mode are frequently used and polivalent at this time—are not given a hint of even the culturally divergent status that is present in Vicente's first play, *Monólogo do Vaqueiro*. Instead, the Salamancans invest their shepherds with thinly disguised nobiliary status; in short, in the Salamancans the courtly use of the pastoral predominates. Courtier psychology is strongly present in their shepherds' makeup, and corresponding language frequently breaks out in their rhetoric, betraying the fact that they do not proceed from any consistent analysis of cultural divergence. The contrast helps to set off and define Vicente's culturalist analysis of the shepherd. The tendency to such analysis becomes greater in the works immediately preceding *Auto da Fé*, the first two of his farces, *Quem Tem Farelos?* (Who has Bran?) and *Auto da India* (Play of India), both obviously benefiting from familiarity with the recently printed *La Celestina*. In the farces, social-class identity codes are dealt with and broadly parodied; proverbs appear in abundance. In short, seen within Vicente's career, *Auto da Fé* would seem to represent a crux of yet another sort: the bringing together of several lines tentatively explored before, the examination of how they work out together, and the following out of the result. I shall return in a moment to touch upon that juncture.

First, let us look to the question of the song that Benito sings at Faith's behest. It reads as follows:

> No no no no no no
> no no no
> que no, que no,
> que no quiero estar en casa;
> no me pagan mi soldada
> no no no, que no que no.
>
> No me pagan mi soldada,
> no tengo sayo ni saya
> no no no, que no que no. (95–96)

> (No no no no no no
> No no no
> No, to be sure, no, to be sure.
> To be sure, I don't want to stay inside;
> They don't give me my just pay,
> No no no, to be sure, to be sure.
>
> They don't give me my just pay,
> I have neither bib nor apron,
> No no no, to be sure, to be sure.)

Aside from the phonic negativity that characterizes the song and provides its chorus, the language is remarkable for its form, incorporating the technique of *leixa-pren* (literally, 'letting drop . . . picking back up') and probably constituting a fragment of the parallelistic song that came from the popular level into upper-level literature during the thirteenth century in the troubadours' *cantiga de amigo* (song of the lover), in which a woman sings of her distant lover. By Gil Vicente's age, however, it had long since passed from literary favor. And, in any case, the text of this example is hardly "literary" in any official-cultural sense. In fact, despite its suggestion of the parallelistic arrangement, the song's content is comically inappropriate. At the same time, however, it appears almost surely because it was associated with the "uso acostumado" of the popular social level in the era. The song thus reaches out referentially beyond the confines of the text to incorporation within a culturalist analysis of an element that has ethnographic and historical resonances connected with that culture. It marks, more forcibly perhaps than any other possible language, the analysis of the shepherds of *Auto da Fé* as culturalistic over and above any other potential mode. The lines that Benito sings are, in the final analysis, a comic parody of popular song functioning as a link to popular-level culture.[6]

Now, if we think back to the fact that what is repeatedly asked for by Vicente's culturally separate and inferior shepherds of the early plays is a *lletrado* as a cultural guide, we can hypothesize in the light of the foregoing considerations that the extratextual reference confirmed in Benito's song is one made to a culture that is precisely not *lletrada*, to one that is orally based. Vicente would not, of course, be invoking our contempoary concept of a modally different oral culture, but it is arguable that the overall representation of the shepherds in *Auto da Fé*—the "concrete" diction; nonlinear, periphrasis-filled language; use of proverb, set phrase, and anecdote; "popular" song—adds up to a bundle that is being presented as different from upper-class culture and that what that presentation attempts to convey is a sense of the presence of what we today would label an oral culture.

It is noteworthy that never again after *Auto da Fé* does Gil Vicente put on stage just "pastores" named Bras, Benito, Gil, and so on. Such names, and aspects of the language that the shepherds of *Auto da Fé* and the other early plays speak, are transferred to the farce—a form being tried out at the time of *Auto da Fé*—in which language-based social typing goes on, growing more and more complex through time. The Christmas shepherd's play too goes on, however, and other devotional plays are written, but with a much more thoroughgoing allegorical structure or like apparatus. In subsequent Christmas plays classical and Biblical prophets appear as shepherds (*Auto da Sibila Cassandra* [Play of the Sybil Cassandra]), seasons of the year as shepherds (*Auto dos Quatro Tempos* [Play of the Four Seasons]), and the shepherd figure serves as cipher for the courtier much as in Encina and Fernández (*Auto Pastoril Português* [Portuguese Pastoral Play]), but no longer do we see plain shepherds and there is certainly no culturalist analysis of them. The one later play that comes close to such a problematic is the *Auto da Mofina Mendes* (Play of Mofina Mendes), of 1534, at the very end of Vicente's career. Although a number of elements of that play are like those of the early plays, much is different, and in the final analysis the shepherds' state of nature allegorizes humanity's forgetfulness of mortality rather than signifying the starting place for a wide cultural problematic. I think that, in the light of that history, one can conclude that in his early sayagués religious-pastoral plays Gil Vicente finds it increasingly difficult to keep culturalist representation from overwhelming argumentation of the subject grounded in traditional hermeneutics, until finally it does exactly that and divides up the shepherd figure—or, rather, what he implied up to that time—reassigning portions of that significance in ways that inform the future work.

The last item to be examined is the source of the pressure that precipitates that division—and the source of the mechanism of the reassignment. I refer to the circumstantial/textual presence of the royal court as articulated in the verbal economy of the play. We have already noted the treble presence of the court. The fact is that the three presences are not isolated from each other; indeed, to the contrary, there is a mechanism that unites them. First, the court provides the sense data for the shepherds. In the nondialogic dialogue its attributes are canvased and named by each side: the shepherds according to their represented cultural paradigm, Faith through engaging in what is presented textually as a transparent renaming, since she reflects the dominant culture, the one shown to be superior. It is clearly at least in part in that role as the voice of culture itself that Faith alone speaks Portuguese. And the entire process, of course, is presented to the Portuguese court as audience. It thus sees its presence and constitution analyzed by the play, and ultimately confirmed. It is in essence given to itself in its own language by an author who in the rhetorical discourse of the play suggests his presence as controller, shaper, and confirmer of all. But in what form does that "self" come? It comes not as God-given pinnacle of homogeneous society ultimately grounded in the Word, as the tradition of the shepherd's play and Vicente's prior career might seem to promise, but rather through the court's own socio-cultural authority, as organizing principle of a society implicitly recognized as heterogeneous. I do not think it at all untoward to see the entire mechanism—court presence leading to definition of the court's implicit participation in the signification process itself and then to re-presentation of that role to the court as audience—as the textual figuration of social forces then at work, as well, correspondingly, as the model of discourse-creation in the play. In a word, I see textual economy, especially given the occasional nature of the work, as representation of social functioning. A degree of homogeneity is by now a necessity for the developing Portuguese state; that necessity leads to analysis of the problematic of real cultural heterogeneity and to efforts to overcome it. The force that needs and seeks to define and create homogeneity and guarantee its viability is the state itself, focused in the royal court. Thus, in the final analysis, *Auto da Fé* is the representation—or rehearsal—of that signifying mechanism to that court itself—a class-bound ideological act. I suggest that it is the circumstantial/textual presence of the court that invokes representation of that mechanism, rendering the traditional movement to anagogy an indefensible proposition. And it is Faith who comes out the prime loser: textually, she is simply inconsistent between her first words and her last.

Now there is one other item that is processed for the court in the same way as are the constitution and role of the court itself – namely, the shepherd figure. It too is posed as material, named, then presented for confirmation to the court as audience. It is named a tangible social category with certain culturally based characteristics. What is happening, in effect, is that a sense of popular-level culture is being propounded and its features are being codified within the text of *Auto da Fé*. Moreover, now-untenable abstract notions of cultural unity are being abandoned in favor of statist mechanisms of unification. While the definition being propounded rests on recognition of cultural difference, its very proposition in this forum constitutes the location of popular-level culture within upper-class, official culture. Thus recognition of difference in the presence of the constituting of authority as organizing principle becomes in effect a homogenizing act: it represents the bringing of the "popular" into a cultural paradigm expanded to include that category, and guaranteed by authority. "Popular" will be characterized as inferior, as grounded in such language as *Auto da Fé* propounds, language based on a metaphorizing of upper-class language, which, in turn, possesses the "true" signifying value – one that, in contrast to the essentially metaphorical discourse ascribed to "popular" language, I would call symbolic.

If we follow the suggestion that the culture being so characterized was primarily oral, according to our contemporary nations of oral culture, with the modal differences from learned culture we now think therein involved, we can glimpse an entire cultural-historical transference being signaled in *Auto da Fé*. Oral culture, which we now think *is* basically discontinuous with learned culture, first is brought into the presence of learned culture – in terms of the text, from the time the two shepherds come in the door, come into contact with the court (i.e., when the first words of the play are uttered) – and then in the play's language it is defined as separate from that culture but in a way that constitutes it as a cultural mode that is not basically discontinuous but only divergent, inferior, idiosyncratic – and whose interchange with what can now be called "high" culture is important, required, indeed guaranteed by state authority.

Now Gil Vicente, court playwright that he is, is notorious for presenting a two-class society; from him we get almost exclusively only *povo* and *nobreza*, little between. The social homogenization project suggested in the structure and language of *Auto da Fé* is pointedly focused in the court. Very clearly the social situation is more complicated than that and rapidly growing even more complex at this precise time: other classes and groups within classes can take up a similar project to similar but hardly identical ends. (I think, as an obvious example, of the Humanists and their circle of influence, who have a very different stake in the representation of the popular.) Furthermore, other groups can be represented linguistically, and other groups can have that representation made to them. And it is precisely theater, of which Gil Vicente is the universally acknowledged primary formal codifier, that will become the first "public" literary medium in the history of peninsular culture. Now, in the case of the representation of the popular, the formal directions Gil Vicente establishes, following the Salamancans and others but setting matters more categorically and in more nearly clear social terms, are more or less followed. Implications of the formal categories, however, will change according to proposer and forum in which the proposal is made. I think specifically of Juan de Valdés's similar representation but very different evalution of aspects of popular language in *Diálogo de la lengua* (Dialogue of the Language).[7]

And the question is not merely limited to a historical object of study. The question "for whom the popular?" here suggested represents a powerful methodological caveat for anyone engaged in studies of "popular culture." Again, Gil Vicente can stand as an example, for by far the majority view of his representation of the popular has it as an unproblematic registering of empirically verifiable "popular material," a view that corresponds to the necessities of the romantic-positivist criticism that initiated, and to some extent still commands, studies of Vicente.

Such are problems ultimately set in motion when Faith tells not only, directly, Bras and Benito but, indirectly, the select audience before which she is performing in a radically new manner "Vos outros tambem cantai por vosso uso acostumado."

Chapter 7
The Stubborn Text
Calisto's Toothache and Melibea's Girdle
Javier Herrero

The Reader and the Text

The tendency of contemporary critics to give considerable autonomy to the reader's interpretation of a text, to the act of reading, requires careful handling. Writing is an act of communication which, among other elements, is compounded of three essential ones: emission, message, and reception. In literature the reception is performed by the reader and through the act of reading.[1] It is obvious that the message is contained in a text that is (or was) sent by an author. It is also obvious that, in most cases, the reader is here, but the author is not; s/he died years, even centuries ago. But even if the author were here, there is no reason to believe that the author's judgment about his/her own work would be any better than the best critic's interpretation of it. This, of course, leaves us with the text and the reader. Is that all? Certainly not. If we accept that the work of art implies an art of communication, it is legitimate to assume that the meaning of the message is somehow shared by the sender and the receiver: such meaning is established through a certain organization of signs, that is to say, to certain signifiers (Calistro's toothache, Melibea's girdle) correspond certain signifieds. But how can we find the signified? This question may seem futile. Is it not clear that any dictionary will give to us for the signifier 'toothache' the signified "Pain in a tooth or in the teeth arising from decay" and for 'girdle' "a sash or belt"?[2] But, as we well know, the essence of the literary message consists of the transformation of literal meaning through the rhetorical manipulation of the semantic value of a word. If a sememe is compounded of semes organized as denotations and connotations, the rhetorical figures of metaphor, synecdoche, metonymy, irony, etc., manipulate such order and, through contextual configurations, bring to the fore semes that would occupy a peripheral position at a purely informative level. I assert, then, that both 'toothache' and 'girdle' can have different meanings from those given by the standard dictionary, although these meanings will be somehow related to them (in this case metaphorically related). But this assertion brings us again to our original question: how can we find out the meaning of these signifiers? The answer, however, is easier than we may expect: to do so is the business of the critic; we find out the meaning of the text through literary analysis.

Popular Tradition and Semantic Roots

There seems to be nothing revolutionary in my conclusion, and I certainly have no intention of being such; in fact, my objective is the much less fashionable action of standing up for a rather rigorous order. All communication is done by signs, and the text possesses a permanent structure based on the interrelationship of these signs: when Quevedo, speaking of a woman who married a *castrato*, writes his poem "De Quevedo a una mujer que viéndole enamorado se casó con un capón" (From Quevedo to a woman who, although he was in love with her, married a castrato) it is obvious that he is introducing a most violent manipulation of the customary use of these words:

> Siendo bella Margarita
> donde el gusto se aniquila
> me espanta que tengais pila
> sin gota de agua bendita,
>
> si es todo vuestro regalo
> el capón que cacarea
> hisopo largo de aldea
> sin barbas y todo palo.
>
> Cuando en vuestro capón piense
> pienso que no pienso mal:
> que teneis cirio pascual
> sin las bolillas de incienso[3]

> (Margarita, being lovely
> where joy exhausts itself,
> I wonder that you have a basin
> without a drop of holy water.
>
> If all your pleasure is
> this cakling capon
> [then, you have] a long, rude, hyssop
> all stick and no beard.

When I think about your capon
I do not think that I am mistaken:
You have an Easter candle,
but without incense balls.

All the images used by Quevedo in this obscene and blasphemous poem are religious. Margarita has lovely genitals ("lovely—where joy exhausts itself"), but
her vagina does not receive the male's semen ("you have a basin—without a drop of holy water"). The male organ of her *castrato* has no scrotum (his
hyssop is "all stick and no beard"; his Easter candle has no "incense balls"). But
a poor critic would be the one who believed that Margarita's frustration was
due to the fact that she could find no holy water with which to purify herself,
no hyssop with which to expel diabolic temptation from her body, and no
incense at Easter to elevate her soul to God! However, nothing could prevent
an unimaginative reader from doing so; but such interpretation would be
wrong. The poem does not mean that. The semantic structure required by the
literary compound of title, metaphor, irony, and related rhetorical devices has
created a system that imposes a meaning. We find such meaning through historical research; through research about the semantic value of the signifiers at
the time and in the society in which Quevedo wrote his poem. Historico-
semantic research forces us to sink our attention on the ambiguities introduced
by popular usage in ordinary meaning; such ambiguities have immense inter-
pretative value. Not only do they allow us to correctly interpret this poem, but
they bring to us the evidence of a profound psyco-sociological conflict. Because
sexuality is expelled from language by religious pressure, it finds revenge by
sexualizing religion's holiest symbols. Metaphor becomes a powerful subversive element.

Calisto's Toothache

We must, then, look deeply into popular semantic manipulations if we intend
to penetrate the veils that hide, from the twentieth century's gaze, the subtle
meaning of the great masters who wrote in an age of conflict. If we do so, the
obscurity is replaced by a radiant clarity that illuminates the text through the
interpenetration of related semantic structures. Two such systems, and their
interrelation, will occupy us here.

Celestina and Melibea: A Dialectic Rape

Celestina goes for the first time to Melibea's house as a go-between of
Calisto. To strengthen her attack she has conjured the Devil and prepared a
charm with which to bewitch Melibea; such charm, with the diabolic power
therein contained, pervades a skein of yarn that she carries with her into

Melibea's house.[4] Melibea soon understands the corrupting aim of Celestina's visit and threatens her with exposure. Celestina retaliates by offering to their conversation a neutral surface that allows for an innocent interpretation of her words; but she will progressively force Melibea to acknowledge her true meaning. It is in this context that we must examine Calisto's toothache. Celestina introduces it as a tactical retreat to answer Melibea's accusations of "alcahueta falsa" (treacherous go-between) and "hechicera" (witch); no, she did not come to seduce Melibea, but to ask for her girdle that has a healing power for having touched the sacred relics of the Holy Land, and for a prayer to Saint Appolonia:

> Yo dexo un enfermo a la muerte, que con sola una palabra de tu noble boca salida, que lleve metida en mi seno, tiene por fe que sanará, según la mucha devoçión que tiene en tu jentileza.

> (I lefte one sicke to death who, only with one worde that should flowe from your noble mouth and descende from thence into this my bosome, I verilie assure my selfe it would save his lyfe, so greate is the devotion which he beares to your gentle disposition, and so greate the comfort he would receave by this kindness.[5])

To Melibea's request for clarification, she answers with the transparent lie that opens the way to a dignified discussion of Calisto's passion:

> Una oración, señora, que le dixeron que sabías de Santa Apolonia para el dolor de las muelas. Assimismo tu cordón, que es fama que a tocado las reliquias que ai en Roma; Jerusalem. Aquel cavallero que dixe pena y muere dellas. Esta fue mi venida; pero pues en mi dicha estava tu airada respuesta, padézcase él su dolor en pago de buscar tan desdichada mensajera. (114)

> (Marrie, a certaine charme, madam, which, as he is informed, your Ladieship hath of Saint Appollonia, which cureth the Toothache, as also that same girdle which you weare there about you. For the reporte goes it hath toucht all the Relique that are in Roome and Jerusalem. Now this gentleman is exceedingly payned with the toothache: he is almost mad, and readie to dye thereof. And this was the whole cause of my cominge. But since it was my ill-fortune to receave so unpleasinge an answer, lett him still for me continue in his paine, as a punishment dewe for sending so unfortunate a messenger.) (113)

Toward the end of the conversation Melibea has accepted Celestina's excuses and, somehow, seems to have felt the undercurrent of meaningful but dark suggestions conveyed by her message, since she gives to the old woman a contradictory message:

¡O cuánto me pesa con la falta de mi paçiencia! Porque siendo él ignorante i tú inocente avéis padecido las alteraciones de mi airada lengua. Pero la mucha razón me relieva de culpa, la cual tu habla sospechosa causó. En pago de tu buen sufrimiento, quiero complir tu demanda; darte luego mi cordón. I porque para escrivir la oraçión no avrá tiempo sin que venga mi madre, si esto no bastare, ven mañana por ella muy secretamente. (116–17)

(O how I am fallen out with mine own impatience! How angry with myself that, he being ignorant and thou innocent of any intended ill, thou hast endured the distemperature of my enraged tongue! But the great reason I had for it, frees me from any fault of offence, urged thereunto by thy suspicious speaches: but in requital of thy sufferance, I will forthwith fulfill thy request and likewise give thee my girdle. And, because I have no leisure to write the charm, till my mother comes home, if this will not serve the turn, come secretly for it tomorrow morning.) (Mabbe-Allen, 81)

Obviously Melibea's answer works at two levels of meaning. At a superficial level, she accepts the excuses of innocence of Celestina and so establishes a pact of apparent respectability. Melibea agrees to accept the convention of Calisto's sickness and of her ability to provide remedies; Celestina must play her role and keep her suggestions at the level of medical metaphors. At another level, the recourse to postpone the writing of the prayer for another day and, above all, the request for great secrecy ("mui secretamente") in her next visit clearly show that she knows very well that such innocent respectability is a game, and that she is agreeing to establish, through a "tercera" (a go-between), an illicit and dangerous relationship with Calisto. That this is true is confirmed by the remark of Lucrecia, Melibea's maid, who on hearing her words exclaims:

¡Ya, ya perdida es mi ama! ¿Secretamente quiere que venga Celestina? ¡Fraude ai! ¡Mas le querrá dar que lo dicho! (117)

(Now, now, is my mistress quite undone. All the world cannot save her; she will have Celestina come secretly tomorrow. I smell a rat. . . . I fear me she will part with something more than words.) (Mabbe-Allen, 81–82)

Wonderful intuition! Indeed Melibea is ready to give more, although of how much more she is not even aware, and most certainly will vigorously refuse to be made so:

Melibea.   Más haré por tu doliente, si menester fuere, en pago de lo sufrido.

Celestina.   Más será menester; más harás, i aunque no se te agradesca.
Melibea.   ¿Qué dizes, madre, de agradeçer? (117)

(Melibea.   I will do more for your sick patient than this, if need require,
              in requital for your great patience.
Celestina.   We shall need more, and you must do more than this, though
              perhaps you will not so well like of it, and scarce thank us for
              it.
Melibea.   Mother, what's that thou talkest of thanks? (Mabbe-Allen,
              82).

'Toothache': A Popular Metaphor

Celestina has spoken in an aside. Melibea is not yet ready to allow the frail
surface of meaning to crumble and the powerful, erotic reality implied by
Celestina's profound language to emerge with full clarity from the level of the
vaguely perceived to that of the consciously and willfully comprehended and
accepted. She must remain, at that time, in a twilight in which meaning is only
figuratively suggested and darkly understood. But Melibea is a character in a
book: she did not see what the reader was supposed to see. And the reader was
assumed to understand Rojas's suggestion because Celestina's allusions are
clothed in strong and vivid images taken from an underworld to which she
belonged and whose sublanguage, formed to a great extent through the semantic
manipulation of the ordinary one, was well known to the literate reader of the
late fifteenth century.

The toothache as a sexual metaphor surfaces occasionally in popular literature, in texts of an erotic or occult character. In a poem printed in Valencia
between 1589 and 1602, entitled *Cuarto cuaderno de varios romances*, we find
a song that was danced to the famous music of *La Chacona*. *La Chacona*, an
immensely popular dance that replaced *La Zarabanda* when this second dance
was forbidden because of its immorality, became an immediate success that
lasted throughout the seventeenth century. The zeal of the moralists was certainly defeated, because *La Chacona* was even more lascivious that *La Zarabanda*. This is how a contemporary describes it:

> All such movements and gestures that can move to lust, everything that
> can corrupt an honest soul, is presented to the sight in the most vivid
> colors. She and he feign sweet regards and kisses, swing their hips, meet
> with their chests, closing their eyes, and it seems that, dancing, they arrive
> at the last climax of love.[6]

The song that I shall quote here shows how right the moralists were in their
furious wrath. The theme of the song is the effort of a lover to slow his

movements during intercourse, so that the woman could achieve orgasm simultaneously with him. Obviously, no poet could develop this idea in the seventeenth century in direct and straightforward terms: the travel toward sexual fulfillment is described, certainly not too originally, as a ride on a too slow horse. The woman complains of her lover's delay:

> Al son del rumor sabroso,
> y al rechinar de las aguas,
> me dijo mi niña a voces:
> "Traidor, ¿para qué te tardas?"
> (*Floresta*, 198)

> (To the sound of the delicious
>   murmur,
> and the moaning of the waters,
> my girl cried to me:
> "Traitor, why do you tarry.?")

Obviously the sweet murmur and the creek's noises are not the conventional elements of a *locus amoenus* but metaphorical expressions of their lovemaking. The lover answers that when, in their journey, he sees the "sweet mine of France," his horse runs away, rushes forward, and he loses control, since "no hay hombre cuerdo a caballo" (there is no sane man on a horse). When the horse calms down, of course, he must again proceed slowly. But, he says, if she becomes impatient, she can pull out three teeth:

> Si, cuando en el juego estamos,
> de otro engaño te recelas,
> sacarte puedes tres muelas,
> mientras que a Francia llegamos.
> (*Floresta*, 198)

> (If, when we are playing,
> you suspect another snare,
> you can pull out three teeth,
> until we arrive in France.

A most astonishing advise! But not if we can penetrate the apparent opacity of signifiers. "Llegar a Francia" (to arrive in France" is a well-established euphemism for the "armónico acuerdo final" (harmonious final accord) in sexual fulfillment (*Floresta*, 200). The sense of these verses, then, is that if the woman grows impatient, she can "pull three teeth out," that is to say, induce in herself three orgasms. This interpretation is obvious, but we do not need to speculate:

another poem, this one in the form of a dialogue of two *comadres*,[7] provides a transparent confirmation of the meaning of this image. The *comadres* say that since their husbands are away, they should prepare to have a pleasant day. The choice of their enjoyment would seem very surprising to a reader who had not been made aware of the nuances of meaning that we have just explored: they would ask the barber to pull out a tooth from each of them:

A. Comadre, la de Tortuera.
B. ¿Qué queréis, la de Garrido?
A. ¿Donde fue vuestro marido?
B. Con despachos a Cervera.
    Decidme, ¿el vuestro do es ido?
A. Entiendo la misma vía.
B. *Pues démonos un buen día*

A. Pues llamemos al barbero
    que nos saque sendas muelas,
    y arrimalle las espuelas
    si no anduviere ligero;
    y pues no cuesta dinero
    que nos haga una sangría:
B. *Darémonos un buen día*
    (*Floresta*, 170)

(A. Neighbor, wife of Tortuera.
B. What do you want, wife of Garrido?
A. Where did your husband go?
B. With errands to Cervera [Deerland].
    Tell me, where has yours gone?
A. I believe the same way.
B. Then, let us have a good day.

A. Let us, then, call the barber
    and have him pull from each of us a tooth,
    and let us spur him on,
    if he does not ride fast enough;
    and since it does not cost money,
    let us have him bleed us.
B. We shall have a great day.)

The context clarifies the sense of "que nos saque sendas muelas." "To make a *sangría* (to bleed) is a well-known popular expression for deflowering a virgin and, by extension, for the sexual act.[8] The husbands are going to *cervera*, a toponym that means "the place of the deer" and, consequently, of horns. Finally, if the barber is too slow, they will spur him on.

'Toothache' And Lust: The Devil's Bite

The sense, then, is clear; but, is it possible to penetrate the origins of such a puzzling metaphor? I think it is. In Sebastián Cirac Estopañán's *Los procesos de hechicerías en la Inquisición de Castilla la Nueva*,[9] we are told that the witches, when they want to awaken lust in a person, make likenesses of him or her and pierce them with an arrow; these arrows must touch first the book of Barrabas and then cut through the heart of their victim:

> Al monte Tabor iréis,
> y nueve varas de mimbre negro arrancaréis,
> en las muelas de Barrabás las hincaréis,
> y luego las quitaréis
> y en el corazón de fulano las hincaréis.

> (To the Tabor mountain you will go
> and nine black osier-twigs you will tear out,
> and into the teeth of Barrabás you will thrust,
> and then you will pull them off,
> and you will pierce with them the heart of so and so.)

Barrabas and Satan are equivalent in these charms, that is to say, the witches must take the poison of lust from the teeth of the Devil and bring it into the heart of their victim.

> El cuchillo de las cachas negras me buscaréis,
> por las muelas de Barrabás buscaréis y en Satanás
> lo amolaréis,
> tres varicas de mimbre negra me cortaréis,
> tres clavos, sean los dos en el corazón de *fulana*
> y el otro en la cabeza para que siempre se acuerde de mí.

> (You will look for the knife of the black handle
> you will look for it in Barrabás's teeth and in Satan's
> you will sharpen it,
> three black osier-twigs you shall cut for me,
> three nails, two to pierce so and so's heart,
> and the other her head, so that she will always remember me.)

In some cases the arrows must be not only sharpened in the teeth of Barrabás, but also wetted in the caldron of Pedro Botero (the Devil):

por las muelas de Barrabás las afiléis
por las calderas de Pedro Botero las pasaréis.
(*Estopañán*, 110)

The brutal sexual character of these spells is shown in the following *conjuro* used by the witch *la Gómez*; in it *la Gómez*, enclosed in the magical circle, and placing her legs over the arrows, so that her own sex could exercise a lustful influence on them, pronounced the following words:

> Ven diablo
> Ven, barba de chivo,
> que mas vale mi coño
> que tu barba
>
> . . . .
>
> vayas a la muela de Lucifer
> y agúzame estas nueve varigas.
> (*Estopañán*, 117–18)

> (Come, Devil
> come, goat's beard,
> that my cunt is better
> than your beard
>
> . . . .
>
> go to Lucifer's tooth
> and sharpen these nine twigs.)

Satan as Serpent; The Poisonous Bite

For the sake of clarity, I shall present here a provisional interpretation of these references to Satan's teeth. These arrows, poisoned in the teeth of Satan, or wetted in his caldron, convey to the heart of the victim the bite of the Devil, that is to say, the irresistible passion of lust. That the person bewitched by *philocaptio* (by magical capture of the heart through lust) was supposed to have been bitten by the serpent (Satan) is a well-known topic in medieval and Renaissance witchcraft. In the *Malleus Maleficarum* (The hammer of the witches), the textbook that served as doctrinal bases for the brutal persecution of witches unleashed by the bull of Innocent VIII of 1484, we are carefully instructed in how the Devil, the Biblical serpent, uses lust as a means for universal corruption:

> There is in them (the devils) a natural madness, a rabid concupiscence, a wanton fancy . . . from witches they usurp to themselves the worship of God, and by this means magic spells are made. . . . And although they have a thousand ways of doing harm . . . and in every way to subvert and perturb the human race; yet their power remains confined to the privy

parts and the navel. . . . For through the wantonness of the flesh they
have much power over men; and in men the source of wantonness lies in
the privy parts, since it is from them that the semen falls, just as in women
it falls from the navel.[10]

The root, then, of Satan's corruption of humankind is found in lust, and witches
are usually his chosen instruments because, as we know from the history of the
Fall, they are more likely to commit the sins of the flesh than men are ("all
witchcraft comes from carnal lust, which is in women insatiable") (*Malleus*, 4).
The destruction of humankind is a continuation of the work that the serpent
started in Paradise:

> Since the first corruption of sin by which man became the slave of the devil
> came to us through the act of generation, therefore greater power is
> allowed by God to the devil in this act than in all others. Also the power
> of witches is more apparent in serpents, as it is said, Than in other ani-
> mals, because through the means of a serpent the devil tempted woman.
> (*Malleus*, 48)

Lust is the result of the bite of the serpent; the poison with which its venum
affects the victims of the penetration of Satan's fangs. This is why the witches
must sharpen and wet their nails, twigs, and arrows with the Devil's teeth and
immerse them in his caldron; in this way the poison of lust is conveyed to their
magical instrument and consequently to the heart of their victims. Against this
semantic background the meaning of the 'toothache' seems clear. Lust is metaphorically signified by the poison that flows from the serpent's fangs (from
Satan's teeth); the bite is magically conveyed by witches through the nails or
arrows that, wetted and sharpened in Satan's teeth, pierce their victims. Infected
by lust, they fall under the Devil's influence and are overcome by his poison that
produces in them the same effect as in their master: a desire to bite (a blind passion toward intercourse). The toothache, then, is simply the image of the presence of lust, of a poison that infects and overflows, that painfully calls for
release.

This maleficent use of Satan's poison is present in *La Celestina* and serves,
in fact, as the background of Melibea's seduction. When Celestina is preparing
the charm that will break Melibea's will, she conjures the Devil and wets the
skein with which she will bewitch her in a caldron in which oil made with poison
of vipers has been poured (Criado de Val, 102); and, when Melibea tries to
explain the passion that it has provoked in her and that has broken her chastity
and shame ("rompimiento de mi honestidad y verguenza") (Criado de Val, 173),
she describes it as a "terrible pasión" that had began with "el ponçoñoso bocado,
que la vista de su presencia de aquel cavallero me dió" (the poisonous bite that
the sight of that gentleman gave me) (Mabbe, 174). This bite of lust has become
irresistible through Celestina's witchcraft.[11] We could multiply the examples; in

fact, so widespread was the image of lust as signified by the serpent's bite that in the portico of the church of Moissac the power of the Devil over his victims is expressed as a sculpture of Satan watching a woman whose breasts are bitten by two serpents and her sex covered by a frog.[12]

The Serpent's Coils: *Lazo; Soga; Cordón*; Witchcraft and Folklore

It will not surprise us, then, to find out that in other spells the three arrows are replaced by three serpents that not only bite but also tie up the beloved (the victim of the charm) to the lover. In the "conjuro de doña María de Vergara para enlazar a su amante Pedro" (Incantation performed by doña María de Vergara to tie up her lover Pedro), the witch enters a circle drawn with coal and recites the following verses:

> Embíote tres sierpes
> y tres serpientes
> e tres galgas diligentes
> e la soga calamera
> que te trave
> del lazo, e del corazón
> (*Estopañán*, 119)

> (I sent three serpents to you
> and three snakes
> and three diligent bitches
> and the hemp-made rope
> to bind the heart with a knot.)

This sense of fastening is present in multiple spells, in which both the emotional and the sexual aspects of the knot are explicitly mentioned and its strength is emphasized:

> . . . aquí me lo traigais
> bien asido, bien prendido,
> asido de su coxón,
> de su pulmón,
> de las telas de su corazón
> (*Estopañán*, 122)

> (. . . bring him here
> well caught, well bound,
> caught from his balls,
> from his lung,
> and from the core of his heart.)

Celestina: a Diabolic Seamstress

The development of the metaphor of the serpent, then, has brought us to an awareness of its double function: it bites; but it also ties its victims up in unbreakable knots, it chains them to each other. This second aspect of the serpent's function brings us directly to Melibea's girdle and to the heart of the *Celestina*. Let us not forget that our *alcahueta* is a seamstress and that it is under this guise that she gains entrance in her victim's houses. She carries a skein of yarn, an instrument and emblem of her trade. This yarn is like the string of a fishing rod: with it she lets the bite sink into her victims. She describes her profession to Sempronio in these terms:

> Aquí llevo un poco de hilado en esta mi faltriquera, con otros aparejos que conmigo siempre traigo, para tener causa de entrar, donde mucho no soi conocida, la primera vez. . . . Porque donde me tomare la boz me halle aperçebida para les echar çebo, o requerir de la primera vista. (99–100)

> Heere in this pockett of mine I carrie a little parcell of yarne and other such trinkettes, which I alwayes beare about me that I may have some pretence at first to make my easier entrance, where I am not throughly knowne . . . to th'intente that which wage soever I turne my tale, or whose part soever I take. I may have a bayte readie, which uppon the first sight therof shall worke my acceptance and hold fast the Fish I purpose to take. (Mabbe, 163)

Peter Russell has shown how the first editors of the *Celestina* had already seen that there was a close relationship between Celestina's spells, the yarn, and the Devil as serpent. In a very early illustrated edition of the book, in which the arrival of Celestina to Melibea's house is depicted, the yarn, divided into several circular skeins, is seen as a coiled serpent.[13] Since this yarn had been soaked into the brew where the viper's oil had been poured, it is easy to see how the two functions just mentioned, biting and binding, are fused: the serpent, as thread, pierces (with its needle) Melibea's heart and sex, and becomes in this way the bite that catches the fish; as *cordón*, it ties her up to Calisto. The text makes quite clear that the stitching that Celestina has in mind is the sexual act. When Melibea has told her that she has been bitten by the poisonous serpent, Celestina answers that she has a needle that can cure her: "Pues si tu quieres ser curada, y que te descubra la punta de mi sotil aguja sin temor" (Criado de Val, 176) (If you be willing to be cured and that I should discover unto you the sharp point of my needle without any fear at all [Mabbe-Allen, 158]). She insists almost immediately that Melibea needs "desta invisible aguja que, sin llegar a ti, sientes en sólo mentarla en mi boca" (178) (this invisible needle, which before it comes at you to stich up your wound, you feel it, only by having it in my mouth and naming it to you [Mabbe-Allen, 161]). When Melibea finally surrenders to Celestina's entreaties, she does so by avowing her need and acceptance of the needle: she offers in exchange her girdle: "cerrado han tus puntos mi llaga, venida soy a tu querer. En mi cordón llevaste embuelta la posesión de mi libertad" (179) (With thy needle you have stitched up my wound; I am come to thy bent; it is in thy power to do with me what thou wilt [Mabbe-Allen, 162]). Melibea, though, is only one case among the many that Celestina has accomplished in her long career. Celestina says that her multiple stitches have covered the city with a spider's web in which innumerable victims have been imprisoned:

> Pocas vírgenes, a Dios gracias, as tu visto en esta ciudad que ayan abierto tienda a vender, de quien yo no aya sido corredera de su primer hilado. En naçiendo la mochacha, la hago escribir en mi rejistro, y esto para que yo sepa cuantas me salen de la red. (Criado de Val, 97)

> (Few virgins [I thank fortune for it] hast thou seen in this city, which have opened their shops and traded for themselves, to whom I have not been a broker to their first spun thread, and help them to vend their wares; there was not that wench born in the world, but I writ her down in my register, and kept a catalogue of all their names, to the intent that I might know how many escaped my net.) (Mabbe-Allen, 55)

It is clear, then, how the iconic structure of the *Celestina* is established: through her powers of witchcraft, Celestina brings the Devil, under his Biblical shape of the serpent, into the skein, converging in this way to the yarn the power of inflaming her victims with lust. This yarn, in a second poetical elaboration, is seen as the thread that, thanks to the work of the needle that stitches the young virgins of the city, is the means to create a vast net of victims tightly fastened by Celestina's spells. In this manner the image of Celestina as diabolical spider is impressed upon her apparently innocent disguise of seamstress. I sustain that Melibea's girdle should be interpreted as an emblem of her acceptance to be so bound. Her offering of it to Calisto, as well as her surrender to the needle, becomes an obvious submission to the Devil's bit, to lust. She will relieve Calisto of his toothache; she is willing to be *enlazada*, fastened to him by the girdle that so closely touches her "relics."

The Cordón in Witchcraft

It seems to me that, after my analysis of the iconic structure of the book, not much evidence is needed to clinch my argument. I shall, however, present some texts that will dispel, I hope, any doubts that could linger in our minds. When Celestina has finally obtained the girdle, she takes it to Calisto exclaiming: ¡Ai cordón, cordón! ¡Yo te haré traer por fuerza, si bivo, a la que no quiso darme su buena habla de grado" (120) (O my prettie girdle, lett me hugg thee a little!

O how my harte leapes in lookinge uppon thee, o brave girdle! I will make thee bringe her unto me by force who would not come to me of her owne accorde [Mabbe, 181]). And Calisto, when he receives it, immediately asserts that the cloth that fastened her now binds him with passionate knots: "O bienaventurado cordón, que tanto poder i merecimiento toviste de çenir aquel cuerpo, que yo no soi digno de servir! ¡O ñudos de mi pasión, vosotros enlazastes mis deseos" (Criado de Val 133) (O happy girdle, which hast had such power and worth in thee, as to hedge in that body, and be its enclosure, which myself am not worthy to serve. O ye knots of my passion, it is you that have entangled my desires [Mabbe-Allen, 102]). Melibea herself will acknowledge that she also has been bound to Calisto through the force of her girdle: when she finally submits to Celestina's needle, she exclaims: "En mi cordón llevaste envuelta la posesión de mi libertad" (179) (In my girdle you carriedst away with thee the possession of my liberty [Mabbe-Allen, 162]).

This function of the *cordón* as a magical means of seduction was a most usual form of popular witchcraft. We possess innumerable examples. Estopañán tells us that among the objects found with the witch Josefa Carranza for the practice of her craft was "una cinta con un herrete y tres nudos" (40) (a ribbon with a tip of iron and three knots)—almost certainly a garter, a striking parallel to the girdle). Two witches, "La Larga un cordón con tres nudos" (a rope with three knots) and Isabel "tenía figuras de cera y llevaba encima consigo una bolsa de bayeta verde dentro de la cual había un cordón cabellado" (42) (she had little waxen dolls and brought with herself a bag of green cloth inside which there was a rope—or a girdle—with three knots) used them. The presence of the waxen dolls adds a new element which illuminates the function of the rope in the charms; this is how Juana Ruiz practiced her craft:

> Tenía escondidas doce a catorca figurillas de yeso de una cuarta y con la forma, ojos, narices y cara como de hombre; algunas . . . estaban atadas con hilo o bramante . . . dos pedazos en forma de corazón y estaban atravesados be arriba abajo con tres alfileres, y uno de ellos también por lo ancho, con una aguja. (43)

> She had hidden away twelve or fourteen little dolls made of plaster, of about a quarter and with the shape, eyes, noses and face as of men; some . . . were fastened with string or hemp cord . . . two pieces, with the shape of hearts, were pierced from top to bottom with three pins, and one of them also sideways with a needle.

The *cordón*, then, has the function of binding the lovers, of creating in the heart of the bewitched an irresistible attraction that, through *philocaptio*, destroys her will. That such a passion is essentially sexual is shown by the kind of *cordones* frequently used by the witches for their charms: Leonor de Barzana, to attract a man to a woman, used a *agujeta de su calzas*, that is to say, a girdle from her stockings (81);[14] la Albardera, to attract a woman to a man, tied her up to him using *la pretina de sus calzones*, again, the string that touched his genitals (81). Melibea's girdle, then, is simply one more case of this magical binding which was a commonplace of popular witchcraft in the Spanish Renaissance and Golden Age.

The Reader and the Critic

It has taken the combined effort of a series of distinguished modern critics to make us aware of the important role played by magic in *La Celestina*. This chapter can be considered, in a way, as the development of the work done by such painstaking and thorough work.[15] My research has aimed to establish the system of images that underlies the metaphoric structure of some important icons of *La Celestina*. We have found that some powerful images dominate the book: Celestinas, as a seamstress, binds, through the stitches of her yarn, all the virgins of the city in a web of lust. The yarn and the needle are also the iconic expression of a deeper myth, the serpent, that, magically infused in the yarn, bites and poisons, and binds with her coils, Celestina's victims. Calisto's toothache, Celestina's needle, and Melibea's girdle are, we have seen, a concrete and partial example of this great net with which the serpent and the witch trap their victims into destruction in this world and damnation in the next.

But how have we come to this interpretation? Have I, as a reader, creatively collaborated with the text, producing a new, original reading? Most certainly not. On the contrary, I have done my best to eliminate the reader, as a subject belonging to a particular time and a concrete culture, and replace the reader with a literary critic. I use the term 'critic' here as signifying "a person who practices the craft of literary interpretation." Such a task deals with meaning and, consequently, with semantics, and entails a considerable and old-fashioned kind of work. Without reading the pertinent bibliography and looking through several books on magic, I could not have arrived at this interpretation. But such research brought me finally to the semantic roots of the text's metaphorical structure: to popular magic. Only through immersion in the iconography, language, and practice of popular witchcraft could I find a coherent interpretation of some puzzling problems of the text, an interpretation that unveiled a pervading and unsuspected structure of the book. Not through the intuition of the reader, but through the thorough and patient labor of the scholar, can we cut the knots of Melibea's girdle or find the diabolical roots of Calisto's tooth. In fact the act of interpretation (not the act of reading) implies a ritual murder: we must kill the reader in us to make way for the critic.

Notes

Notes

Introduction: Toward a History of 'Literature'

1. It has been the distinctive feature of Spanish literature to have its history written by foreigners first (Bouterwek, Sismondi, Ticknor, for example).

2. The major theoretical statements are in Hans Robert Jauss, *Toward an Aesthetic of Reception* (Minneapolis, 1983) and *Aesthetic Experience and Literary Hermeneutics* (Minneapolis, 1983).

3. For a rapid sketch of the argument, see W. Godzich, "After the Storyteller . . . Comes the Storyteller," introduction to Ross Chambers, *Story and Situation* (Minneapolis, 1984).

4. Note that such a request is for impersonal information in contrast to information that may be contained in a letter. We have here an indication of the 'objective' status of the *litterae* in medieval times. See Brian Stock, *The Implications of Literacy: Written Language and Models of Interpretation in the Eleventh and Twelfth Centuries* (Princeton, 1983).

5. Ramón Menéndez Pidal, *La 'Chanson de Roland' y el neotradicionalismo. Orígenes de la épica románica* (Madrid, 1959).

6. Michael Merlich, *Kritik der Abenteuerideologie* (Berlin, 1976).

7. José Antonio Maravall, *La Cultura del Barroco* (Barcelona, 1975).

8. Paul Zumthor, *Essai de poétique médiévale* (Paris, 1972).

Chapter 1. From the Renaissance to the Baroque

1. See the various articles on this theme that I am including in my work *Estudios de historia del pensamiento español; serie segunda: La época del Renacimiento*, which will appear shortly.

2. The book was published under the title *Estado moderno y mentalidad social*, 2 vols. (Madrid, 1972). The summary, with the title "The Origins of the Modern State," can be found in the above-mentioned *Cahiers* (or *Journal of World History*) 6, no. 4 (1961).

3. See my article "La imagen de la sociedad expansiva en la consciencia castellana del siglo XVI," in *Mélanges Fernand Braudel*, vol. 2 (Toulouse, 1973). This article will appear in the volume cited in note 1.

4. J. Heers, *Le XVe Siècle européen; aspects économiques* (Paris, 1966).

5. Claude Carrière, "Le Droit d'ancrage et le mouvement du port de Barcelone au milieu du XVe siècle," in *Estudios de historia moderna* 3 (1953).

6. Heers, *Gênes au XVe siècle* (Paris, 1961), pp. 69–70.

7. J. H. Elliott, *Imperial Spain, 1469–1716* (London, 1963).

8. Joseph Pérez, *La Révolution des Communidades de Castille, 1520–1521* (Bordeaux, 1970), pp. 44ff.

9. F. Mauro, "La Peninsule ibérique à la conquête du monde," *Bulletin Hispanique* 65 (1973): 473.

10. P. Chaunu, *Des produits et des hommes* (Paris, 1972), p. 128, cited by J. Pérez.

11. R. Carande, *Carlos V y sus banqueros*, vol. 1 of *La vida económica en Castilla (1516–1556)*, 2nd ed. (Madrid, 1965).

12. J. Vicéns Vives, *Manual de historia económica de España*, vol. 1 (Barcelona, 1959), p. 253.

13. N. Salomon, *La Campagne de Nouvelle Castille à la fin du XVIe siècle* (Paris, 1964), p. 174.

14. Jordi Nadal, *La población española*, 2nd ed. (Barcelona, 1971), pp. 32–33. Translations of all quotations in this chapter are by Terry Cochran.

15. Gonzalo Anes, *Las crisies agrarias en la España moderna* (Madrid, 1970), p. 92. The paragraphs cited belong to an introductory subsection entitled "El auge de la economía castellana durante el siglo XVI."

16. Carande, *Carlos V y sus banqueros*.

17. H. Kamen, *The Iron Century: Social Change in Europe, 1550–1660*, Rev. ed. (London, 1976), p. 22.

18. See the discourse "El Zelador Universal," in the appendix of Alvarez Ossorio's *Discurso sobre la educación popular de los artesanos*, ed. P. R. Campomanes, vol. 1 (Madrid, 1775), p. 278.

19. See Domínguez Ortiz, *La sociedad española en el siglo XVII*, vol. 1 (Madrid, 1963).

20. Included in *Poetas dramáticos valencianos*, vol. 1 (Madrid 1929), p. 129.

21. In *Memoriales y discursos del Conde Duque de Olivares*, ed. J. H. Elliott and J. F. de la Peña, 2 vols. (Madrid, 1978–80); vol. 1, pp. 46–47, 98; vol. 2, pp. 13, 96, 157.

22. See my *Estado moderno y mentalidad social*, vol. 2, pp. 249ff, and my study in the *Mélanges Fernand Braudel*, pp. 383–84.

23. Richard L. Kagan, *Students and Society in Early Modern Spain* (Baltimore, 1974).

24. In my *Poder, honor y élites en el siglo XVII* (Madrid, 1979).

25. See Dahrendorf, *Las clases sociales y su conflicto en la sociedad industrial* [trans. from German] (Madrid, 1962), p. 82; Eng. version, *Class and Class Conflict in Industrial Society* (Stanford, Calif., 1959).

26. In my soon-to-be-published work, *La literatura picaresca desde la historia social*, where I dedicate several pages to these phenomena of professional and cultural dislocation as disintegrating factors in Baroque society.

27. Leone Battista Alberti, *Momus; o, Del Príncipe*, ed. and introd. G. Martini (Bologna, 1942), pp. 73, 230; Latin and Ital. ed.

28. B. Geremek, *Les Marginaux de Paris en XIVe siècle*, Fr. trans. (Paris, 1976), p. 293.

29. Juan de Mal-Lara, *Philosophia vulgar* (Seville, 1568); I am citing from the 1619 ed., folio 149.

30. Kamen, *The Iron Century*, p. 389.

31. Cristóbal Suárez de Figueroa, *El Pasagero*, ed. R. Marín (Madrid, 1913), p. 32.

32. *Relación de lo que han informado los Corregidores de Castilla la Vieja y Nueva, La Mancha, Extremadura y Andalucía, acerca del remedio que tendrá para la conservación de la labranza y crianza*, in *El problema de la tierra en la España del siglo XVI*, ed. Carmelo Viñas Mey (Madrid, 1941), p. 215.

33. Cristóbal Pérez de Herrera, *Discurso al Rey Felipe III* (Madrid, 1610), folio 23; the work is also cited under the title *Remedios para el bien de la salud del cuerpo de la República*.

34. Cristóbal de Villalón, *El Crotalón*, ed. Asunción Rallo (Madrid, 1982), p. 372.

35. This fact, which has been insisted on by Hans Freyer in *Sociología como ciencia de la realidad* (1st German ed., 1930), has already been pointed out by Pedro Mexia in his *Silva de varia lección*, ed. Soc. de Bibliófilos Españoles, vol. 2, p. 36. Other references can be found in my *Estado moderno*, vol. 1, pp. 413-14.

36. Lawrence Stone, *The Crisis of the Aristocracy, 1558-1641* (Oxford, 1966), chapter 3 particularly.

37. K. Vossler, *Lope de Vega y su tiempo* [trans. from German] (Madrid, 1933), p. 95.

38. Vélez de Guevara, *El diablo cojuelo*, in *La novela picaresca*, ed. Valbuena Prat (Madrid, 1962), p. 1647.

39. Stone, *The Crisis of the Aristocracy*, p. 36.

40. Ferdinand Tönnies, *Comunidad y sociedad* [trans. from German] (Buenos Aires, 1947), p. 65; translated as *Community and Society* by Charles P. Loomis (East Lansing, Michigan, 1957).

41. P. N. Dunn, "El individuo y la sociedad en la vida del Buscón," *Bulletin Hispanique* 52, no. 4, 1960, 380.

42. See my *La cultura del Barroco* (Barcelona, 1975), pp. 107ff.

43. Jerónimo de Gracián, *Diez lamentaciones sobre el lamentable de los atheistas de nuestro tiempo* (Brussels, 1611), ed. P. O. Steggink (Madrid, 1959).

44. Boris Porshnev, *Les Soulévements populaires en France avant la Fronde* (Paris, 1972), p. 293.

45. *Memoriales y discursos del Conde Duque de Olivares*. vol. 1, pp. 217, 225.

46. Cited in my book *La oposición política bajo los Austrias* (Barcelona, 1972), pp. 225-26.

47. Cellorigo, *Memorial de la política necesaria y útil restauración a la república de España* (1600). In 1621, the text reappears in the anonymous *Memorial* addressed to Philip IV in the early moments of his reign; it is included in *La Junta de Reformación*, vol. 5 in the *Archivo Histórico Español* (Madrid, 1932), p. 228.

48. Miguel Caxa de Leruela, *Restauración de la antigua abundancia de España* (1631), ed. Le Flem (Madrid, 1975); part 1, chap. 21 and part 2, cause 3, chap. 1.

49. *El problema de la tierra*, pp. 54ff.

50. In my work *La cultura del Barroco* and in my study "Para una revisión del pensamiento político y social de Quevedo," published in *Actas de la Academia Renacentista* [1980 meeting] (Salamanca, 1982).

51. Cited in my *La cultura del Barroco*, p. 162.

52. See the papers published in vol. 5 of the A. H. M., p. 191. A short revindicating study by M. Navarro Latorre, *Aproximaciones a Fray Luis de Aliaga, confesor de Felipe III e Inquisidor general de España* (Zaragoza, 1981), omits these documents.

53. This is the great danger feared by the epoch's rulers. R. Villari called attention to this theme in *La rivolta antispagnola a Napoli* (Bari, 1967). This is what Olivares is seriously warning the king about, in the *Gran Memorial* of 1624, published by Elliott and de la Peña, vol. 1, p. 62. Some view such an occurrence as a denial of the popular movement's revolutionary character. I think, along with Pareto, that it is precisely that contrary—see Pareto's *Trattato di Sociologia generale*, par. 2058.

54. Porshnev, *Les Soulévements populaires*, p. 314.

55. In Robert Forster and Jack Greene, eds., *Preconditions of Revolution in Early Modern Europe* (Baltimore, 1970).

56. Stone, *The Crisis of the Aristocracy*, p. 13.

57. Edmond Préclin and Victor Tapié, *Le XVIIe Siècle monarchies centralisées (1610-1715)* (Paris, 1949).

58. Philip Butler, *Classicisme et Baroque dans l'oeuvre de Racine* (Paris, 1959), pp. 52-54.

59. C. Vivanti, in *Rivista Storica Italiana* 82, no. 1 (1970), p. 240.

60. *Trattato di Sociologia generale*, par. 2057.

61. A group of these articles have been collected in a volume by Trevor Aston, with an introduction by Charles Hill, under the title *Crisis in Europe; 1560–1660* (London, 1965).

62. A summary of the debate in Spain has been given by A. Gil Novales in his article "La crisis central del siglo XVII," in the *Revista de Occidente* 115 (1972).

63. A. D. Liublinskaia, *French Absolutism: The Crucial Phase, 1620–1629*, trans. Brian Pearce (London, 1968).

64. See Felipe Ruiz Martín, "Un testimonio literario sobre las manufacturas de paños en Segovia por 1625," in *Homenaje al prof. Alarcos* (Valladolid, 1966).

65. G. Anes, "La 'depression' agraria durante el siglo XVII en Castilla," in *Homenaje a Caro Baroja* (Madrid, 1978), pp. 83ff.

66. I have already made use of the author's above-mentioned book in my *La cultura del Barroco*, p. 62. This citation comes from the Spanish translation of various of this historian's texts collected under the title *La crisis del siglo XVII y la sociedad del absolutismo* (Barcelona, 1980), p. 22.

67. See my article "La cultura de la crisis barroca," published in *Historia 16*, supp. 12 (Dec. 1979).

68. R. L. Heilbroner, "Reflexiones: más allá del auge y la quebra," in *Perspectivas económicas*, no. 26, pp. 65–66, 70; originally published in *The New Yorker* (Aug. 1978).

69. See J. H. Elliott, "Self-Perception and Decline in Seventeenth-Century Spain," in *Past and Present*, no. 74 (1977).

70. Jerónimo Barrionuevo, *Avisos (1654–1658)*, in *Biblioteca de Autores Españoles*, vols. 221–22 (Madrid, 1968); this citation comes from vol. 222, p. 5.

71. Sancho de Moncada, *Restauración política en España* (1619), ed. and intro. J. Vilar (Madrid, 1974), folio 2 of the original edition.

72. See Barrionuevo, *Avisos, B. A. E.*, vol. 221, p. 58. I have dealth with this diffusion of "dazzling" elements in my *La cultura del Barroco*, 2nd. ed., pp. 461–63.

73. See R. Mousnier, *Fureurs paysans* (Paris, 1967), p. 9.

74. *La cultura del Barroco*, p. 122; the citation comes from Luis Mur, *Tiberio ilustrado* (Zaragoza, 1645).

75. Incorporated by Anes in an appendix to his edition of Martínez de Mata's *Memoriales y discursos* (Madrid, 1971).

76. Barrionuevo, *Avisos*, vol. 222, p. 218.

77. P. N. Skrine, *The Baroque: Literature and Culture in Seventeenth-Century Europe* (London, 1978).

78. C. G. Dubois, *Le Baroque, profondeurs de l'apparence* (Paris, 1973), p. 242.

79. Etienne Thuau, *Raison d'état et pensée politique à l'époque de Richelieu* (Paris, 1966).

80. *La cultura del Barroco*, pp. 99–100.

81. Gabriel Bocángel, *Obras*, ed. R. Bénitez Claros (Madrid, 1946), vol. 1, p. 84.

82. "When one solicits a solution for everything, there is no need to punish anybody," says the last of those cited (in the appendixes of his *Discurso sobre la educación popular*)—a criterion opposed to the majority of the epoch's politicians.

83. Calderón, *El gran mercado del mundo*, ed. E. Frutos (Madrid, 1976), pp. 139, 150 (lines 1111 and 1422–23, respectively). I understand the work to be more a politico-religious *comedia* than an *auto sacramental*.

84. *Memoriales y discursos del Conde Duque de Olivares*, vol. 2, pp. 63ff.

85. Ibid., vol. 1, p. 61.

86. Porshnev, *Les Soulévements populaires*, p. 42.

87. Henri Hauser, *La Pensée et l'action économiques du cardinal de Richelieu* (Paris, 1944).

88. Stone, *The Crisis of the Aristocracy*, p. 35.

89. Ibid., p. 119.

90. Mateo López Bravo, *Del reino y de la razón de gobernar*, ed. H. Mechoulan (Madrid, 1977), p. 162.

91. Quevedo, *Política de Dios*, ed. J. O. Crosby (Madrid, 1966); see my article cited in note 50.

92. *Memoriales y discursos del Conde Duque de Olivares*, vol. 2, p. 177.

93. In *Estado moderno y mentalidad social*.

94. Bartolomé Bennassar et. al., *L'Inquisition espagnole* (Paris, 1979), pp. 13–14, 372.

95. See pp. 124–25.

96. *Cartas de Andrés de Almansa y Mendoza; novedades de esta corte, y avisos recibidos de otras partes, 1621–1626*, in *Colección de libros españoles raros o curiosos*, vol. 17 (Madrid, 1886), p. 92.

97. J. Rousset, *La Littérature de l'âge baroque en France (Paris, 1953)*.

98. See M. Vovelle, *Mourir autrefois; attitudes collectives devant la morte aux XVIIe et XVIIIe siècles* (Paris, 1974).

99. Pérez de Herrera, *Discurso al Rey Felipe III*, see note 33.

100. La Bruyère, *Les Caractères* (Paris, 1688), p. 185; the passage is taken from the fragment "Du souverain ou de la République."

101. *Consultas del Consejo de Estado*, in the *Archivo Histórico Español* (Madrid, 1930), vol. 3, p. 325.

102. The document has been published by F. Aguilar Piñal in the introduction to his *Sevilla y el teatro en el siglo XVIII* (Oviedo, 1974).

103. *Memoriales y discursos del Conde Duque de Olivares*, vol. 2, pp. 72, 88.

Chapter 2. Popular Culture and Spanish Literary History

1. Peter Burke, "Oblique Approaches to the History of Popular Culture," in *Approaches to Popular Culture*, ed. C. W. E. Bigsby (Bowling Green, 1977), pp. 69–106.

2. Marc Fumaroli, *L'Age de l'éloquence: rhétorique et "res literaria," de la Renaissance au seuil de l'époque classique* (Paris, 1980), p. 31.

3. José Antonio Maravall, *La cultura del Barroco* (Barcelona, 1975).

4. Walter Benjamin, *Ursprung der deutschen Trauerspiels* (Berlin, 1928).

5. For a discussion of these collections, see Colin Smith, "Introduction" to *Spanish Ballads* (Oxford, 1964), esp. pp. 8–12.

6. Elizabeth Eisenstein, *The Printing Press as an Agent of Change*, 2 vols. (Cambridge, 1979). Henceforth this book is cited in the text by volume and page number.

7. Luiz Costa Lima, *Dispersa demanda: ensaios sobre literatura e teoria* (Rio de Janeiro, 1981), pp. 16ff. See also Eric Havelock, *A Preface to Plato* (Cambridge, 1963).

8. Michel de Certeau, *L'invention du quotidien, I: Arts de faire* (Paris, 1980).

9. D. W. Cruickshank, "Literature and the Book Trade in Golden-Age Spain," *Modern Language Review* 73 (1978): 800.

10. Ramón Menéndez Pidal, *Romancer hispánico. Teoriá e historia* (Madrid, 1953), vol. 2, pp. 66–67.

11. Cruickshank, "Literature and the Book Trade," p. 806. See also Augustin González de Amezúa y Mayo, *Opúsculos históricas-literarios*, 3 vols. (Madrid, 1951–53), vol. 1, pp. 371–73.

12. José Ignacio Tellecha, "Bible et théologie en 'langue vulgaire.' Discussion à propos du Catéchisme de Carranza," in *L'Humanisme dans les lettres espagnoles*, ed. Augustin Redondo (Paris, 1979), p. 230.

13. Fray Luis de León, *De los nombres de Cristo*, ed. Cristóbal Cuevas (Madrid, 1977), p. 140.

14. Antonio Márquez, *Literatura e inquisición en España, 1478–1834* (Madrid, 1980), p. 148.

15. Bartolomé Bennassar, *Un Siècle d'Or espagnol*, vers 1525 – vers 1648 (Paris, 1982), p. 260.

16. Peter Burke, *Popular Culture in Early Modern Europe* (New York, 1978), p. 63.

17. Maria Corti, *An Introduction to Literary Semiotics*, trans. Margherita Bogat and Allen Mandelbaum (Bloomington, 1978), p. 152, n. 20.

18. Antonio Rodríguez Moñino, *Construcción crítica y realidad histórica en la poesía española de los siglos XVI y XVII* (Madrid, 1968), p. 14. Subsequent references to this book are cited in the text by page number.

19. See Rodríguez Moñino, ibid.; E. M. Wilson, *Some Aspects of Spanish Literary History* (Oxford, 1967); F. J. Norton and E. M. Wilson, *Two Spanish Verse Chapbooks, A Facsimile Edition with Bibliographical and Textual Studies* (Cambridge, 1969); María Cruz García de Enterría, *Sociedad y poesía de cordel en el Barroco* (Madrid, 1973). Subsequent references to these works are cited in the text by page number.

20. Giuseppe Di Stefano, "*I pliegos sueltos* della Biblioteca Colombina nel Cinquecento. Note a un inventario," *Romance Philology* 34 (1980): 79-80, 91.

21. Cristóbal de Castillejo, "Represión contra los poetas españoles que escriben en verso italiano," in *Obras de amores. Obras de conversación y pasatiempo*, ed. Jesús Domínguez Bordona (Madrid, 1926, Clásicos Castellanos, vol. 79, pp. 233-34.

22. Juan Luis Alborg, *Historia de la literatura española, I: Edad media y renacimiento*, 2nd ed. (Madrid, 1970), pp. 665-66.

23. Burke, *Popular Culture in Early Modern Europe*, p. 23.

24. Maxime Chevalier, *Lectura y lectores en la España de los siglos XVI* (Madrid, 1976), p. 99.

25. María Cruz García de Enterría, *Literaturas marginadas* (Madrid, 1983), p. 33.

26. Mercedes Agulló y Cobo, *Relaciones de sucesos* (Madrid, 1966). See also Cruickshank, "Literature and the Book Trade," p. 816.

27. María Cruz García de Enterría, "Un Memorial, casi desconocido, de Lope de Vega," *Boletín de la Real Academia Española* 51 (1971): 139-60; reprinted in *Sociedad*, pp. 88-89.

Chapter 3. Toward a Nonliterary Understanding of Literature

1. See Paul Zumthor, *Introduction à la poésie orale* (Paris, 1983), p. 23: "Some ambiguity in the adjective 'popular,' in combination with terms like *culture, literature*, or, especially, *poetry* and *song*. Referring to a vague criterion of belonging, the word has no concept behind it: rather than a quality, it indicates a viewpoint, and a particularly unclear one in the world we live in. When I use it, do I allude to a mode of transmission of a cultural discourse? or to some persistence of archaic traits that reflects more or less correctly an ethnic personality? or is it to the class of repositories of these traditions? to supposedly specific forms of reasoning, discourse, and behavior?"

2. See Maxime Chevalier, *Lectura y lectores en la España del siglo de Oro* (Madrid, 1976), p. 19.

3. It is important to distinguish between writing and reading, for it is not necessarily true that someone who does not know how to write also does not know how to read (see "La terre est bleue comme un roman. Entretien avec Daniel Roche," *Révolution*, 175 [8-14 July 1983]: 38-43.)

4. Chevalier, *Lectura y lectores*, pp. 167-97.

5. See Robert Escarpit, "La définition du terme 'littérature,'" in *Le Littéraire et le social. Eléments pour une sociologie de la littérature*, ed. R. Escarpit (Paris, 1970), pp. 259-72.

6. For the term 'popular literature' see Zumthor, *Introduction à la poésie orale*, pp. 45-47.

7. For the term 'genre' se ibid., pp. 47-49.

8. See *Antología de la poesía española. Poesía de tipo tradicional*, ed. Dámaso Alonso and José María Blecua (Madrid, 1956).

9. See Ramón Menéndez Pidal, *Romancero hispánico (hispano-portugués, americano y sefardí). Teoría e histora,* 2 vols. (Madrid, 1953).

10. See Louis Combet, *Recherches sur le "Refranero" castillan* (Paris, 1971).

11. See Maxime Chevalier, *Folklore y literatura. El cuento oral en el Siglo de Oro* (Barcelona, 1978).

12. I do not here wish to approach the problem of other, nonfictional texts that perhaps played a "popular" role in Spain during that time (see, for example, Joseph-Claude Poulin, "Entre magie et religion. Recherches sur les utilisations marginales de l'écrit dans las culture populaire du moyen âge," in *La culture populaire au moyen âge,* Etudes présentées au Quatrième colloque de l'Institut d'études médiévales de l'Université de Montréal, 2–3 April 1977, ed. Pierre Boglioni (Montreal, 1979), pp. 121–43.

13. *Folklore y literatura,* p. 62. Translations of all quotations in this chapter are by Colleen Donagher.

14. El Marqués de Santillana, *Obras,* ed. A. Cortina (Madrid, 1956), p. 33.

15. *Cancionero y romancero español,* ed. Dámaso Alonso (Estelle, 1972), p. 19.

16. Chevalier, *Folklore y literatura,* p. 62.

17. See Werner Bahner, *Beiträge zum Sprachbewusstsein in der spanischen Literatur des 16. und 17. Jahrhunderts* (Berlin, 1956), pp. 36–46.

18. Juan de Valdés, *Diálogo de la lengua,* ed. J. F. Montesinos (Madrid, 1928), p. 13.

19. Ibid.

20. Ibid., p. 12.

21. Ibid., p. 13.

22. José Antonio Maravall, *Antiguos y modernos. La idea de progreso en el desarrollo inicial de una sociedad* (Madrid, 1966), p. 411.

23. José María Blecua, "Introducción," *Antología de la poesía española,* pp. LI–LII.

24. Ramón Menéndez Pidal, "Proemio," *Flor nueva de romances viejos* (Madrid, 1928), p. 39.

25. Ramón Menéndez Pidal, "La primitiva poesía lírica española," in *Estudios literarios* (Madrid, 1957), p. 263.

26. See José Antonio Maravall, *El mundo social de "La Celestina"* (Madrid, 1964).

27. María Rosa Lida de Malkiel, *La originalidad artística de "La Celestina"* (Buenos Aires, 1962).

28. For this, see Chevalier, *"La Celestina* y sus lectores," *Lectura y lectores,* p. 146.

29. Menéndez Pidal, *Flor nueva,* p. 35.

30. Ibid., pp. 35–36.

31. Menéndez Pidal, "La primitiva poesía lírica española," p. 263.

32. Romón Menéndez Pidal, "Poesía popular y poesía tradicional en la literature española," in *Los romances de America y otros estudios* (Madrid, 1948), pp. 76–77.

33. José Antonio Maravall, *Menéndez Pidal y la historia del pensamiento* (Madrid, 1960), p. 127.

34. Ibid., p. 127.

35. Menéndez Pidal, *Romancero hispánico,* p. xv.

36. Ibid., p. 46.

37. Menéndez Pidal, *Poesía juglaresca y orígenes de las literaturas románicas. Problemas de historia literaria y cultural* (Madrid, 1957), pp. VII–VIII.

38. Wolf-Dieter Lange, "El concepto de tradición en la crítica literaria de Don Ramón Menéndez Pidal," *Actas del Coloquio hispano-alemán Ramón Menéndez Pidal,* 31 March–2 April 1978, ed. W. Hempel and D. Briesemeister (Tubingen, 1982), pp. 150–71.

39. Menéndez Pidal, *Romancero hispánico,* p. 58.

40. Ibid., p. 62.

41. Ibid., p. 17.

42. Menéndez Pidal, *Poesía juglaresca*, p. 364.

43. See Michael Nerlich, *El homber justo y bueno: inocencia bei Fray Luis de León* (Frankfurt/Main, 1966).

44. Against the notion of "simplicity" in popular (oral) poetry, see Zumthor, *Introduction à la poésie orale*, pp. 80–81.

45. Menéndez Pidal, "La primitiva poesía lírica española," p. 269.

46. Ramón Menéndez Pidal, "caracteres primordiales de la literatura española," in *Historia general de las literaturas hispánicas*, ed. Guillermo Díaz-Plaja (Barcelona, 1949), p.XX.

47. Menéndez Pidal, "La primitiva poesía lírica española," p. 268.

48. Menéndez Pidal, *Romancero hispánico*, p. 61.

49. Ibid., p. 46.

50. "Poesía tradicional en el romancero hispano-portugués," in *Castilla. La tradición. El idioma* (Madrid, 1955), pp. 41–73.

51. Menéndez Pidal, *Romancero hispánico*, p. 59.

52. Menéndez Pidal, "Carácteres primordiales," p. XX.

53. Maravall, *Menéndez Pidal*, p. 114.

54. Maravall does not follow Mendéndez Pidal's doubtful venture of speculating on the "ultraindividualism" of the Spanish people. In order to stay on the level of rational-positivist reflection, he introduces the term 'plurindividualism', saying that Menéndez Pidal had told him that in a colloquium in Poitiers "his 'traditionalist' theory had been called 'plurindividualism.' " It is also interesting that Diego Catalán, in a recent essay ("El modelo de investigación pidaliano para el futuro," *Actas del coloquio hispano-alemán*, p. 50), also wisely replaces the term 'ultraindividualist' with 'pluriindividualist'.

55. Menéndez Pidal, *Poesía juglaresca*, p. VIII.

56. Menéndez Pidal, *Romancero hispánico*, p. 50.

57. Ibid., p. XVIII.

58. Menéndez Pidal, *Romancero hispánico*, p. 60.

59. Diego Catalán ("El modelo de investigación pidaliano," p. 53) expresses it thus: "in the course of this heroic task of putting Spanish philology on an equal footing with those of France and Italy, Menéndez Pidal was forced to crown his constructs with theoretical arches that were ever higher and more ambitious."

60. "Menéndez Pidal y la actual crítica acerca de las literaturas románicas," *Actas del coloquio hispano-alemán*, pp. 65–75.

61. See Zumthor, *Introduction à la poésie orale*, p. 125.

62. Menéndez Pidal, *Romancero hispánico*, p. 60.

63. Ibid., pp. 60–62.

64. Ibid., p. 61.

65. See Zumthor, *Introduction à la poésie orale*, pp. 141–44.

66. "Conventionalité linguistique et altérité idéologique dans la littérature des 'derniers'," *Neohelicon* 7, no. 2 (1979–80): 99.

67. Eventual ideologization depends on the "context" (for example: where, by whom, and with what voice a song is sung): see Zumthor, *Introduction à la poésie orale*, p. 229 ff.

68. Ibid., p. 231.

69. Among recent works, see especially Paul Bénichou, *Creación poética en el romancero tradicional* (Madrid, 1968); and Diego Catalán, "La creación tradicional en la crítica reciene," in *El romancero en la tradición oral moderna*, ed. Diego Catalán et al. (Madrid, 1972), pp. 153–65.

70. Menéndez Pidal, *Romancero hispánico*, pp. 43 and 46.

71. See Menéndez Pidal, "El primer estado de una canción oral es inasequible," *Romancero hispánico*, pp. 39-40. See also Zumthor, *Introduction à la poésie orale*, p. 246.

72. Gian Luigi Beccaria, *Conventionnalité linguistique*, p. 100.

73. José Ortega y Gasset, *La deshumanización del arte* (Madrid, 1950), p. 3.

74. Ibid., pp. 7-8.

75. Ibid., p. 10.

76. Ibid.

77. See Georges Duby, *Les trois ordres ou l'imaginaire du féodalisme* (Paris, 1978).

78. Combet, *Recherches*, p. 53.

79. For the dialectical relationship between realism and "abstraction" (mysticism, etc.), constantly discussed in Spanish literature, see the famous essay by Dámaso Alonso, "Escila y Caribdis de la literatura española," in his *Ensayos sobre poesía española* (Buenos Aires, 1946), pp. 9-27.

80. "El romancer nuevo," in *De primitiva lírica española y antigua épica* (Madrid, 1977), p. 85.

81. Karl Kohut, "La teoría de la poesía cortesana en el Prólogo de Juan Alfonso de Baena," *Actas del coloquio hispano-alemán*, p. 129.

82. See Pierre Bourdieu ("Comment peut-on être sportif," in *Questions de sociologie* [Paris] 1980: 183): "sports, which come from games that are truly popular, that is to say, *produced by the people*, return to the people through folk music, in the form of spectacles *produced for the people*." I should add that the *passive* role conceded or attributed to the "people" seems to me exaggerated.

83. Menéndez Pidal, *Romancero hispánico*, pp. 438-39.

84. See Zumthor, *Introduction à la poésie orale*, p. 84.

85. Ibid., pp. 286-87.

86. Ibid., pp. 86-99.

87. Ibid., p. 84.

88. Studies on "trivial literature" are most often done by Germans. The reason for this seems to me evident: the notion of popular culture or popular literature does not exist in German (a sport, a politician, a method of administration, or an actor can be popular, but culture—despite some learned attempts at "naturalization"—cannot be so: such a thing is inconceivable). The term previously used to indicate something more or less similar, *volkstümlich* (or *völkisch*) was ruined by the Nazis. This also corresponds to an evident semantic logic: *Volk* is not the same as the "people" (the Spanish *pueblo*) (from this arose numerous misunderstandings in the interpretation of German texts, especially during the Romantic period). Whereas the notion of "people" (*pueblo, popolo, peuple*), despite all the changes, and despite its positive and negative connotations within modern ideological currents, always retains something of its etymological origin *populus (populus romanus*, the body of Roman citizens, which during the last days of Rome include both patricians and plebeians), *Volk* is situated in a nebulous cloud of biological and/or spiritual being. Although there have been many attempts to define the term more reasonably, it has never lost that ambiguity, from which the Nazis were able to derive terrible profit for their racist ideology. Today the term *volkstümlich* "survives" almost exclusively in the German Democratic Republic (at least it is used in the terminology of cultural politics). But it is an obvious misunderstanding. The republican bourgeoisie rebelled against the Nazis' racist perversion of the term, opposing to the perverted term the same one, reanimated through recourse to the republican current that had also played an important role in the history of the ideology of *Volkstümlichkeit* during the eighteenth and nineteenth centuries. The spokesperson of this antifascist *Volkstümlichkeit* current was Georg Lukács, but his error and that of his political successors in the GDR was the failure to see that no attempt at ideological reanimation could prevail against the perversion of the Nazis (in the name of the *Volk* and its supposed "purity," millions of innocents had been killed: what could possibly be accomplished through recourse to the liberal tradition of the "Enlightenment"?). Brecht, however, had understood: his definitions of *Volkstümlichkeit*

constitute the strongest force (also vain) in favor of substituting the semantic field of *Volkstümlichkeit* for that of "popularity," understood in a Marxist sense. (For the history of *Volkstümlichkeit* ideology, see Wolfgang Emmerich, *Zur Kritik der Volktumsideologie* [Frankfurt/Main, 1971]). All this explains why studies relating to the *Volk*, which previously abounded in German research (and in official ideology), have become so rare in German research since the Second World War, at least in the Federal Republic of Germany. It also explains the predominance of research on the so-called trivial literature (see Jochen Schulte-Sasse, *Literarische Wertung* [Stuttgart: Sammlung Metzler, 1976]; G. Fetzer and J. Schönert, "Zur Trivialliteraturforschung 1964-1976," *Internationales Archiv für Sozialgeschichte der deutschen Literatur* 2 [1977]: 1-39; and *Trivialliteratur*, ed. A. Rucktäschel and H. D. Zimmermann [Munich, 1976], etc.) and the problem of cultural dichotomy (see, for example, *Zur Dichotomisierung von hoher und niederer Literatur*, ed. Christa Bürger, Peter Bürger, and Jochen Schulte-Sasse, [Frankfurt/Main, 1982]).

89. See Georges Charbonnier, *Entretiens avec Claude Lévi-Strauss, 10/18*, no. 441 (Paris, 1961), p. 53.

90. For the problem of dichotomy in the context of popular culture, see the fundamental work of Alberto M. Cirese, *Cultura egemonica e culture subalterne. Rassegna degli studi sul mondo tradizionale* (Palermo, 1972).

91. Zumthor, *Introduction à la poésie orale*, p. 41.

92. See Jacques Leenhardt and Pierre Józsa, *Lire la lecture. Essai de sociologie de la lecture* (Paris, 1982).

93. On the *social* formation of individual aesthetic sense, see Michael Nerlich, "Von der Notwendigkeit der Aktfotografie," *Tendenzen* 139 (1982): 30-37.

94. "Popular poetry always flourishes as the result of literary cultivation, when for whatever reason a style takes hold among cultivated poets and inclines them toward a genre that really belongs to the people" (Menéndez Pidal, "Poesía popular, p. 79).

95. For changes in proverbs used in literary text, se Elisabeth Schulze-Busaker, "Eléments de culture populaire dans la littérature courtoise," *La culture populaire au moyen âge*, pp. 81-101.

96. Michael Nerlich, "Zu einigen Problemen der 'nichtkanonisierten Literatur' und des sozialen Realismus in 19. Juhrhundert in Anschluss an Neuschäfers Studien zum Populärroman," *LENDEMAINS*, 7-8 (1977): 215-16.

97. "In art all repetition is worthless," writes Ortega y Gasset, in *La deshumanización del arte*, p. 12.

98. Michael Nerlich, *Kritik der Abenteuer-Ideologie. Beitrag zur Erforschung der bürgerlichen Bewusstseinsbildung, 1100-1750*, 2 vols. (East Berlin, 1977).

99. Menéndez Pidal, *Romancero hispánico*, p. 61.

100. Maravall, *Antiguos y modernos*, p. 27.

101. It is true that medieval authors also used forms from popular-traditional poetry to express other intentions, for example, revindicative ones (see, for example, Julio Rodríguez-Puértolas, *Poesía de protesta en la Edad Media castellana. Historia y antología* [Madrid, 1968]). But in these cases, the material ceases to be popular-traditional poetry.

102. Valdés, *El diálogo de la lengua*, p. 102.

Chapter 4. Gender Markers in Traditional Spanish Proverbs

1. The standard authority on such definitions is Archer Taylor, *The Proverb* (Hatboro, Pa., 1962). Also helpful are B. J. Whiting, "The Nature of the Proverb," *Harvard Studies and Notes in Philology and Literature* 14 (1932): 272-307, and for the Spanish tradition specifically José María Sbarbi, "Disertación," *Monografía sobre los refranes, adagios y proverbios castellanos* (Madrid, 1891), pp. 13-44. The most searching definitional statement on the Spanish *refrán* is Louis Combet, "Le *refrán*: Essai de délimitation," *Recherches sur le "refranero" castillan*, Bibliothéque de la Faculté

des Lettres de Lyon, Fasc. XIX (Paris, 1971), pp. 11-105. Throughout my discussion I use the word *refrán* to refer generally to the traditional Castilian popular proverb. All translations to English are my own.

2. Useful distinctions between oral and written culture and a discussion of literacy levels in society can be found in Franz H. Bäuml, "Transformations of the Heroine: From Epic Heard to Epic Read," in *The Role of Woman in the Middle Ages*, ed. Rosemarie Thee Morewedge (Albany, N.Y., 1975), pp. 23-40. For the effects of societal changes on oral culture, see Pierre Crépeau, "The Invading Guest: Asome Aspects of Oral Transmission," *Yearbook of Symbolic Anthropology* 1 (1978): 11-29. A good overview of theories of mass and popular culture is Jean Franco, "What's In a Name? Popular Culture Theories and Their Limitations," *Studies in Latin American Popular Culture* 1, no. 1 (1982): 5-14.

3. Combet, *Recherches* pp. 93-105, denies "moral" validity and the "truth" of proverbs while stressing the sociological value of *refranes* for reflecting life and the general conservatism of the form. William R. Bascom, "Four Functions of Folklore," in *The Study of Folklore*, ed. Alan Dundes (Englewood Cliffs, N.J., 1965), pp. 279-98, points out the social functions of oral folklore, including behavior control; see also Michael R. Marrus, "Folklore as an Ethnographic Source: A 'Mise au Point'," in *The Wolf and the Lamb: Popular Culture in France from the Old Regime to the Twentieth Century*, ed. Jacques Beauroy, Marc Bertrand, and Edward T. Gargan, Stanford French and Italian Studies, III (Saratoga, Calif., 1977), pp. 109-25; Lucienne A. Roubin, "Savior et art de vivre campagnard," in *The Wolf and the Lamb*, pp. 93-100. Some contemporary folklorists and symbolic anthropologists seem to reject any societal function in proverbs beyond that of individual verbal strategy. See Wolfgang Mieder and Alan Dundes, ed. *The Wisdom of Many: Essays on the Proverb* (New York and London, 1981); J. David Sapir and J. Christopher Crocker, eds. *The Social Use of Metaphor: Essays on the Anthropology of Rhetoric* (Philahelphia, 1977); E. Ojo Arewa and Alan Dundes, "Proverbs and the Ethnography of Speaking Folklore," *American Anthropologist* 66, part 2 (1964): 70-85.

4. Bäuml, "Transformations of the Heroine," pp. 23-30; Julian Pitt-Rivers, *The Fate of Shechem or The Politics of Sex. Essays in the Anthropology of the Mediterranean*, Cambridge Studies in Social Anthropology, 19 (Cambridge, 1977); J. G. Persitiany, ed. *Honour and Shame, The Values of Mediterranean Society* (London, 1965). The on-again, off-again literate class's interest in the speech habits of the common people of Spain, particularly their proverbs, is traced in parts 2 and 4 of Combet, *Recherches* pp. 109-77 and pp. 289-335.

5. A Plethora of anthropological studies on Spain document the recent dates of significant change in that society. Among the best are Susan Tax Freeman, *Neighbors: The Social Contract in a Castilian Hamlet* (Chicago, 1970); Michael Kenny, *A Spanish Tapestry: Town and Country in Castile* (Bloomington, Ind., 1862); Carmelo Lisón-Tolosana, *Belmonte de los Caballeros: A Sociological Study of a Spanish Town* (Oxford, 1966); Juan F. Mira, "Sociedad rural y cambio social: notas para un planteamiento," in *Primera reunión de antropólogos españoles*, ed. Alfredo Jiménez, Publicaciones del Seminario de Antropología Americana, XIII (Sevilla, 1975), pp. 211-13; Joseph B. Aceves, Edward C. Hansen, and Gloria Levitas, eds., *Economic Transformation and Steady-State Values: Essays in the Ethnography of Spain*, Queens College Publications in Anthropology, 2 (Flushing, N.Y., 1976); David Gilmore, *The People of the Plain: Class and Commmunity in Lower Andalusia* (New York, 1980). See also *Estudio sociológica de la familia española*, by the Instituto de Sociolgoía Aplicada de Madrid (Madrid, 1976). Michelle Riboud, "Labor Force Participation and Earnings of Women in Andalusia," in *Women and the World of Work*, ed. Anne Hoiberg (New York and London, 1982), pp. 256-66, gives literacy statistics for Andalusian males and females in 1979; María •Angeles Durán, *El trabajo de la mujer en España* (Madrid, 1972), states that statistics published by the Franco regime were misleading and mentions the difficulties posed therein for sociological analysis.

6. See the enlightening essays on the subject in A. Sánchez-Romeralo, D. Catalán, and S.

Armistead, eds., *El Romancero hoy: Nuevas fronteras*, I (Madrid, 1979), especially Jesús Antonio Cid, "Recolección moderna y teoría de la transmisión oral: 'El traidor Marquillos,' cuatro siglos de vida latente," pp. 281–359. The changing nature of festivals is discussed in Enrique Luque, "La crisis de las expresiones populares del culto religioso: Examen de un caso andaluz," in *Expresiones actuales de la cultura del pueblo*, ed. Carmelo Lisón-Tolosana (Madrid, 1976), pp. 87–113.

7. The novels of Miguel Delibes frequently portray proverbialist peasants, and the only collection of Castilian proverbs in popular editions today still insists that the speech of the common people (*el pueblo*) abounds in *refranes*: José Bergúa, ed., *Refranero español*, 9th ed. (Madrid, 1981).

8. For an example of this, see Robert A. Barakat, *A Contextual Study of Arabic Proverbs*, Folklore Fellows Communications, 226 (Helsinki, 1980). Social hsitorians, however, do appreciate the folklorists' documentation; see Natalie Zemon Davis, "Introduction: The Historian and Popular Culture," in *The Wolf and the Lamb*, pp. 9–16.

9. International paremiologists whose research traces specific proverbs through many cultures also seem to deny cultural uniqueness of proverbs to any particular society. See, for example, Archer Taylor, "Sunt Tria Damna Domus," *Hessische Blätter für Volkskunde* 24 (1926): 130–46, reprinted in Archer Taylor, *Selected Writings on Proverbs*, ed. Wolfgang Mieder. Folklore Fellows Communications, 216 (Helsinki, 1975), pp. 133–51, and Matti Kuusi, *Regen bei sonnenschein. Zur Weltgeschichte einer Redensart*, Folklore Fellows Communications, 171 (Helsinki, 1957).

10. Dundes and Mieder, *The Wisdom of Many*, p. 257. Parker's essay appears on pp. 257–74.

11. Ibid., p. 243. Among the contextualists are Arewa and Dundes; Peter Seitel, "Proverbs: A Social Use of Metaphor," *Genre* 2 (1962): 143–61, and "Saying Haya Sayings: Two Categories of Proverb Use," in *The Social Use of Metaphor*, pp. 75–99; and Barbara Kirschenblatt-Gimblett, "Toward a Theory of Proverb Meaning," *Proverbium* 22 (1973): 821–27.

12. Analysis of proverb use in the manuscript dictated by Madre Isabel de Jesús, an illiterate lower-class Spanish mystic (1587–1648), would prove useful. See Electra Arenal, "The Convent as Catalyst for Autonomy: Two Hispanic Nuns of the Seventeenth Century," in *Women in Hispanic Literature: Icons and Fallen Idols*, ed. Beth Miller (Berkeley, Calif., 1983), pp. 147–83, for Arenal's description of that recently discovered manuscript.

13. José Bergúa, "Al lector," *Refranero español*, pp. 6–17, makes definite class distinctions. A historical overview of the Western idea of "the people" is George Boas, *Vox Populi: Essays in the History of An Idea* (Baltimore, 1969), esp. p. 85. See also the distinctions made by María Cruz García de Enterría, *Sociedad y poesía de cordel en el barroco* (Madrid, 1973); Américo Castro, *El pensamiento de Cervantes* (1925; Barcelona, 1972), p. 184; Ian MacLean, *The Renaissance Notion of Woman. A Study in the Fortunes of Scholasticism and Medical Science in European Intellectual Life* (Cambridge, 1980), p. 4.

14. Combet, *Recherches*, pp. 441 and 299–314, esp. p. 309.

15. The *Seniloquium* has a modern edition in Combet, *Recherches*, pp. 461–71; Combet, *Recherches*, p. 130, summarizes the debate on the authorship of *Refranes que dizen las viejas tras el fuego* (Sevilla, 1508).

16. Castro, *El pensamiento de Cervantes*, p. 184.

17. Marcel Bataillon, *Erasmo y España*, trans. Antonio Alatorre, 2nd. ed. (Mexico, 1966), pp. 609–98.

18. Pedro Vallés, *Libro de refranes* (Zaragoza, 1549; Facs. ed. by M. García Moreno, Madrid, 1917); Juan de Mal Lara, *Filosofía vulgar*, ed. Antonio Vilanova, 4 vols. (Barcelona, 1958–59).

19. Gonzalo Correas, *Vocabulario de refranes y frases proverbiales* (Madrid: 1st ed., 1906; 2nd ed., 1924). The best edition is by Louis Combet (Bordeaux, 1967).

20. Juan de Valdés, *Diálogo de la lengua*, ed. José F. Montesinos (Madrid, 1928), p. 12.

21. Quoted in Antonio Vilanova, Introduction to Juan de Mal Lara, *Filosofía vulgar*, vol. 1, pp. 21–22. Subsequent citations of this edition appear in the text as ML and give volume and page.

22. Great care must be taken to use either the original texts (or a copy thereof) or a scrupulous

modern edition, like Combet's of Correas, because of postsixteenth-century censorship of Hernán Núñez's collection as well as those of his contemporaries.

23. Miguel Mir, "Al lector," in Correas, *Vocabulario de refranes*, 1906 ed., pp. v–xiii, esp. p. x.

24. Quoted in Combet, *Recherches*, p. 170.

25. The publication in 1906 of the Correas collection created a sensation among Spanish folklorists and paremiologists. It apparently consternated Francisco Rodríguez Marín, all of whose proverb collections after 1890 were presented in comparative, quantitative terms: *Más de 21.000 refranes castellanos no contenidos en la copiosa colección del Maestro Gonzalo Correas* (Madrid, 1926); *Los 6.666 refranes de mi última rebusca . . . no contenidos . . .* (Madrid, 1934); *12.600 refranes no contenidos . . .* (Madrid, 1930); and *Todavía 10.700 refranes más no registrados por el M. Correas* (Madrid, 1941). What makes these collections difficult to work with in historical terms is that Rodríguez Marín counted as a "new" proverb each and every minimally different variant and listed them alphabetically. Beyond that problem, Combet, *Recherches*, pp. 333-34, accuses Rodríguez Marín of "creating" some proverbs and "polishing" others, which, if true, totally distorts the data.

26. "Literatura y folklore: Los refranes," *1616. Anuario de la Sociedad Española de Literatura General y Comparada* (1978): 139-45.

27. Roman Jakobson and P. Bogatyrev, "Die folklore als besondere form des schaffens," *Donum natalicium Schrijnen* (Nÿmegen-Utrecht, 1929), pp. 900-913; Kenneth Burke, "Literature as Equipment for Living," in *The Philosophy of LIterary Form*, 3rd ed. (Berkeley, Calif., 1973), pp. 293–304; Arewa and Dundes, "Proverbs," p. 71.

28. José Gella Iturriaga, "444 refranes de *La Celestina*," in *La Celestina y su contorno social*, ed. Manuel Criado de Val (Barcelona, 1977), pp. 245-86; "El refranero en la novela picaresca y los refranes del *Lazarillo* y de *La pícara Justina*," in *La Picaresca: Orígenes, textos y estructuras*, ed. Manuel Criado de Val (Madrid, 1979), pp. 231-55.

29. Arewa and Dundes, "Proverbs," p. 71.

30. Luis Martínez Kleiser, *La mujer en el refranero* (Madrid, 1931); José Jara Ortega, *Más de 2.500 refranes relativos a la mujer (Soltera, casada, viuda y suegra)* (Madrid, 1953).

31. *Refranes famosíssimos y provechosos glosados* (Burgos, 1509; fasc. ed. Madrid, 1922). Chapter 3 begins this way:

> De aquel animal imperfecto fragile y variable muger que huyas hijo mío como del fuego te consejo. Y si del todo apartarte della no podras; a lo menos que no te allegues mucho: mas en tal manera que hayas temor así como si fuese pestilencia. Y de todas ellas solo aquella te quiero aceptar que Dios habrá ordenado que sea tu muger. De la qual te digo tal nueva: que por virtuosa que sea será tal que te hará caer las alas: y colgar las orejas sobre los hombros. Perderás buena sombra y cobrarás mala gracia, huirá de ti todo placer y reposo, y allegarse te han diversos trabajos y ansias continuas: según que dize el refrán: *Casarás y amansarás*. Mas recuérdate que *Al enhornar: se hazen los panes tuertos*. No consientas que cabalgue ni te señoree: y avísote que todas vienen proveídas de consejos de algunas malas viejas para que todo se haga a voluntad dellas: mas a ti recuérdesete del proverbio que dize: *En la casa del mezquino: manda más la muger que el marido*. Que peor sería que mula de se lo desuezar: si una vez se lo comportas. Por mi ha pasado y bien es *Quien por mal de otro se castiga*. E mira bien hijo que aunque la veas andar llana y estar algun poco reposada: ni por eso te fíes: que por tales reposas se dixo *Del agua mansa te guarda*. Que muchas vezes se contrahacen y se muestran simples y dulces: porque las amargas intenciones puedan traer a su propósito para haber lo que quieren; por eso dize el refrán, *Becerreta mansa: todas las vacas mama*. Por tanto cuando tu loas alguna de aquellas de humilde y mansa que parece que visten piel de oveja dize aquel que mejor que tu la ha conocida. *No la habéis tenido*

el pie al herrar. Y por esto yo querría que si te casas que del mal lo menos escojiesses y no tomes moza de pocos días: porque quanto más amor le tengas menos te estimará, y bien lo sabe el que dixo *Amor de niña, agua en cestilla.* No tomes muger que en nada sea infamada porque todos tiempos *En el aldea que no es buena, más mal hay que no se suena.* No sea fruta de mal árbol, ni verga de mala raiz, porque *De mala berenjena nunca buena calabaza.* Y el labrador en su proverbio da buen consejo cuando dize *De buena planta, planta la viña, y de buena madre toma la hija.* Por esto hijo mío te ruego no poses amor en mala muger, porque con dificultad te podries retraer de amarla. Primero ablandan, y después con falsas artes hazen lo que quieren, y entonces no será en tu poder te apartar, que *Quien bien ama, tarde olvida.* E tu comportarás lo que aquella hará en vergüenza tuya, diciendo por escusa *Lo que la muger quiere, Dios lo quierre.* E en las malas obras que aquella hará, las cuales tu no sabrás, tus vecinos presumirán que *Lo que la loba hace al lobo le place.* No creas que por un solo yerro se pierda la buena opinión en que es tenida la muger, mas dizen las gentes que *Quien hace un cesto hará ciento.* Y pues comienzan a perder la vergüenza, no dudan atrevidamente continuar en el vicio, en qualquier edad o estado en que se hallan, que *La muger enlodada ni viuda ni casada.* Hijo mío agradecerás mucho a dios omnipotente si te da buena muger, mas ni por eso no pierdas el temor y la recelosa sospecha, que por las semejantes se dixo *De la mala muger te guarda y de la buena no fíes nada.* Que son veletas que a todos vientos se vuelven, y son enemigas de firmeza. No he por bueno que te muestres celoso de aquella, mas si licción le querrás dar, seas maestro en artes y esto es que con discreción digas, *A ti lo digo hijuela, entiéndelo tú nuera.* Y si ves que a cada parte ligeramente vuelve los ojos, di no a ella mas a la moza, *La muger que mucho mira, poco hila.* Y si ves que tu muger mucho a menudo se peina y toca, demándale, porque se dize *En cabeza loca no se tiene la toca.* Y si vieres que vasquea mucho por irse a pasear, di a la esclava que cierre el gallinero que *La muger y la gallina, por mucho andar se pierde ayna.* Y aun se puede recitar de aquellas dos comadres que dixo la una a la otra, *Comadre andariega, donde voy allá os hallo.* Y la otra respondió *Si vos comadre estuviéssedes en vuestra casa con la pierna quebrada, no me veríades en cada casa.* Y no te olvides dezir el peligro del *Cántar o que muchas vezes va a la fuente,* etc. Y si por ventura tu muger fuere muy cantadora, dile la fábula de la cigarra y de la hormiga, y aun fingirás que una muger pasa por la calle que dixo *Bien canta Martha después de harta.*

32. See MacLean, *The Renaissance Notion of Women,* and Edward Shorter, *A History of Women's Bodies* (New York, 1982).

33. See Freeman, *Neighbors;* and Susan Mosher Stuard, ed., *Women in Medieval Society* (Philadephia, 1976), especially Heath Dillard, "Women in Reconquest Castile: The *Fueros* of Sepulveda and Cuenca," pp. 71–94 and David Herlihy, "Land, Family, and Women in Continental Europe, 701–1200," pp. 13–45.

34. Mary Beard, *Woman as Force in History. A Study in Traditions and Realities* (New York, 1946); reprint 1976), pp. 57–64; Wendy Martyna, "The Psychology of the Generic Masculine," in *Women and Language in Literature and Society,* ed. Sally McConnell-Ginet, Ruth Borker, and Nelly Furman (New York, 1980), pp. 69–78.

35. The proverb texts quoted subsequently are taken from the 1967 Combet edition of Correas, *Vocabulario de refranes,* and the Vilanova edition of Mal Lara, *Filosofía vulgar,* with volume and page indicated in the text.

36. Seitel, "Saying Haya Sayings" and "Proverbs: A Social Use of Metaphor"; also Heda Jason, "Proverbs in Society: The Problem of Meaning and Function," *Proverbium* 17 (1971): 617–23.

37. In addition to the works cited above in notes 4, 5, and 32, see Beard, *Woman as Force in History;* Jessie Bernard, *The Female World* (New York, 1981); Martine Segalen, *Mari et femme*

dans la société paysanne (Paris, 1980); and Yvonne Verdier, *Façons de dire, façons de faire: La laveuse, la couturière, la cuisinière* (Paris, 1979).

38. For a good example of this new emphasis in folklore studies, see Alan Dundes, "On the Structure of the Proverb," in *The Wisdom of Many*, pp. 43-64.

39. José Gella Iturriaga, *Refranero del mar*, 2 vols. (Madrid, 1944); Nieves de Hoyos Sancho, *Refranero agrícola español* (Madrid, 1954).

40. Combet, *Recherches*, p. 149.

41. See Susan Harding, "Street Shouting and Shunning: Conflict Between Women in a Spanish Village," *Frontiers: A Journal of Women Studies* 3, no.3 (Fall 1978): 14-18, and "Women and Words in a Spanish Village," in *Toward an Anthropology of Women*, ed. Rayna R. Reiter (New York, 1975), pp. 283-308. Also important is Verdier, *Façons de dire*; and Ruth Borker, "Anthropology: Social and Cultural Perspectives," in *Women and Language in Literature and Society*, pp. 26-44.

Chapter 5. Literature versus Theatricality

1. See Hans Robert Jauss, *Aesthetic Experience and Literary Hermeneutics* (Minneapolis, 1983).

2. Wolfgang Iser, *The Act of Reading* (Baltimore, 1983).

3. V. N. Voloshinov (Bakhtin), *Marxism and the Philosophy of Language* (New York, 1973).

4. Much of the subsequent develoment is indebted to Paul Zumthor, *Essai de poétique Médiévale* (Paris, 1972). Translations of quotes from that volume are by Nicholas Spadaccini and Wlad Godzich.

5. Cesare Segre, *Crítica bajo control* (Barcelona, 1970).

6. Zumthor, *Essai, passim.*

7. Walter Benjamin, "The Storyteller," in *Illuminations* (New York, 1969). p. 239.

8. M. M. Bakhtin, *The Dialogic Imagination* (Austin, Tex., 1981).

9. M. M. Bakhtin, *Rabelais and His World* (Cambridge, Mass., 1968).

10. M. M. Bakhtin, *The Dialogic Imagination.*

11. Benjamin, "The Storyteller," p. 87.

12. Zumthor, *Essai*, p. 42. See also p. 37.

13. Julia Kristeva, "Modern Theater Does Not Take (A) Place," *Sub-Stance* 18-19 (1977): 131-34.

14. Zumthor, *Essai*, p. 74.

15. Jacques Derrida, *Of Grammatology* (Baltimore, 1976).

16. Henri Meschonnic, *Pour la poétique*, I (Paris, 1970).

17. Benjamin, "The Storyteller," p. 95.

18. Jurij Lotman, "Problème de la typologie des cultures," *Social Science Information* 6, no. 2 (1967): 29-38.

19. Henri Focillon, *Art d'Occident*, 2 vols. (Paris, 1965).

20. Juan Oleza, "Hipótesis sobre la génesis de la comedia Barroca," in *La Génesis de la teatralidad Barroca*, Cuadernos de Filología, III: Literaturas: Análisis (Valencia, 1981), p. 18.

21. A number of issues discussed in this essay were touched upon in Jenaro Talens, *La escritura como teatralidad* (Valencia, 1977).

Chapter 6. "Vos outros tambem cantai por vosso uso acostumado"

1. I have greatly benefited from discussion of this paper, in preliminary version, in a graduate seminar at the University of Minnesota led by Professors Wladyslaw Godzich and Nicholas Spadaccini. I should like here to thank both them and their students.

2. For dating and other documentation, I follow the standard Jack Horace Parker, *Gil Vicente* (New York, 1967), which does not significantly diverge from critical opinion on any major issue that comes into question in this paper.

3. Gil Vicente, *Obras Completas*, preface and notes by Marques Braga (Lisgon, 1942), vol. 1, p. 84. Subsequent references, not only to *Auto da Fé* but also to other works dealt with in this essay that are also contained in this volume, are incorporated into the text by page number only. All translations are my own and aspire to literal status only.

4. This is by no means a surprising connection, of course. In Portuguese texts from this era and before, *letrado* seems virtually synonymous with *cleric*, a synonymy that probably bespeaks an actual social division of labor—i.e., there were very few lay people who were "lettered." That lexical interrelationship continues through the eighteenth century, presumably becoming decreasingly descriptive and increasingly prescriptive during that time.

5. See, e.g., Parker, *Gil Vicente*, p. 139.

6. I here differ with the reading of Eugenio Asensio, *Poética y realidad en el cancionero peninsular de la edad media* (Madrid, 1957), pp. 143-46, who sees the passage as palace lyric. Indeed, although I agree with the general thesis of the section of his book that runs from p. 133 to p. 180 (not to mention other sections as well), I find that Asensio's argumentation is often weakened by failure to read passages against a defensible reading of the entire work from which they are taken. The shepherds' song of *Auto da Fé* is a case in point: there can be no doubt that it is designated as "popular" by the terms of the text itself. If Asensio's proposal has any validity whatsoever—a question about which, given the anachronism upon which the argument depends, frankly I am undecided—then it must reside at a metalinguistic level. The entire passage might, accordingly, be read in a manner like the "cruz" passage commented on above. Its implications for communication between author and audience would, then, be similar to those that I propose for the "cruz" passage—indeed, in the light of Asensio's commentary, even more obviously so. Such a reading of the two passages might well pave the way for an attempt at a reading of metacommentary in Vicente's work.

7. I have used the version printed by Gregorio Mayans y Siscar in *Orígenes de la lengua española*, 2nd ed. (Madrid, 1873), pp. 1-148.

Chapter 7. The Stubborn Text

1. As is well known, the leading theorist among those who emphasize the autonomy of the reader is Wolfgang Iser, who in two major works, *The Implied Reader* (Baltimore and London, 1974) and *The Act of Reading: A Theory of Aesthetic Response* (Baltimore and London, 1978), set the theoretical bases for a justification of centering the interpretation of a text on the act of reading and on the reader's response. A careful analysis of *The Act of Reading* (a book more enthused about than studied) would show that Iser's tenets are based much more on authority than on argument: chapter 1 on an assertion of Henry James, chapter 2 on quotes from Walter Slatoff and Northrop Frye, and so on. There is no denying of Iser's importance as a critic and the great and useful influence that his ideas have exercised; but it is necessary to insist that his theories are based more on rhetorical manipulation than on solid semantic and hermeneutic reasoning. For general information on the contemporary theories on reader-oriented criticism, see *The Reader in the Text*, ed. Susan R. Suleiman and Inge Crosman (Princeton, N.J., 1980).

2. These meanings are given in *The Living Webster Encyclopedic Dictionary of the English Language of America*, 1971 edition.

3. Francisco de Quevedo, *Obras Completas* (Madrid, 1943), p. 109.

4. In a recent article, Otis Handy discusses the rhetorical devices through which the seduction takes place; his very careful analysis leaves no doubt about the double level of the conversation of Celestina with Melibea and fully clarifies the erotic character of the double entendres: "The Rhetorical and Psychological Defloration of Melibea," *Celestinesca* 7.1 (1983): 17−27. That this seduc-

tion is helped by diabolical influences is well established: the role of magic in *La Celestina* has been the object of lively controversy in recent years. For theoretical and bibliographical information, see P. E. Russell, "La magia como tema integral de la *Tragicomedia de Calisto y Melibea*" (Studia Philogica, *Homenaje ofrecido a Dámaso Alonso* 3[1963]:337–54); rewritten and expanded, this article appeared again in his book *Temas de la Celestina* (Madrid, 1978), pp. 241–76. See also Elisabeth Sánchez's "Magic in *La Celestina*," *Hispanic Review* 46 (1978):481–84.

5. I quote from *La Celestina*, ed. Manuel Criado de Val (Madrid, 1977); for this quote see p. 111; and from James Mabbe's translation *Celestine or the Tragick-Comedie of Calisto y Melibea*, ed. Guadalupe Martínez Lacalle (London, 1972), see p. 172. When the 1972 edition is incomplete, I shall quote from the reproduction from Mabbe's 1631 edition, ed. H. Warner Allen (London, 1923); such quotes will be indentified as "Mabbe-Allen." I shall use the Mabbe-Allen text only where absolutely necessary since it is so unfaithful to the original that at times it becomes useless.

6. *Floresta de poesía erórtita del Siglo de Oro*, ed. Pierre Alzieu, Yvan Lissorgues, Robert Jammes (Toulouse, 1975), p. 200; my translation. Henceforth this book will be cited as *Floresta*. The sense of erotic passion as a possible meaning of *toothache* has been indicated by M. Dominica Legge in "Toothache and Courtly Love," *French Studies* 4 (1950):50–54. More recently Geoffrey West (*Celestinesca* 2, no. 1 [1979]:3–10) has shown that a "neat symmetry is . . . established between Calisto's supposed toothache and his sexual frustration" (p. 3). I intend to present an interpretation of the metaphorical roots of this image, an interpretation that would explain the close semantic relationship of this image with the *cordón*.

7. *Comadre* is an untranslatable term: it is the name given reciprocally by the mother and godmother of a child. But, by extension, it means the close friendship existing among the women, and, often, among neighbors. For this reason, I translate it as "neighbor."

8. See *seguidilla* 5, *Floresta*, p. 264. These poems are quoted by West in *Celestinesca*, p. 6.

9. Sebastián Cirac Estopañán, *Los procesos de hechicerías en la Inquisición de Castilla la Nueva* (Madrid: C.S.I.C., 1942). Quotations from this book are cited in the text by short title (*Estopañán*) and page number; translations are my own.

10. *The Malleus Maleficarum* was written by the Inquisitors Fr. Henry Kramer and Fr. James Sprenger; I quote from the edition of the Rev. Montague Summers (New York, 1970), pp. 23–24. Subsequent quotations are cited in the text by short title (*Malleus*) and page number.

11. Russell, *Temas de la Celestina*, p. 259–63.

12. Julio Caro Baroja, *Las brujas y su mundo* (Madrid: Alianza, 1969), p. 99.

13. Russell, *Temas de la Celestina*, p. 260–61. The *hilado* as a net in which Celestina snares her victims has been suggested by F. M. Weinberg in "Aspects of Symbolism in *La Celestina*," *MLN* 86 (1971):144–47; recently Alan Deyermond, in two important articles, analyzed the erotic value of the images, as well as the connection between *Hilado — Cordón — Cadena — Serpiente*. Obviously, there is common ground between Deyermond's interpretation and mine; the main difference would be the paramount importance given in this chapter to the serpent as the final center of the metaphorical structure of *La Celestina*; through it *Hilado*, *Cordón*, and *toothache* become icons dominated by the higher archetype of the Devil-Serpent, the master of Celestina, who, through her, displays his net over her city.

14. The *agujeta* was a string with metallic tips at the end; it was used to fasten the hose. The metal points were used to pass the string through the holes in the top of the hose (very near the groin, obviously). Because of this, the *agujeta* was a subject of obscene jokes. In the *Floresta de poesía erótica*, it appears with the meaning of "dildo" in a poem about the games of two lesbians (p. 46).

15. Apart from the articles of P. E. Russell and Elisabeth Sánchez quoted in note 4, considerable attention has been given to the theme of magic in *La Celestina*. Menéndez y Pelayo saw clearly the importance of Celestina's bewitchment of Melibea for our understanding of the plot but failed to fully appreciate the importance of the Devil's intervention and of Celestina's role as a *hechicera*. For some time after Menéndez y Pelayo, *La Celestina*'s critics showed interest only sporadically in

its magic and diabolic aspects: in 1928, Julius Berzunza, in "Notes on Witchcraft and Alcahuetería" (*The Romanic Review*) 19 [1928]:141–150), studied the fate of witchcraft in the early Renaissance as well as the medical and magical properties of the remedies used by Celestina in her incantations. In 1932, F. Rauhut ("Das Damonische in der Celestina," *Festgahe zum 60 Geburtstag Karl Vosslers Munich* [1932]:117–48) concentrated on the philosophical significance of the Devil's presence in *La Celestina*. In 1952, José Bergamín, in a somewhat vague and loose essay, made some assertions of merit: he insisted on the importance of magic for our understanding of the *tragicomedia* and of Celestina's *hilado* (yarn) as the instrument by which the Devil is introduced as an active agent into the plot. But the work that, above all others, gave to the subject of magic the paramount importance that it has acquired in contemporary scholarship was that of P. E. Russell (see note 4). More recent studies are Fernando Toro-Garland's "Celestina, hechicera clásica y tradicional," *Cuadernos Hispano Americanos* 180 (1964):438–45; the chapter "La idea de Fortuna y la visión mecánica del mundo. El papel de la magia," in José Antonio Maravall's *El mundo social de "La Celestina"* (Madrid, 1972), pp. 134–52; and the already quoted article of Elisabeth Sánchez, "Magic in *La Celestina*."

Contributors

Contributors

Canet, José Luis. Professor of Spanish literature at the Universidad de Valencia, Spain. Author of studies on Renaissance and Baroque drama. His research interests include the Valencian theater of that period.

Godzich, Wlad. Professor of Comparative Literature and French Studies at the Université de Montréal; Professor of Comparative Literature and Eastern European Studies, and Director of the Center for Humanistic Studies at the University of Minnesota. Coeditor of the series "Theory and History of Literature" at the University of Minnesota Press; coeditor of *The Yale Critics: Deconstruction in America* (Minnesota, 1983); author of the forthcoming *An Essay in Prosaics* (with Jeffrey Kittay) and *The Culture of Literacy*.

Herrero, Javier. William R. Kenan Professor of Spanish and Comparative Literature at the University of Virginia and former Mellon Professor at the University of Pittsburgh. Author of numerous essays on the Generation of 1898, the nineteenth-century novel, the picaresque novel, eighteenth century reactionary thought, and Spanish Golden Age drama. His books include *Fernán Caballero: un nuevo planteamiento* (1963), *Angel Ganivet, un iluminado* (1966), and *Los orígenes del pensamiento reaccionario español* (1971). More recently he has written on *Lazarillo* and Calderón, combining traditional scholarship and erudition with modern semiological theory.

Maravall, José Antonio. Professor emeritus at the Universidad Complutense de Madrid and member of the Real Academia de la Historia. A historian of social mentalities, he has authored more than thirty books and over one hundren articles. His books include *Teoría del saber histórico* (1958), *El* *pensamiento de Velázquez* (1960), *Antiguos y modernos. La idea de progreso en el desarrollo de una sociedad* (1962), *Estado moderno y mentalidad social*, 2 vols. (1972), *La cultura del Barroco* (1975; soon to appear in English from the University of Minnesota Press), *Utopía y contrautopía en el Quijote* (1976), *Poder, honor y élites en el s. XVII* (1980), and *La picaresca vista desde la historia social*, (forthcoming).

Nerlich, Michael. Professor of Romance Literatures at the Technische Universität Berlins. Editor-in chief of *Lendemains*. Author of *Untersuchungen zur Theorie des Klassizistischen Epos in Spanien (1700–1850)* (1964), *El hombre justo y bueno; inocencia bei Fray Luis de León* (1966), *Kunst Politik und Schelmerei* (1969), *Kritik der Abenteuer-Ideologie. Beitrag zur Erforschung der bürgerlichen Bewusstseinsbildung 1100–1750*, 2 vols. (1977; soon to appear in English from the University of Minnesota Press).

Sousa, Ronald. Professor of Luso-Brazilian Studies; Professor and Chair of Comparative Literature at the University of Minnesota. He is the author of a book, *The Rediscoverers* (1981), and has written numerous essays on authors ranging from Camòens to Fernando Pessoa to José Rodrígues Migueis. Recent investigations have taken him into the area of oral performance and reception.

Spadaccini, Nicholas. Professor of Hispanic Studies and Comparative Literature at the University of Minnesota. He has written especially on the picaresque novel and Spanish Golden Age drama and has edited a number of Spanish classics including Cervantes' *Entremeses* (1982), and in collaboration *La vida y hechos de Estebanillo González*, 2 vols. (1978), and two of Cervantes' *comedias*: *El Rufián dichoso* and *Pedro de Urdemalas* (forthcoming). Recent investigations have taken him into the area of popular culture and reception.

Sullivan, Constance. Associate Professor of Hispanic Studies and Chair of the Department of Hispanic and Luso-Brazilian Literatures and Linguistics at the University of Minnesota. She has written articles on contemporary Spanish narrative and drama, and her current research interests are focused in the area of popular culture, especially the way proverbs function in speech and written texts.

Talens, Jenaro. Professor of Literary Theory at the Universidad de Valencia, Spain. He has published several books of poetry, has translated into Spanish a number of European classics, including Shakespeare, and has authored many books of criticism and literary theory. Among them are *Novela picaresca y práctica de la transgresión* (1975), *La escritura como teatralidad* (1977), *Escriptura i ideología* (1979), and *Elementos para una semiótica del texto artístico* (1978).

Index

Index